the "dangerous class" and revolutionary theory

thoughts on the making of the lumpen/proletariat

J. Sakai

KER
SPL
EBE
DEB
2017

The "Dangerous Class" and Revolutionary Theory: Thoughts on the Making of the Lumpen/Proletariat
by J. Sakai

copyright J. Sakai, 2017

this edition copyright Kersplebedeb

ISBN: 978-1-894946-90-2

Kersplebedeb Publishing and Distribution
CP 63560, CCCP Van Horne
Montreal, Quebec
Canada H3W 3H8

www.kersplebedeb.com
www.leftwingbooks.net

Table of Contents

the "dangerous class" and revolutionary theory

thoughts on the making of the lumpen/proletariat

J. Sakai

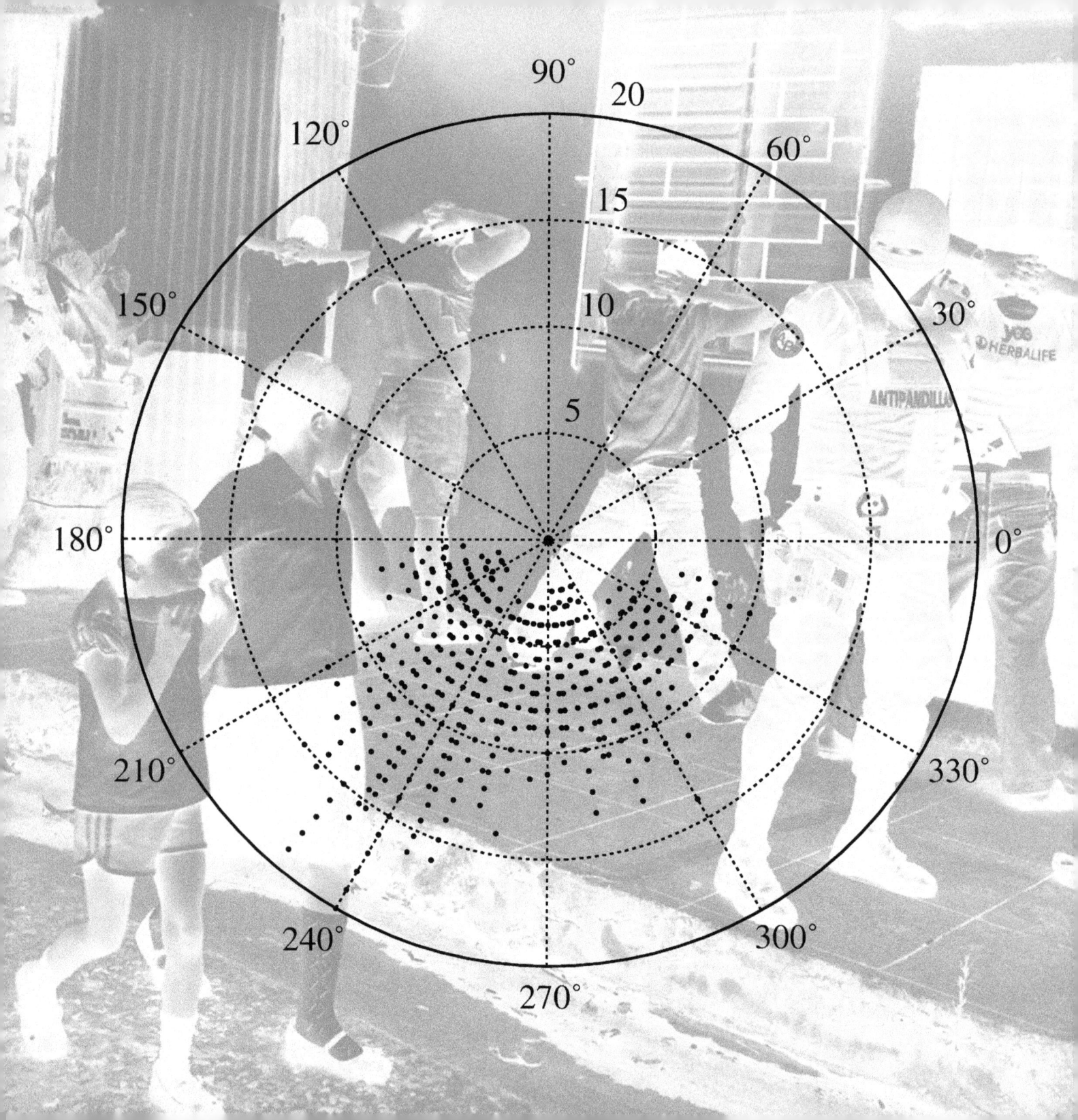

prologue:
"science" and "theory"

The crisis of revolutionary theory right now is that it's plain too old and obsolete. Meaning that in practice it's largely unusable. This is understood as a practical reality, and we usually leave revolutionary theory behind us in the attic when people go out to play. Nowhere is this more true than when it comes to the lumpen/proletariat, that most dramatic, most elusive of maybe-or-maybe-not "classes." This matters because the revolutionary movement and the lumpen have a much longer and more involved relationship than we've fully owned up to. *Whether revolutionaries think it's good or not, the lumpen are going to play a big part in everyone's future.* No better place, then, to start remaking the tool of theory.

Society is made and controlled by classes; that's why classes are so critical politically. To not understand classes is to not get how human society transforms and gives birth to itself over and over again. That's where we are right now, mostly, not getting it as Rome burns. Hating capitalism doesn't mean that we automatically understand it.

When we think of class we are conditioned to involuntarily think of dull textbooks and dusty social science courses. When it's the reverse that's on target. It's hard to get class in part because it's always too new, too threatening, as we maybe are threatened with switching classes personally or are constantly drafted to be raw material for remaking classes around us. Class is too revealing to easily confront. Plus, under capitalism the ruling class itself doesn't want to be identified, and so is always mystifying classes and its own class structure.

Class is also a human dimension where we are both hammer and anvil, when most want to be neither. On this primal level of human society there is nothing but class and class elements, where classes are simultaneously the user of the tool, the hammer itself, and the object being changed. Just as class is the wielder of the knife, the weapon itself in its arc, and the present being cut open. Everything is made of classes and class strata, and class is the landscape and those moving on it and the atmosphere itself all at once. Our goal is simple, to improve our ability to identify the broken up class terrain that we are moving across, so that our step is more sure.

The lumpen are so critical as a subject to us today because they are a wildcard in the process of change, in every society worldwide. Radicals of all varieties usually talk mostly of the working class against the capitalists, or maybe indigenous peasants versus the corporate elite. Seldom of the lumpen, that most masked and marginalized of "non-class" formations. But whether we are seeing the coming end of straight-up capitalism in its shocking decay, or globalization's instant rag-tag armies scourging civilizations in ways we never expected, it is the lumpen who are everyone's first weapons of change and then reaction to change. They are the catalysts in the motions of major classes, the first doers, the apostles and the true believers, the risks of change personified.

SOMETHING BECOMING ITS OPPOSITE

Revolutionary theory in form has too often in essence become its opposite.

One part or aspect of revolutionary theory falling into disuse, is that it's mostly decoration right now. Maybe like an old sword hung on a tavern wall. *Real, but not real.*

Once it was genuinely revolutionary, startling even, cutting edge in describing a new world coming into being. But now? The little black and white tv screen of revolutionary theory has a mighty dull resolution, and to feel the new everyone turns to mediums like hip-hop, manga, to illegal fiction, or to just checking out the latest street fighting.

The main use of established revolutionary theory now is maybe even *conservative*: as recycled propaganda, or as an ideological stage prop to claim that someone's triumph is "inevitable" or that someone's politics must be "correct."

The dysfunction of old theory has only led to the more and more popular belief that revolutionaries don't really need any theory or science at all. Untrue to the extreme, this one.

Being real, all areas of human endeavor need science. We not only use it, but expect it and demand it every day without a moment's question. Even those clowns who scoff at science. It's completely woven into the fabric of our reality.

If a "pilot" in our jetliner announced that he didn't believe in any aeronautical science and never bothered to study flight, but just wanted to pull the throttle back all the way and improvise—we'd all be fighting to get out that exit. If a "surgeon" told us that she never bothered learning anatomy or physiology or any other part of medical science, but only wanted to cut people open and see what spontaneously she could create, we'd be looking for restraints and handcuffs. Same with engineering cars, putting up skyscrapers, formulating biochemical compounds, planning an ambush to free prisoners, etc. You can fill in the blanks. No less, then, with analyzing the complex flow of societal politics, and building an alternative social power to overthrow existing civilization in all its aspects.

The skeptics on a leash, well-trained in the capitalistic viewpoint, always say that revolutionary science is merely a fantasy, and that the only true sciences are the "hard" sciences like physics and chemistry and medicine; which have proven their value with a world-changing flow of practical results, like hydrogen bombs and synthetic fabric yoga pants. We on the other hand have only created popular illegal conspiracies and destroyed governments. Much harder (but much more satisfying).

Remember that our word "history" comes from the Greek root word *historia* or *istoria*, which meant "research" or "knowledge gained by inquiry." Their scholars used the term for the study of human society as much as the study of physics and biology.[4]

WHICH SCIENCE?

The ruling classes of any age own and therefore shape the sciences of that society, as surely as they own the land and the factories and the laws. But their possession is never uncontested, as we continually struggle to remake it into its opposite. The main difference between our science and theirs is that the science of revolution by its very nature is meant for different hands, to be used by the exploited and oppressed. The other big difference is that *ours is so very young*, so undeveloped, historically speaking.

After all, we know medicine and physics are "real" sciences. They even give Nobel prizes and big paydays for them. Those sciences were many slow centuries developing, over 2,000 years old. Our science of revolutionary change is a mere several centuries old, a child still finding its feet.

For most of that 2,000 years, though, the "hard" sciences this civilization worships had only one after another totally untrue or fantastical theory to explain most aspects of the real universe. Turns out that was only part of the crawling before you can walk, walking before you can run, type of thing. Even in our own day, these supposedly superior sciences have proven clueless and confused time after time (and they are getting the big bucks, don't forget, they're not doing the messing up for free).

We don't have to look at the Ebola epidemic or the AIDS plague to get it, for instance, how crude and sometimes murderous ruling class medical science still is.

Check out the first "heart healthy" diet introduced by the American Heart Association and the Food & Drug Administration in 1950. Not 1750 or 1850, but 1950. The American Heart Association gave their new diet plan the cutesy, pun-able name, "The Way to His Heart." As you

might guess, that's because their "heart healthy" diet was designed only for white men, but would be actually executed (to use an irresistible pun) by the subordinate women who supposedly would be cooking their meals in 1950s America.

But where was the "heart healthy" diet for women? The cardiologists and medical researchers of the American Heart Association and the federal government didn't bother even writing one up. They firmly "knew" that no such diet was needed, since only white *men* were victims of heart disease they said. No cardiac resources were needed for white women or any people of color, their Bozo the patriarchal capitalist scientist had decided. And, yet, no one doubts that medicine despite all its pratfalls is a scientific discipline. It's only that it should be a world different.

And physics, what about that most theoretical of the capitalist sciences? Which in the Western tradition started with the ancient slave-owning Greek philosophers many, many centuries ago.

It's symptomatic of its theoretical uncertainty that at a July 1999 conference on quantum physics at Cambridge University, a poll of the physicists on whether the present *theory* of quantum mechanics was true or not, found little support for it as is. Only four physicists supported the standard, completely dominant theory of quantum mechanics as presently taught at universities. Thirty physicists there would have agreed with the standard theory only if the additional theory, straight from science fiction novels, of an infinite number of parallel universes was attached to it. The great majority, fifty physicists, simply expressed doubts or serious uncertainty about today's accepted theory as scientific explanation. Nobel prize-winning theoretical physicist Gerard t'Hooft said present quantum theory is "inaccurate." In the words of prominent British physicist Sir Roger Penrose, "present-day quantum mechanics is fundamentally incomplete." Relatively speaking, that was an endorsement, which shows you something.[5]

This is only in keeping with scientific tradition, since the *whole history* of Western physics has been of theories one after another held up and then discarded, superseded or just tossed in the dumpster. And yet, no one doubts that their incomplete, uncertain physics is a "science." Our record of theoretical thinking in our short beginning is if anything much better than theirs.

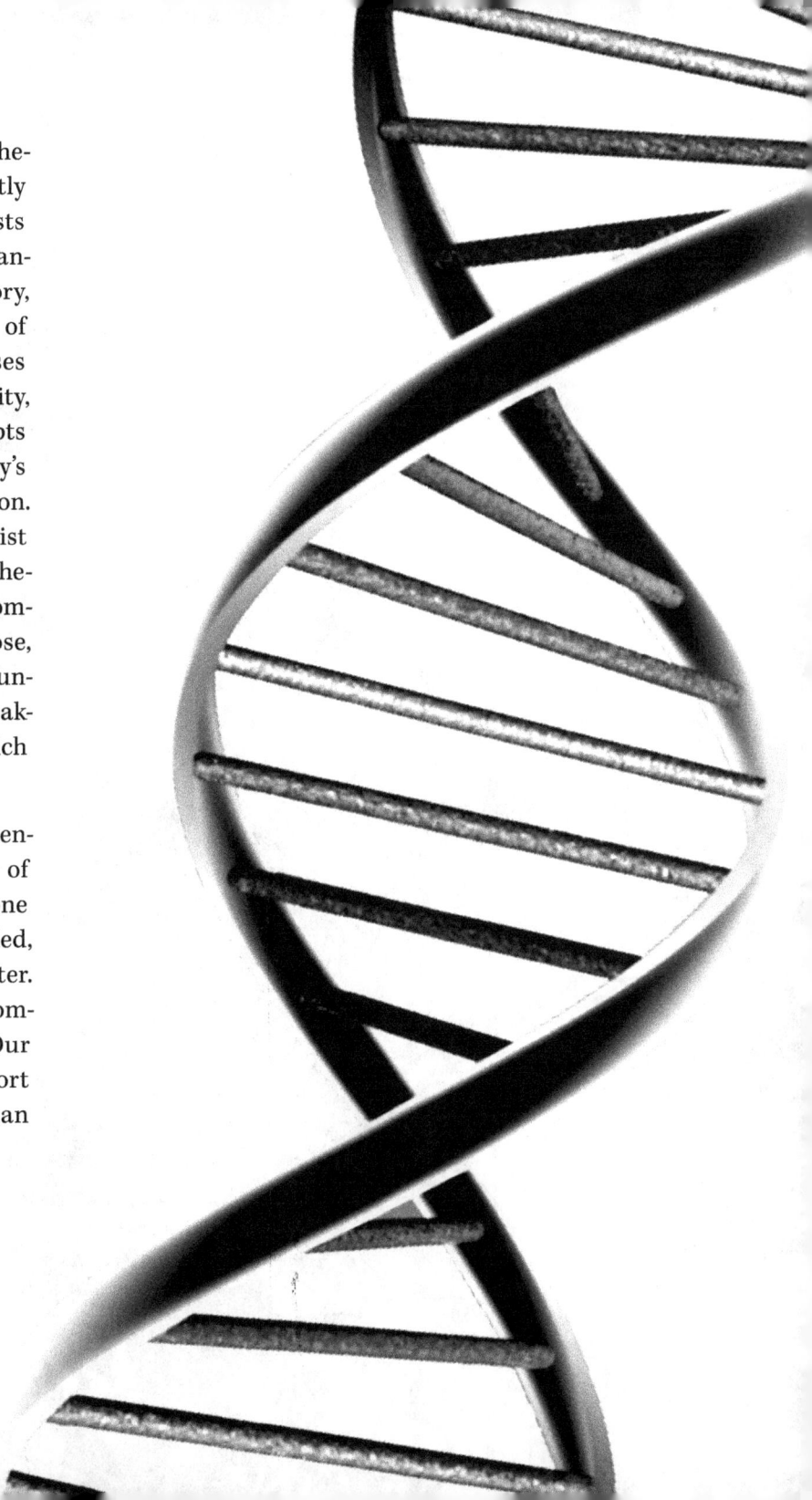

1. re-starting at the margins

This is the book that i always looked for when i first came into the movement, but never found. Instead, was always told by old socialists how the unionized steel-workers and dockworkers and like that were going to make the revolution—it was all we had to know about "class." Never could figure out why the radical biggies never explained about the lumpen. Never explained anything about the semi-outlaw communities many of us came from.

Even today, left literature is so often celebrating male industrial workers, though right here they're an evaporating minority in our imperial metropolis. When the cards get so worn and dog-eared that no hand is a surprise, players got to change the deck. Same with the violently radical truth of understanding classes. Cause real is always a surprise.

Revolutionaries have always pointed to the industrial working class as our main instrument of change, but in this lifetime it has just as often been the lumpen/proletariat that has surprised us, has been the force of disruption. Even in the raising of unexpected new social orders. Whether that's good or ill, whether anyone likes it or not. Whether it's the Black Panther Party for Self-Defense in the 1960s, explicitly proclaiming the lumpen/proletarian leadership over the entire Black community—or the many thousands of death commandos from all over the world, drawn to the lumpen warlord banner of the Islamic Caliphate's shifting state of fugitives. If NATO, the White House, the Great Russian stalinate, and most of the Arab capitalist regimes of the Middle East, all have to declare war on you, you gotta be repping something XL.

Don't get me wrong. It isn't just about some latest big thing, and workers are definitely at the heart of the liberation we need ... It's just that there are several ideas we were critically mistaught. One of which was to settle for the old, oversimplified, stick-figure picture of class structure that anti-capitalist pioneers such as Marx and Bakunin and Engels had hurriedly drawn in the sand, so that nobody would admit that in real life, "class" is much more complex and has a specific gravity to it.

My old left generation was mistaught that men's industrial labor was really important, but that women's unwaged labor in production and reproduction, work carried out by half the human race, was unimportant. Didn't know that gender could have class attributes, or that an oppressed inner colony could be the most radically conscious part of the proletariat. So clueless us were surprised when it was women breaking out of marriage and unwaged labor, following in their own way the Black Nation as it burned cities, that seemingly changed everything.

Radicals explain actually-existing capitalism's class structure as formed by everyone's roles in economic production and distribution; that's true but is also *not the only way classes are made*. Classes do not grow "naturally" or easily out of simple economy without further ruling class engineering and genocides. **Capitalism, for example, can give forced birth to outcast class strata by criminalizing people, by repressing them out of their old social-economic roles and drying up their livelihoods and niches in humanity.** Criminalization isn't mere prejudice or just racism, nor is it only ruling class propaganda; criminalization once realized in people's lives can become a material force. It actually remakes and changes who we are.

Criminalization is a basic condition of our paradoxically growing yet collapsing, glittering but increasingly decaying late capitalism. Shaping the zone of the poorest and most exploited in postmodern society, the zone of the dispossessed that everyone knows of. Here it's often called the inner city or the rez. Same same as elsewhere it's called the *favela* or the ghetto, the bantustan or *banlieue*. Every capitalist nation or society has its own name for it; it's always different and always the same, because it is where the dispossessed have to gather, to live and struggle to survive. It's where criminality is out front and **where the lumpen/proletariat are mass produced as jagged fragments or strata of "partial-class."** While the lumpen fall from all classes, it is in these zones of the dispossessed that they reach an open and mass character. That they themselves can take over the life of parts of the neighborhood and make it "home."

The unspoken feature of these zones of the dispossessed, is that they are not mono-class but charged by the duology of the lower working class and the

2

lumpen/proletariat living together ambidextrously side by side, being family, being inside each other's lives and struggling with and against each other to stay alive. A class difference that's in large part a gender-class difference. Survival itself, living, is the bar of success.

Out of this enduring culture and criminalization of the zone, lumpen/proletarians are constantly being made in larger and larger numbers even in the most technologically advanced and affluent nations of imperialist "civilization." Of all the classes of capitalist society, it is the lumpen/proletariat that has the most outdated theory attached to it. Just scraps of theory, really. Still pictured by many socialists as a small and marginal maybe-or-maybe-not "class," wretched and largely unimportant to revolutionary change. But today the lumpen have become major players in the political crises of both left and right. This is something that has to be picked up, no matter how white-hot to the touch.

Karl Marx was the first to popularize the term "lumpenproletariat" in any current sense, in his and Engels' historic *Communist Manifesto* of 1848. Describing these people as: *"The 'dangerous class', the social scum, that passively rotting mass thrown off by the lowest layers of old society."* Later, in his famous work, *Capital,*

Marx referred to the *"vagabonds, criminals, prostitutes, in a word the lumpenproletariat proper."* Obviously, his own take on the lumpen/proletariat was largely negative. Within that was both an insightful contribution but also the visual obstruction of a confused class bias.

While seldom used by radicals here, the "L" word has slowly become more popular with intellectuals in general, like a prideful flashing of university erudition. As by journalist Mary Anne Weaver, who

NOTE: The standard spelling in translations of Marx and Engels' writing is the familiar "lumpenproletariat," or sometimes with a hyphen, "lumpen-proletariat." I prefer and use here "lumpen/proletariat," because it conveys the essential ambiguity of this "non-class." In grammar a slash can join two related things or link two opposites, or both (such as "black/white," "on/off," or "interrogation/torture"). And I say simply "lumpen" most often because in daily usage most of us use that instead of the fuller term that's maybe problematic on the tongue and mind.

3

wrote the celebrated report on how more British Muslims numerically have run away to join Al Qaeda and ISIS than have joined the British army. She wrote sarcastically about the Western-educated young jihadists from comfortable middle-class homes—*"This is not a movement of the lumpenproletariat."* Exactly wrong she is, since that is just what it is.

Or the dismayed political column in my local *Chicago Reader* free weekly, after the Trump election juggernaut: "The only guy I know who predicted this was a former Chicago alderman who told me Trump would win by bringing out the *lumpen-proletariat*—people who had never believed in the system enough to vote." So intellectuals aren't using the term in any definite way, vaguely meaning those marginalized in some sense or another.[1]

The lumpen/proletariat cannot be defined as simply the poorest of the poor, or the ever-unemployed. Nor can it be pictured simply as career criminals and beggars, as many believe. Although these categories often find themselves within the lumpen. It is identified by its central characteristic: as a "partial-class" or "non-class" of peoples who have voluntarily or involuntarily left the "regular" classes of economic production and distribution. Who are "unplugged" if you will from regular class society. Of those declassed

fragments or strata fallen out of the class structure, who are then forced to find a living from parasitism or outlaw activities. An increasing sharpness will be steadily thrown on this definition as we go on.

Marx's theory on the lumpen/proletariat, identifying it as strata distinct from the working class itself and other full capitalist classes, was a valuable starting insight. He didn't invent the terms *proletariat* and *lumpen/proletariat*, but he was the first to discover their modern identities within the then-new industrial capitalist class structure. On the other hand, while carefully disclaiming being a learned "social scientist" like Marx, his contemporary the anarchist Mikhail Bakunin flipped those class identities right over. Criticizing Marx's language about the declassed as only contemptuous snobbery, Bakunin saw those poor rebels who were already criminals, fighting the laws and the propertied, along with desperate peasants dispossessed from their lands, as the most radical and anti-capitalist groupings of all. The social explosive that revolutionaries needed.

Criminal activity is hardly limited to the lumpen, since we know that poor workers and rural peasants are always doing "crimes of survival" to say nothing of class warfare. Recall that it is bloody capitalism itself that is always defining what's a crime. Just as during the massive New Afrikan women's labor strike in the ex-Confederate states right after the Civil War 1, being an unemployed Black woman was made an illegal "crime" punishable by unwaged forced labor by most of the Southern states, for the next century. All classes do crime, remember, the capitalists most of all.[2]

Perhaps due to confused stereotypes, there has been little theoretical analysis of the lumpen and crime. Also, the lumpen/proletariat as a highly criminalized "partial-class" is generally wary of exposure—a trait also shared by revolutionaries, to be sure. While most mainstream news about crime centers narrowly on cops vs. perps, the lumpen have always played a class role in the survival activity of the oppressed. In 1852, for instance, when the journalist Frederick Law Olmstead (later the famed designer of New York's Central Park and other public spaces) investigated the u.s.a. "Slave South" on assignment for the *New York Times*, he found settler criminals as indispensable illegal business partners of New Afrikan en-slaved workers. Those lumpen outlaws their only local white allies, in fact. Carry that in your pocket.

"A sugar estate in Louisiana," Olmstead wrote, where "... the slaves themselves appropriated food and equipment from their master's sugarworks, and then sold their ill-gotten gains to white men who plied the Mississippi River in boats, called 'chicken thieves'." He found the same high-risk nighttime dealings in the coastal South Carolina rice plantations. "These slaves too persisted in illegal trafficking with white traders." Trading their own handicrafts secretly made along with agricultural goods which supposedly didn't belong to them, in return for valued things such as forbidden bibles with which the New Afrikan women taught themselves to read.

Trafficking in stolen goods, white and New Afrikan outlaws meeting on secret lumpen terrain was a survival mechanism for the oppressed. You don't have to be friends to be allies, just saying. We could also note that *all* classes in capitalism have a need for crime and thus for lumpen, not only as the illegal catspaw which carries out certain necessary tasks of a risky nature. The dime bag didn't materialize on our kitchen table all by itself.[3]

In our neighborhood in the 1970s and 1980s, some doctors had little dusty storefront clinics, where women with medical green cards from the Welfare would get "scripts" for antibiotics they didn't need. They'd "crack" these at the pharmacist, who would look the other way as the women exchanged them for Pampers, skin lotion, food and other things. So everyone got something they needed out of it—the doctor and the small neighborhood drugstores most of all (who were losing to the big drugstore chains like Walgreens, and needed every sale they could get). Women used nickel & dime crime for survival commodities, in keeping their precarious balance walking the line between working class and falling into the lumpen. All classes from bottom to top were tacitly cooperating in little crimes, hidden in the hum-drum activities of daily life. Like in the 1990s, young New Afrikan and Latino messengers in New York City—many fresh outta a year or two in juvie—would be regularly jumping the subway turnstiles. The brass subway tokens they were given for deliveries would be saved up, and then spent on cigarettes or sandwiches at little mom & pop *bodegas* which accepted the tokens as legal-to-us currency. Again, different classes were hand-in-hand surviving through daily criming the state in little chips, just as the capitalists and their state do it to us.

The lowest layers of the working class, the proletariat proper, keep being forced over the line of criminality, and have been since the birth of the Western capitalist order. It's a basic. In a paradoxical way, seeing the outcast lumpen/proletariat helps us better understand the working class itself at a time of profound political confusion.

In the late 1960s, the u.s. government experimented with hiring the Blackstone Rangers and Disciples street organizations in Chicago as mercenaries. Paid with "poverty grants" to violently repress "riots" and all other Black community anti-capitalist activity. They even put a stop—at gunpoint—to spontaneous looting and burning after the Rev. Martin Luther King, Jr. was assassinated. It worked very effectively for euro-capitalism, abruptly ending all protests in the designated test area. But also got in the way of the much greater machinery of straight-up police repression, and so had to be discontinued.

Taking what they had learned, the police and government made a more sophisticated and "deniable" counter-insurgency program. Remaking massively unemployed street youth into loose mafias under tacit police supervision, to de-politicize oppressed communities and set things in motion for the even bigger wave of mass incarcerations. Capitalism once caught napping by anti-capitalist revolutionaries had now woken up to the future of recycling lumpen as instruments of mass social repression against their own, and even against their own selves. We could say that all sides are playing with rigged decks now.

Why is an understanding of the lumpen so important now?

The absolute and relative growth of the lumpen/proletariat is due to basic changes in world capitalist development. Rural areas of the periphery long under capitalist hegemony are being intensively reconquered, with millions of families driven off the land. Local industries are either being expanded worldwide or else are being ruined, as everything is replaced by world industries and world agriculture whose cheaper products seem always to be made elsewhere. More and more people are separated from nature, unable to sustain themselves independently from capitalism's cash nexus. Increasingly, youth all over the world are brought into a Western imperialist culture which offers them endless commodities, but denies their own identities as people. As growing up Muslim and Asian in "tighty-whitey" Britain, for example.

These are not simply world changes in a linear sense but are changes in dimension and identity. The world has suddenly morphed. Better class analysis and theory is so necessary to our struggle because the neo-colonial merging/separation of the globe into imperial metropolis and periphery is at the heart of politics, as the great 2016 refugee crisis of millions migrating illegally together across the Mediterranean and into *"Festung Europa"* proved. A renewed far right has sharply spread there and here, itself joining arms across old national borders, based on the mass politics of imperialist parasitism. Indeed, mass parasitism has become such an institutionalized phenomenon in late capitalism that it bends and confuses everything.

The "right" or privilege of patriotic parasitism becomes a program for industrial workers and youth just as with capitalists, whether it's the white settler nationalist Trump campaign or the nominally left Occupy Wall Street. As parasitism itself continuously increases within rotting capitalism. The defined parasitism of the armed robber seems confusing compared to the parasitism of the suburban white high school students. Who is the parasite—the unionized crane operator putting up the condo highrise downtown or the young sex worker a block away from where I'm writing this tonight? If we really have it, you know, our class analysis is a weapon.

EVEN PRIOR TO THE *MANIFESTO,* MARX AND ENGELS HAD BELIEVED THAT THE LUMP-
EN NOT ONLY EXISTED AS DISTINCT "CLASS" STRATA OR SPLINTERS, BUT HAD A REAL
PRESENCE IN EVERY EARLIER EUROPEAN CLASS SOCIETY. AS FAR BACK IN HISTORY AS
THE ROMAN EMPIRE, THEY WROTE IN 1845 IN *THE GERMAN IDEOLOGY*: "THE PLE-
BEIANS, MIDWAY BETWEEN FREEMEN AND SLAVES NEVER SUCCEEDED IN BECOMING
MORE THAN A LUMPEN-PROLETARIAT." THEY CONTINUED, SEEING THE LUMPEN EX-
ISTING IN LATE FEUDAL EUROPE AS A VISIBLE POPULATION *AND* A POLITICAL FACTOR:
"**THE LUMPENPROLETARIAT IS, GENERALLY SPEAKING, A PHENOMENON EVIDENT
IN A MORE OR LESS DEVELOPED FORM IN ALL PHASES OF SOCIETY TO DATE. THE
NUMBER OF PEOPLE WITHOUT A DEFINITE OCCUPATION AND A STABLE DOMICILE
INCREASED GREATLY AT THAT PARTICULAR TIME, DUE TO THE DECAY OF FEUDALISM
IN A SOCIETY IN WHICH EVERY OCCUPATION, EVERY SPHERE OF LIFE, WAS STILL
FENCED OFF BY COUNTLESS PRIVILEGES. THE NUMBER OF VAGABONDS IN ALL
THE DEVELOPED COUNTRIES WAS NEVER SO GREAT AS IN THE FIRST HALF OF THE**

SIXTEENTH CENTURY [I.E. EARLY 1500s—EDITORS]. IN WARTIME SOME OF THESE TRAMPS JOINED THE ARMIES, OTHERS BEGGED THEIR WAY ACROSS THE COUNTRYSIDE, AND OTHERS STILL EKED OUT A MEAGER LIVING ... ALL THREE GROUPS PLAYED A PART IN THE PEASANT WAR; THE FIRST IN THE ARMIES OF PRINCES, WHICH OVERPOWERED THE PEASANTS; THE SECOND IN THE PEASANT CONSPIRACIES AND PEASANT TROOPS, WHERE ITS DEMORALIZING INFLUENCE WAS EVIDENT AT ALL TIMES; AND THE THIRD IN THE CLASHES OF THE URBAN PARTIES."

AS EARLY IN THEIR WORK AS THIS WRITING WAS—WHICH REMAINED UNPUBLISHED IN MARX'S LIFETIME AND ONLY BECAME AVAILABLE IN ENGLISH IN THE LATE 1960s— WE CAN SEE CONFIRMATION OF THEIR THINKING ABOUT THE LUMPEN/PROLETARIAT. AND A ROUGH OUTLINE POLITICALLY: OF THOSE LUMPEN NOT HAVING ANY SINGLE "CLASS" AGENDA, SEPARATING TO FIGHT ON A MULTIPLICITY OF SIDES BOTH WITH AND AGAINST EACH OTHER. THIS IS A PATTERN WE WILL RUN ACROSS AGAIN.[7]

2. lumpen—german: shred, damaged, miscreant, as in *broken-proletariat* or *feral-proletariat*

Revolutionary theory explaining the lumpen/proletariat began in public with Marx and Engels' historic *Communist Manifesto*, which was propelled by the wave of revolutionary insurrections across Europe in 1848. In those pages, Marx magisterially hurled down the bright lightning and thunder of both recognition and moral scorn:

> *"The 'dangerous class', the social scum, that passively rotting mass thrown off by the lowest layers of old society, may here and there, be swept into the movement by a proletarian revolution; its conditions of life, however, prepare it far more for the part of a bribed tool of reactionary intrigue."*[6]

This now-famous passage set revolutionaries on alert, to guard against the activity of this usually extremely poor but largely untrustworthy class intruder in the normal social strata.

In that light, the lumpen/proletariat is often thought of as the poorest of the poor, the permanently unemployed and outcast, or equally often as the hardened criminal elements—all partly true but off target. Marx repositioned himself on this almost immediately, but his artful misimpression still lasts. For what distinguishes the lumpen/proletariat is that they have been cast out of or have left or are excluded from the functioning classes of patriarchal capitalism. Though many of them are among the very poorest and the most desperate, the step that distinguishes them as lumpen is that they have fallen out of class. They're "unplugged" socially. That is, the lumpen/proletariat has no regular role as a grouping in "legal" production and distribution, and to survive must often devise immediate if short-term ways to get their livelihood from others.

This is not one "class" but a "partial class" in Engels' words, or a "non-class" as some label them now. It's important to keep in mind that parasitism alone cannot define them, since capitalist society itself is by its nature supremely parasitic. Marx underlined this himself, and was literarily up there with the Anne Rices and Sookie Stackhouses when he described Capital for all its apparent vigor as "dead" and "vampire-like." View him as a pioneer horror writer. Who is in this "partial class," then?

3. uncertain cast of characters

Shortly after scribing the *Manifesto*, Marx further identified what he considered typical component parts of his lumpen/proletariat, in denouncing a new type of reactionary French regime. Louis Bonaparte had fashioned a mock retro-aristocratic facade for early financial & industrial capitalism, pretending to be the great Napoleon's imperial successor:

> "Alongside decayed roués with dubious means of subsistence and of dubious origin, alongside ruined and adventurous offshoots of the bourgeoisie, were vagabonds, discharged soldiers, discharged jailbirds, escaped galley slaves, swindlers, mountebanks, lazzaroni, pickpockets, tricksters, gamblers, pimps, brothel keepers, porters, literati, organ-grinders, rag-pickers, knife grinders, tinkers, beggars—in short, the whole indefinite, disintegrated mass, thrown hither and thither, which the French term *la boheme* ... A 'benevolent society'—in so far as, like Bonaparte, all its members felt the need of benefiting themselves at the expense of the laboring nation. This Bonaparte, who constitutes himself *chief of the lumpenproletariat* ... here alone rediscovers in mass form the interests which he personally pursues ... recognizes in this scum, offal, refuse of all classes the only class upon which he can base himself unconditionally ... ."[8]

Brilliant as Marx's social insights could be, and powerful as his stormy pen was, it's hard to escape the feeling that his middle-class prejudice was staining his "laundry list" view of those scrabbling in various ways for survival in the streets, some ingenious and admirable, some reasonable, some perhaps ugly. Why should an escaped slave or a rag-picker be condemned out of hand? Today we revolutionaries don't in either case, and haven't for some time.

Keep in mind, it wasn't Marx's or anyone else's job to be right 100% of the time, but only to start the process off, to approximate the new capitalist crazy landscape best that they could, reporting back as advance scouts to our line of march.

It is also true that his categories, of his early industrial capitalist world not today's, did not always have the same meaning as they would in ours now. i don't view a returning army veteran as anyone out of the ordinary, but in the England of that time military veterans were being frequently hanged or imprisoned. The problem they had and posed was most evident in the Irish. This background: Despairing of a means of bare survival in Britain's harshly ruled Irish colony, between the years of the early 1700s and the great Irish potato famine of 1848, as Irish were increasingly robbed of their farmlands, young Irish men in droves left Ireland to find bread as mercenaries. Peter Linebaugh writes of the heart of this in *The London Hanged*:

> "Eight per cent of the Irish hanged at Tyburn had been soldiers. Many had served apprenticeships as tailors, weavers or shoemakers. Others were laboring country people. Such men comprised the 'wild geese' who left their homeland to form Irish regiments in European armies. It has been estimated that between 1691 and 1745, 450,000 Irishmen entered French military service—an exaggeration certainly, yet the number was significant. 'A good many became highwaymen and robbers.' William Mcklaughlane, a Belfast man, fought with the French regiments in the West Indies. James Carter, hanged in 1727 for stealing a silver tankard, had served in the French armies for five years. John Mahoney, hanged for stealing a watch in 1722, had fought in Sicily and Messina for the Spanish. John Norton, hanged in 1705 for stealing a piece of damask, had fought all over Europe for twelve years."[9]

Those surviving veterans discarded after killing for Britain or France or other states in their colonial wars, came with nothing to England's streets, where at least they saw a bare chance of survival, trying to use their few skills. Armed robbery and burglary and snatch-and-grab crimes often accounted for their executions. Still, today we would be more moved to try to defend these desperately and violently dislocated, difficult as that may be, rather than distance them as so-called class enemies.

At the other end of the street were men like the "literati." Which then as now simply means one trying to scratch out a living from being educated or literate (a book critic or a music critic today in our daily newspaper might be still referred to as being in the literati), but at a time when that was uncommon. We have to keep in mind that there wasn't really much public education then. Handfuls of children from affluent families were educated, often by household tutors, while the Church trained boys to have educated roles within their large structures. Reading the bible, doing correspondence, and reading property documents and various laws was the main thing. But those who had fallen out of these career tracks had to survive using their literacy for anyone's hire. Which might mean forging all kinds of documents, or publishing slanderous street flyers against someone's political or business or even romantic rivals.

When we look at that list of Marx's, questions only naturally come to mind about labeling people like tinkers or knife grinders or many others as "scum" and "offal." Tinkers were among the lowest of the low; itinerant fixers for small household metal items, tools or utensils, for working families of modest means, usually traveling a circuit or slow route through neighborhoods and towns.

One popular assumption in the England of Marx's day, was that tinkers were not respectable or legitimate but rather a "degenerate" people, who were really natural thieves, or worse, using the cover of being traveling workingmen to justify looking for easy pickings in people's homes. Of course, helping propel that judgment along was the fact that tinkers in England then were often assumed to be largely Irish or Welsh, thought to be untrustworthy and inferior "races" of resentful colonial subjects, eager to do ill to their English racial "betters." Sound familiar? Although we still hear folk songs about the "jolly Irish tinker," by the later 20th century tinkers in England were no longer so Irish but often Roma. Another group also widely mis-believed in euro-capitalist culture to be born ready-made criminals by race.

Since i was a child in the 1940s, i can remember how in this country the Irish tinker or the knife grinder (who was Italian, in our case) would make his way down our alley. Their harsh cries repeated over and over loudly announcing their services. Since they hadn't been there for many weeks, women burst out their back doors with kitchen things needing their hands. They were much appreciated, among us poor people, anyway—it was during and right after World War II and civilian goods were not being adequately produced. They were just thought of as ordinary working people plying their small trade. (Maybe our repairing the weapon of theory could be called tinkering, too?)

4. theoretical split: who is on the edge of rebellion or betrayal?

Marx and Engels' scathing identification of the lumpen/proletariat did not go unchallenged in revolutionary circles in Europe at that time. Mikhail Bakunin, once an aristocratic cadet in the Czar's military and then a world famous pro-democracy exile, had become one of the political founders of anarchism. He strongly thought that Marx and Engels were misguided about the lumpen. In fact, Bakunin questioned their basic analysis and didn't use the term. Rather than the worst, those stigmatized as "lumpenproletariat" were to be among the best in terms of revolutionary roles. To him the urban workers without regular jobs, together with street rebels already experienced in crimes against property, and most especially the great mass of completely destitute and now rootless peasants pushed off their lands, were the cutting edge of the world struggle.

"By the flower of the proletariat, I mean above all, that great mass, those millions of non-civilized, disinherited, wretched and illiterates ... I mean precisely that eternal 'meat' for governments, that *great rabble* of the people ordinarily designated by Messrs. Marx and Engels by the phrase at once picturesque and contemptuous of 'lumpen proletariat', the riff-raff, that rabble which, being nearly unpolluted by all bourgeois civilization carries in its heart, in its aspirations, in all necessities and the miseries of its collective position, all the germs of the Socialism of the future, and which alone is powerful enough to-day to inaugurate the Social Revolution and bring it to triumph."[10]

Bakunin didn't disagree that there was a meaningful outlaw strata, a marginalized and sometimes violent social element that was divorced from the labors and to some degree from the day-to-day concerns of the peasantry and working class. It's just that he concluded that they were an indispensible political blasting cap needed to trigger off the larger revolutionary upheaval. As he wrote in a June 2, 1870, letter to Sergei Nechaev, about their setting up "*the collective dictatorship* of a secret organization":

> "There are two basic facts in popular life and popular thought which we can build on: frequent uprisings and the free economic commune. There is a third basic fact, and that is the Cossack world of thieving brigands, which contained in itself a protest both against the State and against the restrictions of a patriarchal society, and, one might say, contains elements of the first two ...

> "The frequent risings, although always caused by casual events, nevertheless were due to general conditions and expressed the deep and widespread dissatisfaction of the people. They form, as it were, the everyday or natural phenomenon of Russian popular life ...

> "I am deeply convinced that one of the chief means of attaining this aim should be through the free Cossacks in all parts of the country, and through the enormous number of vagabonds, both 'holy' and otherwise, through 'pilgrims' and '*beguny*', thieves and brigands—the whole of that widespread and numerous underground world which, from time immemorial, has protested against State and sovereignty and against a knouto-Germanic civilization ..."*

* *Beguny* were a much-discussed social phenomenon in Czarist Russia then: wandering vagabonds who often claimed religious visions or pilgrimages, but who were in fact illegally "dropping out" and refusing to bear the yoke of semi-slave agricultural life in being serfs for the landowners. They were possibly of special interest to Bakunin because their survival as semi-fugitives was often due to the sympathetic aid and shelter they got from many peasants. They were a spark of anti-ruling class resistance in the Russian countryside.

He then adds, with his own characteristic sense of forewarning:

> "Whoever wants to preserve his ideal and virgin chastity had better remain in his study, dreaming, thinking and writing dissertations or poetry. Whoever wants to become a real revolutionary activist in Russia should pull off his gloves, for there are no gloves that can preserve him from the Russian mud which goes on forever in all directions. The Russian world, whether it be the world of State privilege or the people's world, is terrible. Inevitably the Russian revolution will be a terrible revolution. Whoever is frightened of horrors and mud better get away from this world and this revolution; but whoever wants to serve the revolution should know where it will lead him, and must brace himself and be ready for anything."[11]

To me, Marx at that moment was a step too distant from the "street," from lower working-class life, to accurately grasp who made up what. And Bakunin was on to something about his beloved "destitute proletariat" and the "rabble" of the streets, if too hopefully simplistic about a complexly evolving world.

In practice, after sifting through the results of actual struggle, there is something real about what Marx was bringing impatiently up from the depths to the surface of our class vision. But despite this, we have to say that Marx and Engels should have been more open to seeing shades of gray about the lumpen/proletariat. Instead, their view was completely negative.

It has been pointed out that the two were well aware that "lumpenproletariat" was a German language phrase, not English. In their lifetimes, in their English translations, they usually didn't say "lumpenproletariat" but substituted an English term. Employing not literal but evocative English phrases, such as "scum," "mob," "lumpenmob," "dangerous class," "lazzaroni," "offal," "refuse" and the like. More neutral usable terms such as "declassed" or "marginalized" took a second seat to hurled insults by the pair, who pictured these peoples not merely as negative but as degenerate humans.

When you think about it, it's amazing. This wretched layer had caused a complete angry divergence of basic class analysis among European revolutionaries. From taking it as very negative to taking it as very positive, a 180 degree zig-zag difference.

Apart from any error and distortion of partial clues, there is also the factor of time, you know. We are constantly following time's arrow here. Marx and Bakunin wrote those words while young guys, when those classes and strata were young, and when the anti-capitalist movement itself was politically very young. That was only starters, and we shouldn't blame any of them if something they said isn't the last word. Everything was still learning, developing, still forming itself. Society has not simply changed, but morphed since then. And still is.

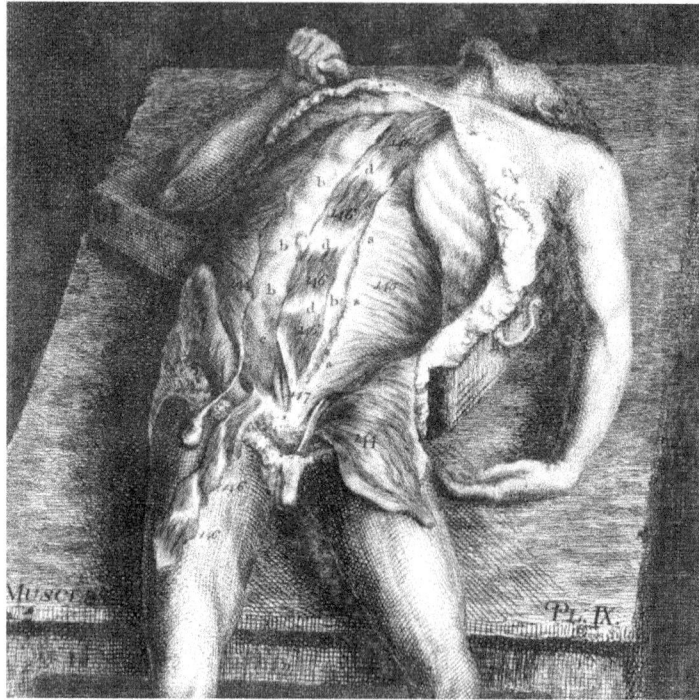

5. forensic analysis of suspect: k. marx

Was talking to a comrade about this work, and she broke in: "I don't see why you're writing about Marx at all? To me he's real 19th century, a stuffy, middle-class white man, and his writings are difficult to read."

That's obviously a popular opinion, but there's also something singular about this situation. The real old dude, Karl, is different here because he was present at the instant of creation. He was the co-discoverer back then of not one but two significant class formations in capitalism: both the lumpen/proletariat and the industrial proletariat itself. He wasn't like an astronomer who discovers a comet; he was more like a scientist who discovers how the solar system is structured. Though he was wrong about some bodies in motion, i'd believe.

We need to scope out his theory about the lumpen/proletariat, not so much to applaud it or diss it, but because all groundbreaking scientific endeavor has an inescapably high "did not work" rate. And we need to understand all the re-search theories and the methodology, so we can avoid the same dead ends and big potholes on the highway. Just because he was a pioneer, estimating and pushing the test results in one direction rather than the other, and lived way back in the 19th century, doesn't mean that any mistakes from back then aren't still being passed along in the political atmosphere. And need to be cleaned up.

Again, we know that most scientific exploration, most theory, is imperfect and often turns out to be not as hoped for under one condition or another. Whether that's some new cancer therapy or new strategies of teaching kids, or the latest "computer security" software patch, or ... you know. This is just reality. So in getting the benefits of any theoretical explorations or discoveries, we need to also know what ideas didn't work as well as what did. And why. Even imperfect theories, even failed theories, are important, because they help fill in blank areas in the map. Guide us away from dead ends and towards the more productive directions. That's pretty useful. Think of this as research, experimental theory, not so black or white, "incorrect" or "correct."

Marx tried to emphasize the *separateness* of the lumpen/proletariat from the industrial proletariat, how *different* the two were, as a major theme in his analysis. In his writings on how the class struggle in France led to the making of a lumpen paramilitary, the regime's *Garde Mobile*, Marx puts his full weight down on this cleavage:

> "... the lumpenproletariat, which in all big towns forms a mass *sharply differentiated* from the industrial proletariat, a recruiting ground for thieves and criminals of all kinds, living on the crumbs of society, people without a definite trade, vagabonds, people without hearth or furniture, unapologetically with no fixed address, varying according to the degree of civilization of the nation to which they belong, but never renouncing their lazzaroni character."[12] [our emphasis]

There are few theoretical overviews of the lumpen which have caused greater misunderstanding than this one.

Because, for starters, the industrial proletariat and the lumpen were born *together*, in the same act of creation and at the same location in society. That is to say: in the same mix of people, at the same address. Marx knew this full well, in fact, but wanted to brush over it for tactical reasons in this one discussion. However, in *Capital* he wrote of the whole historical sweep in Europe which led to the development of a mass of desperately impoverished urban workers, unmoored within a relentlessly violent social cataclysm, without the medieval safety belts of hereditary rights to farm tenancy or being practitioners of restricted guild trades such as locksmithing or textile dyeing or prostitution. This was a big chunk of the transition to full-blown modern capitalism.

> "The proletariat created by the breaking up of the bands of feudal retainers and by the forcible expropriation of the people from the soil, this 'free' proletariat could not possibly be absorbed by the nascent manufactures fast as it was thrown upon the world. On the other hand, these men, suddenly dragged from their wonted mode of life, could not as suddenly adapt themselves to the discipline of their new condition. They were turned en masse into beggars, robbers, vagabonds, partly from inclination, in most cases from stress of circumstances. Hence at the end of

the fifteenth and during the whole of the sixteenth century, throughout Western Europe a bloody legislation against vagabondage. The fathers of the present working class were chastised for their enforced transformation into vagabonds and paupers ...

"Thus were the agricultural people, first forcibly expropriated from the soil, driven from their homes, turned into vagabonds, and then whipped, branded, tortured by laws grotesquely terrible, into the discipline necessary for the wage system."[13]

That is, Marx understood how in making today's capitalist wage labor system, becoming an anonymous laboring class without economic rights or position and being forced for survival into mass criminality were really one and the same event. Being remade involuntarily by the same cutting machinery.

It wasn't that Marx was just some grumpy old guy with a patriarchal beard—his negative view of the lumpen went deeper than that, which is why it still so influences socialists. He had hoped that the new industrial proletariat, however, reduced to "wage slaves," was still in embryo a new scientific-minded class. Forced to be technological, used to innovation and working collectively. Bringing together many different peoples in honest and needful daily labor. This was to him the pioneering, groundbreaking class of men that could remake society. The assorted lumpen were just bad news people you wanted to get lost, in Marx's hopeful futuristic view.

But Marx and Engels didn't see how we always need some outliers to creatively cross lines and go against laws and customs. To be rule-breakers. Finding new shortcuts and paths for the most oppressed and those without hope. That liberation needs Huey Newtons as well as Fannie Lou Hamers. Needed Malcolm X and Eazy-E as well as Jesse Jackson (oh, wait, nobody ever needed Jesse). That the surprise outlaw creativity of the lumpen might be a necessary ingredient, too, to make the mix.

What was most ironic about his righteous diatribes about "thieves and criminals of all kinds, living on the crumbs of society, people without a definite trade, vagabonds," is that Karl himself didn't seem too far from that description. A Jew growing up in Aryan and anti-Semitic Northern Europe, his adult nickname among friends, all his life, was "the Moor."

A battered but game participant in the class struggle, Marx airily dismissed "vagabonds," but he himself had just a few years earlier been arrested for violent treason, had been narrowly acquitted at criminal trial while some of his rappies got life sentences in maxi-maxi, and then was deported permanently from Germany as an unemployed, officially "stateless" alien. Our Karl once in fiscal desperation did apply for a straight job as a railroad clerk (rejected for having illegible scrawl for handwriting), but essentially never did a regular day's labor in his entire life. So Karl was kind of "vag" his own self.

What he was up to theoretically late at night, after office hours, with the lumpen/proletariat becomes clearer when we look at the proletariat itself.

The urban proletariat that had a lusty existence just as industrialization dawned, was no secret to anyone in Europe at that time. Very poor, owning nothing, ever-growing, unable to survive often even with plying a real trade or skilled craft, sometimes criminal and sometimes not, the so-called "swell mob" of the proletariat was infamous to the propertied classes. To them, to educated opinion of the 18th and 19th centuries, it was a rootless class of hereditary criminals that hid behind doing crude hire tasks, living all mixed up in the urban slum streets. As Nicholas Thoburn says about the very word "proletarian":

"… from the fourteenth century up until Marx's era, 'proletarian' was a derogatory term akin to 'rabble' and 'knave'. In Samuel Johnson's 1755 *Dictionary* for example, the proletariat was described as 'mean, wretched, vile, or vulgar', and later in the 1838 *Histoire des classes ouvrieres et des classes bourgeoises*, Granier de Cassagnac described it as a subhuman class formed of a cross between robbers and prostitutes. Haussmann characterized the proletariat as a 'mob of nomads', and in 1850 Thiers spoke of 'this heterogeneous mob, this mob of vagabonds with no avowed family and no domicile, a mob of persons so mobile that they can nowhere be pinned down'."[14]

Marx, whose German Communist League had started life significantly enough calling itself "The Outlaws League"—a sexier name, in my humble opinion—and was made up in large part by migrant clothing makers from the Germanic states, saw in that impoverished mass the birth of a new world-historic class to come.

Marx decided to best frame this new rebel class by calling it the "industrial proletariat." Instead of the old model, of a laboring poor still bound up in the old culture of feudal fealty and mutual loyalties—as in a lord of the land and his hereditary tenants, or a master tradesman and his apprentices and servants who all lived with him—Marx saw a truly modern class forming, bound only by the mass, anonymous cash hiring which brought them inescapably face-to-face with the capitalists as their oppressors. Taught cooperation as workers together in a complex industrial process as well as by urban life. Becoming the new majority as the countryside inexorably kept emptying out, and the industrial cities became the centers of the new civilization.

Seen in this light, a positive vision no less romantic in its own way than Bakunin's "destitute proletariat" and "landless peasants," Marx's scan picking up a discordant "partial-class" of lumpen strata all mixed in with the urban poor was brilliant intuition. The professional robbers and thugs and other trades of committed criminals, who didn't expect or even want to be workers in mundane production and distribution anymore, hardly fit into the moral class culture of the new industrial proletariat, Marx thought. Even though back in the real world they all knew each other, sometimes intimately or warily, as neighbors of the slums, family members, friends and lovers, and landsmen.

It worked out conveniently, then, that Marx's political campaign to rewrite the soiled political image of the "proletariat" into a modern working class, responsible, honest, and forward-looking, was made much easier by a clean theoretical backhand swat. By consigning the violent outlaws, prostitutes, fences, transporters, con-men and other conspirators of the professional criminal trades, all into a different "partial class" altogether. Yes, the "rabble" existed, but it was in the waste bin of the soon to be discarded lumpen/proletariat. Tra-la!

From my very small point of view, growing up half in the lower working class and then struggling politically in the lower depths of capitalism, identifying the lumpen/proletariat as itself, as plainly different folks, makes only common sense. *The real question is what this means politically.*

To identify the lumpen, Marx was sensibly using already-established social markers that came from the eye of his own semi-feudal culture. Three to be precise: living by crime, having no recognized trade or occupation, and being rootless without an established residence, i.e. being a vagabond. In practice, these tell-tale markers made sense, but are by themselves too scattered a blunderbuss shot. Okay for Marx or anyone to put together a rough theoretical scan on unknown ground, maybe in a first approximation. Not, however, good enough now a hundred and fifty years later. To do our revolutionary work, we can't think that simplistically. What was good enough a hundred and fifty or two hundred years ago, as starters back in dinosaur times, isn't good enough now.

Stepping aside here, just a moment, we gotta say something: For some reason, radicals are often encouraged to think that Marx and others of his times were writing ... just to you and me, and speaking about an eternal "now." No, Marx absolutely wasn't writing to you or me. He wasn't writing to any people of color, or anyone who used the internet. Not to women, either, whom he scarcely mentions. And he sure wasn't analyzing today's mutant world which he didn't come close to seeing. Not his fault, that. He was speaking to his own people, men who were politically active in the culture of the mid-1800s European civilization, and he was first crudely trying out various ideas to capture the essence of what was a new reality for him. But it shouldn't be "new" or "unknown" to us.

On the one hand, Marx and Engels were emphasizing how far apart the proletariat and the lumpen/proletariat were, and how—as Fred Engels famously put it—"The lumpenproletariat, this scum of the depraved elements of all classes, which establishes headquarters in the big cities, is the worst of all possible allies. This rabble is absolutely venal and absolutely brazen. If the French workers, in every revolution, inscribed on the houses: *Mort aux voleurs!* Death to thieves! And even shot some, they did it, not out of enthusiasm for property, but because they rightly considered it necessary above all to keep that gang at a distance. Every leader of the workers who uses these scoundrels as guards or relies on them for support proves himself by this action alone a traitor to the movement." Marx's co-writer was sincere, but in my view it was the sincerity of the prosperous bourgeois businessman with socialistic ideas, which Engels also was.[15]

On the other hand, four years before *The Communist Manifesto*, Marx had been sizing up the lumpen/proletariat, although he wasn't publicly calling them that. Speaking particularly about former workers or other insurrectionary veterans, who had enjoyed the exciting movement life so much that they had lost all interest in going back to working-class jobs or civilian life in general. Instead, they now spent their days hanging out in the cafes and bars, hustling the rent money, gossiping and talking up the latest conspiracies:

"It is they who throw up and command the barricades, organize the resistance, plunder the arsenals, lead in the seizure of arms and munitions in homes, and in the midst of the insurrection carry out those daring coups which so often cause disarray in the government ranks. In a word, they are officers of the insurrection."[16]

Marx spoke quite frankly. He then went on to severely criticize that mixed scene of what had become professional conspirators, of lumpen militants and what he felt were dissolute workers, for their bad politics. Which, he pointed out, lead them to be so eager for action that they prematurely start fighting at the first hint of unrest, misjudge political situations, and overestimate the role of technical military factors as against the whole of the workers' movement. At a guess, Marx could well have been right, since these are common errors in revolutionary struggle right now as well as then.

But what is revealed is that in the working-class rebellions of those very tumultuous mid-1800s times, "officers" from the lumpen/proletariat in Marx's own view were right in the thick of things, playing critical roles leading the workers' uprisings—and doing it with full commitment and at least some competence. Not bad for "scum of the depraved elements."

Marx's frustration back then is understandable, but today we wouldn't piss and moan about the need for the lumpen/proletariat to *lead us better* in armed engagements (which, if you boil it down, is one meaning of Marx's somewhat grumpy complaint). Today, we'd emphasize our need to raise the *general* political level of everyone's understanding and competence about how force is needed in groundbreaking ways for revolutionary social change.

When he denounces the lumpen/proletariat, Marx so often talks about the "lazzaroni" and the "lazzaroni character," that he makes this peculiar word sound like the most evil of evils. Which at first confused me, since all i dimly could recall of that was some kind of maybe Italian pastry? Was Marx using some old 19th century leftist argot—like, "The army knew they were in trouble, 'cause they were facing the real 'cookie'!"? But, no, it turns out that lazzaroni were legendary in those times, as the political, criminalized street mobs of Naples in Italy. Made up of many semi-criminal crews of beggars and street workers and hustlers, each crew under the leadership of a chief, the lazzaroni helped repress the bourgeois democratic fever of the 1848 uprisings in Naples, supposedly because of their strong nationalistic loyalty to the reigning royalty (which was apparently loyal to them in turn). This is what caused Marx to demonize them.

But later, in 1860, when Garabaldi was waging his historic military crusade to force out foreign occupiers and unify Italy as one country, that same nationalism caused the lazzaroni to open the streets of Naples for his revolution. They had politics, but it wasn't as simple as left or right, but had an orientation of their own class viewpoint from the street.

When he was explaining the French state using some lumpen for a new counterinsurgency militia, Marx threw an around-the-corner curve ball about the lumpen/proletariat which has famously confused radicals to this day: *"... at the youthful age at which the Provisional Government recruited them, thoroughly malleable, as capable of the most heroic deeds and the most exalted sacrifices as of the basest banditry and the foulest corruption."*[17]

Marx wasn't getting the big bucks to make anyone's revolutionary life easier. i mean, i guess he had to report his initial findings and evaluations no matter how headache-producing. What was he really saying? That the lumpen when caught as young teenagers can be brainwashed to do *any*thing and become *any*one, no matter how angelic or devilish? (Which is what his words seem to mean.) In any case, Marx had all the bases covered there; no matter what any lumpen did, good or bad, you could say he predicted it. But you can see how such richly imaginative intellectual advice can be really confusing. i think that Karl had caught a flashing glimpse of something real there, but didn't have enough evidence yet to more fully diagram it. We'll come around to this point again.

The actual political positions of the lumpen do vary much more widely than usual, since this is a "non-class" or some assemblage which fell out of all other classes. It also is oriented by the society or nation they are in. Mainstream working-class politics have a similarity in country after country—trade unionism or workers' associations, fighting against the factory owners and landlords, being for protective social legislation, and so on. Same with the capitalist class, only flipped over in reverse. But not so when it comes to the lumpen/proletariat.

There is a widespread theoretical mistake in the movement, to reify the crude over-simplification of theory understandable for Marx and Bakunin's times an age ago. Which is maybe okay if you are just having a drink and shooting the shit—but which is not functional in thinking out the problems of the struggle. This results in a mechanistic distortion of class politics, a reductionism. Like, believing that everyone who works on factory assembly lines has the same politics. Or that everyone who lives by criminal activity must have similar politics. Class identity being so human, it is a lot more sensual and many-layered and grounded in a specific terrain than that.

It is critical for us all to keep in mind that the actual politics of the lumpen vary widely, shaped by the situation of the society or nation they are in. Marx was trying to do class analysis for capitalism as a system, as a whole. But really he was only able to base his analysis on a small European sample, a small minority of our human race. He couldn't really know anything about lumpen in rural China or Oakland, California. To say nothing about women's relationship to the lumpen/proletariat, which he clearly never even thought about. It be *terra incognita* to him, as they say. It's too bad, since if Marx had thought about women and the lumpen in class terms, which is a startling field, he might have been shocked into the next century or two!

You know, Mumia Abu-Jamal reminds us: *"Prison is the dressing room of America, where everyone is naked. The hatreds are more open, unalloyed. So is the repression. That's often because the state has immersed two distinct populations together, who would not mix in the exterior world—poor whites (guards) and poor Blacks (prisoners)."* He's talking about both sides—the poor white guards and the poor Black prisoners—being the mix at their respective nation's bottom of lumpen/proletarian and lower-working class, but one side earning a modest but respectable living repressing the other as their most hated enemy. As Mumia observes, gazing though the dry gin and tonic of life: *"For many Blacks who don't have historical knowledge, prison is a rude awakening indeed ..."*[18]

What Mumia significantly isn't saying, because he doesn't need to, is that New Afrikan prisoners aren't led by goody-goody organizations like the NAACP, but by lumpen groups like the hunger strikers in maxi-maxi prisons with their radical demands for the abolition of the u.s. 13th Amendment, or the Gangster Disciples or Nation of Islam. While white prisoners, who are absolutely there also though in often smaller numbers, aren't led by respectably dead and stuffed euro-settler organizations like the American Jewish Congress or the Tea Party, but by lumpen criminal groups such as the Aryan Brotherhood. (It isn't that all prisoners are lumpen—far from it, there are many

We mostly only see the clowns and losers, you know, when it comes to euro-settler lumpen. Most white lumpen are "invisible" because they aren't in conspicuous revolt against bourgeois society, no matter how much they privately despise it. To see just one part of these strata: They can get lots of weapons and legal permission to invade and occupy and beat and kill colonized peoples, while wearing tough uniforms and getting a nice salary, too. Why look like a weirdo parading around in a Nazi costume, when you can be a police officer or a guard or a career military professional and do blood sport for real? And their class population spreads far wider than that in this parasitic oppressor society, too.

Military "contractors" in Afghanistan.

working-class prisoners and even middle-class prisoners. But the kind of command organizations which can take power in the permanent war environment of the kamps are not usually civilian ones.) One side is for Black criminal revolt against the oppressor society, while the other side is for doing euro-settler genocide and white supremacist fascism. Both are lumpen populations, forced into the same small arenas, but with different violent politics that can't hardly get any further apart.

When i say that we can't use simplistic markers to chart the lumpen/proletariat as a class, here's an example of what this means:

Back in the old days, one of the small political support things i did briefly was collect cans of food for the struggle down in Cairo. That was a little town on the banks of the Mississippi River, way, way down at the Southern-most tip of Illinois state. What even most Americans don't know, is that those towns and cities on the Mississippi had historically been integrated into the economy and culture of the Slave South, upriver of them but connected to them by trade culture. All the way up to St. Louis, which when i was young still marked the divide between "free" North and Segregated South (That's where when i first got on them, Grey-hound buses on the routes going South all had metal signs by the front steps, politely instructing "Negroes" to sit in the back seats only). Cairo was pronounced not like the Egyptian city but differently, somewhat like the ever-present kay-ro syrup, and was as close in miles to Jackson, Mississippi as it was to Chicago, Illinois—and in culture was a damn sight closer to Mississippi.

The militant freedom struggle in Cairo was fierce, with imprisonment and gunplay being common as tipping your hat. So savage, but so determined on the New Afrikan part, that their local civil rights group, the United Front of Cairo, and their brilliant young leader, the Rev. Charles Koen, were famous in New Afrikan communities coast to coast. Since the klan used to do drive-bys, using rifles and shotguns, blasting away at the Black public housing project every weekend, Rev. Koen's group was unabashed about shooting back in return. The klan was covered for by the local white police, who also liked joining in the "free fire zone," shoot 'em up atmosphere. *It was a war,* to quote one H. Rap Brown.

At one South Side apartment where i dropped off the few groceries i'd managed to collect for the embattled Cairo people, there was a teenager, clearly one of those in charge. Can't remember if we ever got his name, but in any case always privately called him "Young General" (a very Asian macho name). He was maybe 16 or 17, and belonged to one of Chicago's main street organizations. What impressed me, was that he had organized weekend car caravans of youth from Chicago's various big "gangs" to go together to deliver support.

Ammo was being packed, too, and it turned out that the primary task the "gang" convoy was doing was to stick around down there every weekend. Adding a number of shooters to the active defenses of the housing project at night. They were pretty proud of driving off the klan and cops on numerous occasions, protecting families—and, by the way, didn't see much difference if any at all between the klan and the cops. Call that a way pre-Ferguson awareness. One weekday night at the food drop-off place, the "Young General" looked at the time, then said to the crew from his organization, *"Time to go to work."* After they left, found out he meant it was time to go do their burglaries of white businesses, which was how he and the guys in his crew made a scant living.

So here's a kid with no trade or occupation, unless you might call it being a soldier, and earning a living from crime. Was he lumpen/proletarian according to some classic definition? Really, the fact

was that he was consciously a solidly lower working-class guy. With you bet'cha working-class politics. Though perilously balanced on the class borders, for sure.

Came from a union family that had worked in the factories and fought the corporations, and was proud of that. Smart as he was, could have made much more money in the drug trade or some other hustle. There were no "legal" jobs for him then, and in his community the drug trade was like the nearby mill or mine was to the early European working-class towns or neighborhoods. It was the community economy. Not his path, though.

He wasn't giving speeches about it, that's certain. However, when i looked at what he was doing, what the practice actually was, there was a pattern so sharply cut you could pick it up and put it in your jacket pocket: he was organizing his street organization brethren to go to the front lines, and do their soldiering defending their People, not throw down killing others just like themselves. And he recruited his nighttime crew on the same principle. Rather than sell poison to your own People, you can forcefully take your survival from the white oppressors themselves, ripping it right out of their wallets. Survival itself can chew so fine. You can see why i called him "Young General," in serious respect.

He was living and working and developing his politics violating the law every step, doing crime and dangerous crime at that, just about as regularly as some of us would punch in at the factory. Wasn't his a real working-class politics, though? It's telling that *his* crimes and *his* group's use of violence were so very different in essence from the crime and group violence that so many lumpen street leaderships were ordering up in their auto-homicidal civil wars over territory and dope. In both cases, poor New Afrikan young males using guns and doing crimes—but in handling the texture of the class politics, your hand knew the real difference. One was pulling people up, the other was pushing them down.

Keep in mind that especially the young, especially those balancing on the borders of one class and another, can and do change classes, voluntarily and involuntarily, even back and forth sometimes. Young General was fighting, was struggling, consciously, to stay working-class in the criminal activity that he was pushed into. Or to be lumpen but in a political and conscious way, even as the pull of the tide moved him. Who knows, later he might have been hijacked by the cops and judges into a "bid" downstate, and after prison pulled down further into the "street." Even when classes remain coherent as they evolve, people in them at the edges come and go in constant motion. And the class is ever changed by what they do.

When Marx was writing that poor street youth in Paris right then were highly impressionable, liable to be led left or right, this is the reality he was grasping only the surface of. Not simply to be pawns or followers of established entities and forces, though. To also make their own way, in new paths of their making. Which is why we also understand class life as so "sensuous," to use a favorite description of his.

Of all this, it is as the poet Wu Cheng'en wisely said: "Locked in tight embrace, the vital powers are ever strong; even in the midst of fierce flames the golden lotus may be planted, the five elements compounded and transposed, and all put to new use."

6. evolution of left views on lumpen

There have been many zigs and zags, bursts of new experiences and new radical theory about the lumpen/proletariat since back then, of course. In the 1920s–30s, the Chinese Revolution recorded an indication of its breakthrough view of lumpen/proletariat through Mao's social investigations and theoretical work. Just as in the 1950–60s, the anti-colonial revolutions against the West made new observations off of Frantz Fanon's writings. These were theoreticians studied worldwide by millions of revolutionaries. Leading to a decisive change by 1960s lumpen/proletarians themselves, such as Huey Newton and George Jackson of the Black Panther Party for Self-Defense and the Black Guerrilla Family, writing their own theory about themselves. Thing is, even the newest of those politics are outmoded now, not working as theory should. Their shiny gleam rubbed off, the short-circuits and cracks in places obvious if we look.

There is one striking thing about how Marx first described the lumpen/proletariat back then. It's all about *men*. If you focus on that list of roués and escaped galley slaves and swindlers and porters and literati and so on comprising his projected lumpen/proletariat, most of the categories were mainly or completely male. This fits right into the constant masculine image of the lumpen/proletariat that crowds our own news today. Whether it's the young adventurers in warlord militias, executing male civilians while seizing their women relatives as slaves, or more commonly young foot soldiers burning their lives up like warning flares in drug mafias and street organizations.

Only one of Marx's 19th century colorful list of examples—brothel keeper—was primarily a women's position. This is a striking imbalance. Actually, when the subject of women and the lumpenproletariat is raised, prostitution or sex work always pops right up. Marx had put "prostitute" in his tattered crowd of "scum" bottom dwellers. Certainly, Marxists worldwide regularly have considered sex workers a conspicuous part of the "reactionary" lumpen/proletariat, as Mao and Lenin did. And many revolutionaries today still do.

To many leftists this has only been a normal kind of assumption, not worth going into in a patriarchal world. What if it isn't "normal," though? It's like a sudden surfacing of the actual structure of society, which lets us see momentarily lit up what the social strata truly are. Those that are pushed aside, judged too insignificant and marginal or even deformed to matter, can be a key to unlocking our understanding of the larger whole. We're going to shift our focus onto this.

7. women interpenetrate lumpen/proletariat

Since we have our teeth into this subject, we might as well really get to the meat of it. Traditional bourgeois discussion of prostitutes has tried to judge them more or less as objects. Are they "immoral" or are they "degenerate criminals," or merely "tragic victims" (the last being the favorite left position)? With it being tacitly understood that their own views do not count. Objects can't judge themselves. Nor do we ask the fox if she is feral.

Instead of this, for revolutionaries it might be more relevant to ask what

their *politics* and *political role* are? Are prostitutes "degenerates" politically, too? Do their lives "prepare" them "far more for the part of a bribed tool of reactionary intrigue"? Are they likely police informers and agents, enemies of the oppressed? Which is what i was told when first joining the old socialist left as a teenager. There may be social investigations that factually verify these now quite ancient but still commonly repeated charges, but, you know, i have never seen one.

So what little do i know about this?

When one of my sisters entered the ninth grade, she was still a skinny kid without sexual experience or romantic experience of any kind. But she got an offer to become a sex worker, in which she would be paid as a live-in companion, providing sex for a well-known businessman, every weekend. For a quite poor working-class child, the money was important and she would still be able to stay in school. That was a difficult decision for her to make, though. Finally, she went for it—which changed her life, of course.

The point here is, what happened when we flip the clock forward over a decade. In the late 1960s, my sister was living in California. In the same state, two part-time community college students named Huey Newton and Bobby Seale started an armed anti-police organization with revolutionary aims, which they named the Black Panther Party for Self-Defense. My sister was an early local supporter, coming before the start of their demos so that she could paint placards for the young teenage Panthers to carry. At that time, she was also active in the brand new Asian-American consciousness-raising movement. She wasn't any "heavy" or any kind of leader, but was a serious supporter of whatever liberation was breaking out.

My sister was certainly lumpen, definitely a material girl (having a nice Benz was a life goal to her), and no fan of the straight working life. But where did she stand then *politically* in the struggle? Was she "scum of the depraved elements of all classes," as Engels charmingly put it? i would say that what she really *did*, her actions when the struggle broke out and everyone had to take a stand on one side or the other, was the answer.

We noted how Marx wrote that brothel-keepers in France were part of the "indefinite, disintegrated mass" of criminalized social discards who were so eager to be parasites on the "laboring nation" and serve the ruling class in repressive ways. This was not necessarily unrealistic on his part. In general, there are no secret brothels except in novels and male fantasies. It isn't social work agencies who regulate brothels, after all, but the police apparatus. This is a regular and quite profitable job of theirs. Particularly in the France of Marx's day, where brothels were often licensed and routinely officially inspected by the police, the brothel-keepers were assumed to gather information for them.

But how should that translate for us here? Back in our times, a member of my family was the operator of an escort service, which is a functional though not cultural equivalent to the brothel in our digital age of Craigslist. The idea to start her escort service came from some of the sex workers themselves, who knew her at the local business where she had worked.

Corrupt informer and servant of the police? In fact, when a dispute happened between the police brass and some local small businesses, because the officials wanted a bigger "under the table" cut of business income, the escort service got caught up in what weren't even originally her hassles. Her women started getting arrested on the street all the time, and the police wanted to muscle into the business and take more of the profits. She refused to knuckle under. Finally closing the escort service and going back to not earning much and being a wage worker rather than work for the cops. She certainly wasn't going to be any kind of flunky for them. This refusal wasn't even "political," in her own view.

These small examples may puzzle some leftists, since my sister was stone lumpen, but was politically engaged like many university radicals might have been in those rebellious times. And the other relative from a younger generation was deeply involved in the sex trade, in what is usually considered a lumpen class role, but her tough, antagonistic attitude towards the cops was much more what we'd consider working-class. Neither was

necessarily "typical" politically of women in the sex industry, but of those i've known in the life they were certainly in a normal range on the political spectrum.

It isn't that prostitutes or people in the sex trade are all anti-capitalist or rebels, any more than anyone else ordinarily is. Nor can they just be taken as ordinary workers or shopkeepers, since patriarchal capitalism has criminalized them. **It's that the old male left stereotype of their alleged *politics* may be no more real than any of the other patriarchal stereotypes and fantasies placed involuntarily on them all the time.**

Not that lumpen/proletarian women don't hesitate to pull the trigger any more than lumpen men do. Or work every corner of the intersection. When one wanted guy in the old Black Liberation Army was beating on his girlfriend severely, she got scared for her life. So she turned him in to a relative who was a cop. Just dropped that dime and trashed him. That wasn't a bind my sister was ever in, so she didn't have to cross to that corner of the street. Nor was she ever kidnapped and imprisoned in an anonymous brothel in some foreign city. She escaped those types of experiences.

This is how we start, to repair revolutionary theory in the only way we can.

By reexamining previous theory, summing up "book knowledge" and street knowledge, recharging theory with what we learn by interrogating the practical results of the class activity of millions. Which constantly goes on all around us and in which we are immersed.

This is difficult with the lumpen/proletariat, since fragmentary evidence we have shows more than the normal *political* distortions at work. In the epoch-making Paris Commune of 1871, the first successful European socialist revolution, most prostitutes were not on the side of the Commune from what we know. That could have had something to do with the fact that the Commune seemed determined to wipe them out. And not as a figure of speech.

In the tumult of the new revolutionary democratic society, there was a spontaneous patriarchal movement to "clean up" the public life of Paris by eliminating brothels and prostitutes. In the 2nd arrondissement the council closed the licensed brothels, while in the 15th arrondissement they had the prostitutes arrested. New laws were being prepared to imprison all prostitutes citywide. Was it so strange that women involved in the life were more than a little cynical about the left?

Edith Thomas tells us that even at the military infirmary set up at the Hotel de Ville, prostitutes showing up wanting to help care for the wounded were turned away. This was witnessed by Louise Michel, the great anarchist fighter and political firebrand of the Commune. "They were refused this honor, for, Louise Michel noted, the men of the Commune wanted pure hands tending the Federals ... Therefore, she directed them to a committee of women (the 18th arrondissement Vigilance Committee? The *Union des Femmes*?) 'whose spirits were generous enough to let these women be welcomed.' 'We shall never bring shame down upon the Commune,' these prostitutes said. Many, indeed, died courageously on the barricades during the Bloody Week in May ..."[19]

There is an even more famous example, of sex workers intervening in a desperate war against capitalism. In Kenya, during the 1950s anti-colonial rebellion to oust the British empire, Mau Mau freedom fighters in Kenya faced a crisis when their scant initial stores of rifle ammunition started to run out. These they had gotten from the settler estates and colonial police barracks they had overrun in early surprise attacks. But once warned, these easy sources of supply from the enemy were under guard.

Somali woman defends herself
against Islamic men's gang,
who are ripping her clothes off in the street.

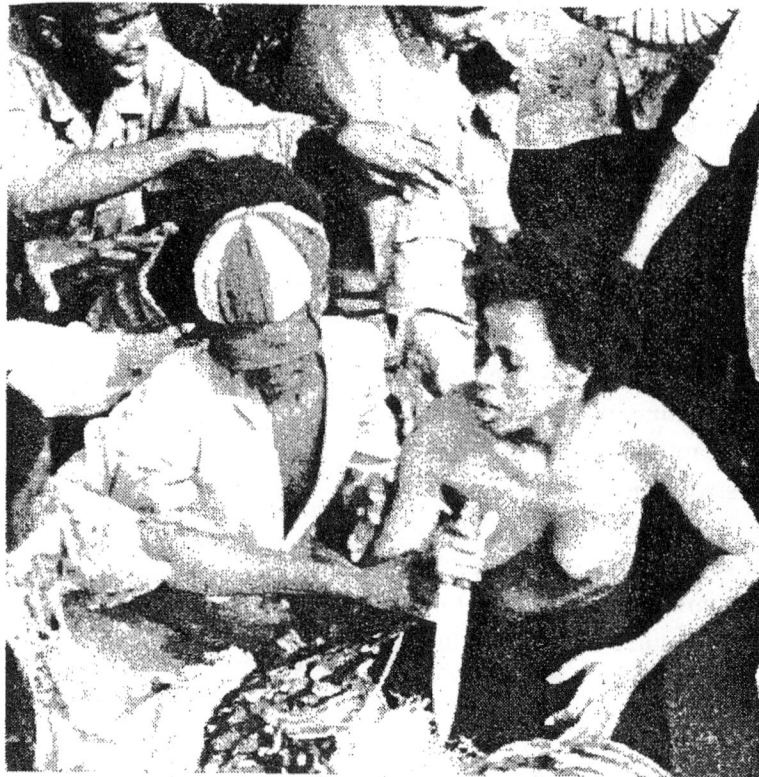

'If we say the world of the man is the state, the world of
the man is his commitment, his struggle on behalf of the
community, we could then perhaps say that the world of the
woman is a smaller world. For her world is her husband,
her family, her children and her home. But where would the
big world be if no-one wanted to look after the small world?
How could the big world continue to exist, if there was no-
one to make the task of caring for the small world the centre
of their lives? No, the big world rests upon this small
world! The big world cannot survive if the small world is
not secure.'

Adolf Hitler, speech to
the National Socialist Women's organization,
Nuremberg Party Rally, 8 September, 1934.

In return for sex, some prostitutes started getting a few bullets at a time from the colonial Afrikan mercenaries serving the British, these precious bullets saved up and then carried at night into the forests for the guerrillas. In a few cases, prostitutes worked "honey traps," where Mau Mau men broke in and snatched weapons and ammunition from British soldiers after they had undressed and had their attention completely diverted. Working women also aided the guerrilla war in other ways, all of which had its own contradictions since the Mau Mau in theory proscribed prostitution, and punished their men who maintained intimate relationships with sex workers. Isn't that how it goes?

In many cases, the sex workers who supported the Mau Mau rebellion had very different circumstances than the capitalist ideology of prostitution would have us believe. As in all countries, in colonial Kenya sex work as a practical trade had different categories, each with its own realities. The *malaya* prostitutes provided workers in the colonial economy, often separated from their homes for long periods of time, with a simulation of being cared for, of having a "home." They entertained men in their small homes, serving tea and providing warm water for baths, serving dinner and spending the night in conversation and sex.

To many *malaya* prostitutes, the life was a refuge from forced marriages. Where they would have to provide sex for a man without any choice, as well as do lifetime unwaged hard labor and bear children to enrich him in a definite kind of enslavement. Runaway wives and young women refusing to obey the authority of their fathers to be traded off as property, were common among them. It was capitalist marriage and the patriarchal family that were life-threatening for them, more than sex work with strangers.

The possible financial independence of these Kenyan prostitutes was most important to them. "At home, what could I do?" one *malaya* woman said. "Grow crops for my husband or father. In Nairobi I can earn my own money, for myself." Those who handled their money well, often saved enough to buy small real estate or livestock. In the 1930s, half of the landlords in Pumwami, a Nairobi suburb where much of the sex trade took place then, were *malaya* women. Fighting off legal challenges by fathers and their patriarchal birth families, these sex workers could take an heir to leave their house and money to. "This is my heir," a prostitute would declare in front of other *malaya* women, designating a younger woman who would help take care of her in her old age and then inherit. Deliberately

41

creating matrilineal families of their own design. There was much group aid and cooperative help in dealing with the police and courts. So some of them were rebels not only in terms of fighting for the ouster of British colonialism, but in stepping outside the colonialism of the patriarchal culture they came from.[20]

What i can see is that old male left views on the *politics* of sex workers have been simplistic and wildly inaccurate. There are also problems of their class positioning, in the lumpen/proletariat. Of fitting them into any male-centered class, maybe. And many people have long asked, how can prostitutes be "parasites on society," if the only person they might exploit in a Marxian sense is themselves? The radical cultural critic Walter Benjamin remarked long ago on capitalism's ambiguous commodity *"fetish ... provided by the whore, who is both seller and commodity in one."*

It's interesting that sex workers are supposed to be a completely marginal phenomena, maybe of interest to the social worker, the feminist intellectual, and the cop, but unimportant to the workings of society. Yet they don't seem so marginal at all, once we pull aside the mental curtains.

For instance, there have been three auto plants in the larger Chicago area, two assembly plants and one stamping plant. (The Chrysler plant is being remodeled; the two Ford factories are notorious for sexual assaults and harassment of women workers, with over a hundred women even making official complaints to the u.s. government about it. And perhaps for that reason one of those plants has had a woman plant manager.) In good years, with added shifts and hot new truck or car models, the total employment at these three plants was still far under 10,000 workers. Still, mayors and governors may attend ribbon-cutting ceremonies for the media when a new model first rolls off the line. Auto factories are big in the economy, everyone knows that.

Then there's this: According to Illinois State Attorney-General Lisa Madigan in 2014, there were approximately 16,000 sex workers in the city of Chicago. Many thousands more than auto workers. For a social category, remember, which cannot be readily counted since it is criminalized and stigmatized and driven into semi-invisibility at the edges of society. Could sex workers be as meaningful in a different way to actually-existing capitalism as workers at automobile factories?

To look at this same question turned inside out: In this same year, lumpen/proletarian warlord movements such as Boko Haram in Nigeria and the Islamic

State in Iraq and Syria, were aggressively looting villages of young women and girls for use and trade as slaves, among the most important commodities for them. Those women were becoming sex workers whether they knew it or not, by one of the ways it historically happens. We are seeing women and the raw creation of transitory societies and shadow states. This is on the cutting edge of actually-existing late capitalism.

It's clear now that existing revolutionary theory has a class analysis of sex workers like we have travel guides to the dark side of the moon. What we need is to better understand just what it is we *don't* know. For one thing, we don't know enough to meaningfully identify the *politics* prostitutes or sex workers have and act on, here and now. In large measure, this is due to the criminalization they exist in. Sex workers, like much of the lumpen/proletariat, live in the constant haze of criminalization, which capitalism denies any responsibility for while at the same time sucking off it and regulating it as an important resource like oil or drugs. Again, we haven't understood this well enough to forge usable class analysis about it yet.

Advocates for the human rights of sex workers have demanded that the decaying proscription around them be blown up. That as one step the term "prostitute" with its heavily negative connotations be replaced in our everyday usage by plain "sex worker." Acknowledging the right of this, i still deliberately use both words here because the old language continues to radiate the malicious patriarchy which is our ruling culture, and still represents their criminalization. Which no one should forget for one minute. This is something a reform of some words won't cure.

45TH PRESIDENT OF THE UNITED STATES OF AMERICA

8. theory mao tossed to us

Like a hand grenade of ideas thrown from the distance into our skirmishes, when Mao's iconic writings from the 1920s–30s were finally translated and widely disseminated here in the 1950s–60s, revolutionary theory on the lumpen/proletariat underwent a major shift. We still haven't come to grips with the confusion of that change, even though the blast zone is far behind us on the highway now.

While appearing to follow the form of the Marx & Engels class analysis of the stormy petrel of the lumpen/proletariat, Mao's theoretical take represented a big remodeling job. A sharper turn, in fact, than i personally could hold onto or understand back then. Mao Z most famously explained the lumpen/proletariat's difference from all other classes in his analysis of Chinese society in 1926:

> "Apart from all these, there is a fairly large *lumpen*-proletariat, made up of peasants who have lost their land and handicraftsmen who cannot get work. They lead the most precarious existence of all. In every part of the country they have their secret societies ... One of China's most difficult problems is how to handle these people. Brave fighters, but apt to be destructive, they can become a revolutionary force if given proper guidance."[21]

This is a sharply abbreviated version of the opening chapters in *Mao Z's Revolutionary Laboratory & The Lumpen/Proletariat,* which is the work in the second part of this book. Readers interested in following up the complex class experience of the Chinese Revolution should definitely read the complete version in our companion article.

Mao Z's terse last line summing up the lumpen for the revolution, became famous among many revs in the 1960s–70s. From Anti-War organizers to the Black Panthers who quoted it frequently, the line reverberating and influencing far beyond the much smaller ranks of those who called themselves "Maoists." It seemed so basic, it didn't occur to would-be revolutionaries like myself that it wasn't anywhere near as simple as it seemed, and that in fact i didn't fully understand it at all.

Mao Z's starting analysis accepted the lumpen as ordinary people, not as primarily "dangerous" or exotic. Our guy wasn't afraid of them. Humanizing them in his analysis, Mao was painting there with broad brushstrokes, in optimistic colors, of the lumpen as victims shaped by poverty and oppression—thus as potential revolutionary tinder. This concise, seemingly easy to understand explanation of Mao's was a pretty radical change of class understanding for Marxists back then. It reflected a newer understanding of realities out in the capitalist periphery.

The other thing that many of us didn't grasp, is that Mao's words weren't just another theory, like Marx or Bakunin had. Mao's theories were in a whole different ballpark from those earlier comrades. Not because he was necessarily any more observant, but because his theory was shaped by the political experiences of millions of lumpen over almost *two generations in China from the early 1900s to the 1940s. These ideas had been reforged over and over on the anvil of oppressed people's experience*, up to and including all-out revolutionary war, year after year. Understanding paid for in many human lives, and which carried that more than one individual's personal weight to it.

What our guy Mao Z knew even then, subtly coloring those first words in 1926 when he called them a potential "revolutionary force," was that the lumpen played a key role in the revolutionary process for him. They weren't just bit players or minor actors on the large stage of overturning society. The lumpen in China were a major, and even at some times and places a *decisive* factor, in the mass revolutionary struggle that actually took place. Whether that fit anyone's theory or not. They burst through all that. That's what becomes clearer when analyzing in depth the class politics of the Chinese revolutionary experience.

THE "VAGABOND ARMY"

Over and over, in the struggle in those early years, Mao Z ran into and found common cause with lumpen/proletarian fighters. Retreating after the disastrous, ambitious, 1927 "Autumn Harvest Uprising" during the first year of the open civil war, the small core of a thousand revolutionary soldiers led by Mao took shelter upon the Chingkangshan mountain range, an elevated and remote plateau that was a traditional refuge for bandits and other fugitives. They were only a tenth of the forces that uprising had started with, and Mao Z had been disavowed by the Central Committee and stripped of his party leadership positions. Not that it had made much difference to those revolutionaries resting and regaining strength on the mountains. They were being schooled in learning how to survive as guerrillas 101.

The "red" survivors ran into two bandit chiefs who were said to be Triad secret society members—Wang Tso and Yuan Wen-t'sai—with their little armies. Both of them former bandits turned army unit commanders of the new modern capitalist national army, turned back to bandit leaders. Their bands quickly became "red" and joined Mao's small army on the mountain, which increased then from one to three "regiments" (later, after Mao's main force left the area, they were rumored to have reverted to banditry again; in any case both chiefs were killed in the constant fighting of that time, as so many were).[22]

Starting the next Spring of 1928, other "red" forces began converging with Mao's as the new Red Army began to take shape. General Chu Teh (*Zhu De* in the new translation system) became the commander-in-chief of the rapidly growing central Red Army, with Mao Z as the chief political officer, in a historic partnership that shifted the center of gravity of the entire revolutionary leadership to the distant universe of mass guerrilla war in the countryside. Chu Teh was then the more famous, as a noted mercenary general, and the force—with its many tens of thousands of soldiers—was often called "the Chu-Mao army" in the Chinese newspapers and by the public.

A career military officer, in difficult circumstances Chu Teh had won battlefield promotion to general, and was a star in Chinese military circles. Holding powerful capitalist government offices that came with a high income from the customary bribes and graft, Chu Teh soon had a mansion, a harem with several wives as well as concubines, and a heavy opium habit. Before he conquered his long-time addiction to put everything else away and become a revolutionary. It's no surprise that Chu Teh was also a senior member of the lumpen/proletarian Elder Brothers, a tie he freely admitted actively sustaining and using in his Communist guerrilla years.[23]

The Elder Brothers were the dominant lumpen secret society in the key Yangtze valley region. Many members came to hold responsible positions in the local revolutionary movement and the insurgent Red military.

In those first years of the Red Army, when the whole democratic movement was reeling on the defensive, retreating under constant attack, forced under that great repressive pressure to transform into an illegal mass movement of undergrounds and partisan organizers and rebel militias and soldiers by the many thousands—or perish—the lumpen/proletariat were the indispensible social base for the revolutionaries. Not simply some useful people, but temporarily the key strata, maybe not according to anyone's admitted political doctrine but in the actual real time situation.

At the party's 1929 Gutian conference, two years after the Red Army's founding, Mao Z's report on their political-military situation bluntly said that their military's "roving banditism" and other such political problems had their root in the reality that *"the lumpen-proletariat constitute the majority in the Red Army"* (while in those years of rebuilding right after the Autumn Harvest uprising, Mao also had reported that *"the soldiers of peasant or working class origin in the Fourth Army in the Border Region constitute an extreme minority."*). Lumpen/proletarian soldiers were the definite *majority* of the many thousands of revolutionary fighters under his leadership. Although neither Mao Z nor the rest of the party leadership were eager to broadcast this heretical and scandalous situation.[24]

PEASANT CHINA THROWS MILLIONS INTO THE GAME

This major revolutionary role for the lumpen was only normal, we should say, in the context of China then. Since the same surprising class configuration had been responsible for the much larger mass movement which the new revolution drew its lifeblood from. A giant peasant rebellion in the form of militant Peasant Associations had broken out in 1926 across Southern China, centered in the expansive rural countryside of Hunan Province and contiguous areas, and comprising at least 4.5 million peasants.

In reporting on the new rebellion in the countryside, Mao Z *didn't* place the Communist Party at the center of events, because they weren't. Although the relatively small numbers of Communist cadres would try to hold village meetings and inspire the peasants to start local branches of the associations, before quickly moving on as they usually had to. Instead, he placed as the key instigators a new grouping of the most oppressed themselves—which he referred to as the *"utterly destitute."*

This was difficult to pin down on the surface, because the party was reporting from the countryside through a filter. Bluntly, closeting the lumpen as much as possible. Because the major role of the lumpen in the revolution was so counter to established Marxist doctrine, both Mao Zedong and the party itself worked to lessen the flashy guest appearances of their lumpen/proletariat on late-night tv. Remember, this was a time when Mao Z was being heavily attacked within the party for recognizing the radical potential of lumpen outlaws. Party leader Li Li-san even explicitly criticized him for the sin of *"guerrillaism infected by the viewpoint of the lumpenproletariat."*[25]

In Mao's 1927 "Report on an Investigation of the Peasant Movement in Hunan," referring to surveys which showed the overall shape of the movement, Mao mentions one in Changsha county, which counted the poor peasants as 70% of the Peasant Associations' membership. Which Mao thought representative for the overall membership of the militant Peasant Associations in Hunan province. Mao then added a significant point, that **there was a sub-category of the very most poor, the "utterly destitute," which accounted for 20% of the peasant movement's total members.**

Even more, Mao goes on to say that almost all the grassroots leadership at the local level were poor peasants and especially the very poorest. In fact, according to Mao, in one of the best-surveyed areas with mature peasant organizations, it was shown that "... of the officials in the township associations in Hengshan County **the utterly destitute comprise 50 per cent** ..." There's no question that this newly identified social strata he named *"the utterly destitute"* played a key leadership role in the militant movement, apparently far beyond their size in the population. But who were they?

In fact, the *"utterly destitute"* were our old friends the rural lumpen/proletariat all over again. The Communist Party central committee editorial group supervising the later republishing of Mao's writings admitted that by the *"utterly destitute,"* Mao specifically meant two groups together: the "rural *lumpen*-proletariat" and the "rural proletariat." The second was only a tiny fig leaf. What was really happening was that the rural lumpen themselves were playing a big grassroots leadership role in the rural uprising that would transform all China. A good day, for outcasts and outlaws.

It seems that everywhere Mao looked in those early days of the 20th century in rural China, the lumpen/proletariat were involved when battles against the rulers broke out. That this was true of the most important mass movement in China's history—the peasant movement which became the popular base of anti-capitalist guerrilla war and eventual revolution—only throws more fuel onto our theoretical camp fire.[26]

It was not all positive report cards. As the revolutionary war developed, in 1939 Mao Z himself warned party cadres that it was in the nature of the lumpen to *"waver"* and *"vacillate"* between revolution and counter-revolution. At the same time, however, he reaffirmed that at the root most lumpen/proletarians still remained innocent victims of oppression who needed the revolution's help in liberating and reforming themselves. Less positively, he warned: *"While one portion is easily brought over by the reactionary forces, the other portion has the possibility of participating in the revolution."*[27]

In general, within the oppressed zone of the periphery, the criminalized world is much larger than the lumpen/proletariat. While in the oppressor zone of the imperialist metropolis, the reverse is true. Their criminalized world is much smaller than their considerable lumpen. And now neo-colonialism is smashing these once-distant worlds into each other, probably just to confuse us.

9. rechecking original code

Karl Marx's quick, off-hand description in *The Communist Manifesto* of the lumpen as "that passively rotting mass" was a dramatic shout from off-stage—but it didn't give anyone much of a practical handle in dealing with the lumpen. Rather, it was in Karl M's post-1848 revolutionary scribbling on the protracted political crisis in France, as well as on the evolution of the early French capitalist state itself, that the question of the lumpen/proletariat was addressed more in depth. In ways that are still daring conceptually. As well as dangerously incomplete. Here our reading gets a little more complex, the ground under our bedtime slippers surprising and uneven.

While everyone associates Marx with his massive and largely unread *Capital*, Marx scholars say that it's his political writings on revolutionary France that have long attracted the most intellectual attention and debate. Which centers strangely enough around the supposedly minor-league lumpen/proletariat itself.

What's so critical for us about searching this large historical warehouse, is that this is where Marx did his most sustained exploration of the lumpen/proletariat's possible roles in capitalist crisis. These are ideas which still strongly influence—and, frankly, confuse—socialist politics. In this location, we find his most searching negative forecasts as well as his most creative questions about the lumpen's role in class evolution. Questions as of now still unanswered. Which we will try to measure.

By the way, Karl Marx's contemporary analysis of French society and politics in general is not our subject here, though we respect its daring. What we are doing is narrowly focusing on what we can learn from certain roles played by that emerging lumpen/proletariat, in both the light and shadows of his view.

Taking in the lumpen in the revolutionary center that was 19th century Paris, in real time for him, brought things to a decisive theoretical point for our guy Karl.

As he and Fred Engels said, it was his first attempt to use their new method of historical and dialectical materialism on a "live" political situation still being fought out. The air still full of smoke. Ironically, his results were too spontaneous, too original and risky to accept, by droning professors and "Marxists" most of all, and so to this day remain carefully dust-covered on the top shelf where children can't reach them.

We have to move closer in, tighter. There is a pretty common misunderstanding about what Marx was doing, in his analysis of the lumpen in mid-19th century France. Which distorts understanding of his words.

Marx was working in an early capitalist era, where like a hot cultural wave, society was taken with science as the new answer for everything. In the new age of industrialization, it was replacing established religion as the ideological and cultural framework. In particular, the development of scientific "systems" to explain everything. From the invisible "building block" particles of the physical universe to Charles Darwin's evolution by natural selection, which continually reshaped all animal and plant species. Marx, who greatly admired Darwin's achievement and once famously wrote him sending him a copy of *Capital* (that copy remains pristine, its pages said to still be uncut, in the preserved Darwin library), was trying to do precisely the same thing. In terms of first systematically understanding, and then reshaping the evolution of society.

In order to do things in what he thought was a scientific way, Marx was first laying a proper foundation to revolutionary anti-capitalist politics. By fully analyzing economics and the inner workings of capitalist production and distribution in theory. This took the thousands of pages of the six known volumes of *Capital*, and more, and preoccupied most of his life's intellectual work. He had wide-ranging and ever multiplying interests, and started many, many studies which he never fully finished. Learning Turkish (since he had already taught himself English and Russian) and a major study of classes, were among these many unfinished projects, when he up and died at age 65.

So his first analyses of French capitalist society caught in revolutionary crisis were *not* the conclusion of intellectual investigation, but only a beginning. They were rich with a new appreciation of previously uncovered class politics, very exploratory in spirit, quite polemically explained based on what was known at the time, all at Karl's top volume, denouncing the ruling classes at every turn. Rather than bending to explain every incident or appearance of the lumpen according to one uniform doctrine, Marx just played it as it came. Concentrating primarily on saying what seemed most evident to him right in the example he was discussing, whether that was consistent with or emphasized a different explanation of the lumpen or not. He was stepping boldly, as an explorer of a seismically shifting political geography.

Two aspects of the new French bourgeois regime in 1848–1852 particularly took his attention. **Both involved the lumpen/proletariat, interestingly enough. Relocating it from the margins of his class analysis to the center of his attention.** The first was the bloody and effective role of the new paramilitary force of the *Garde Mobile* in repressing the Parisian workers, in their 1848 revolution. The second was the special core of the new empire itself, in the rise of the "lumpenproletarian prince," Emperor Louis Napoleon III, and his close followers as denizens of a new, thoroughly "parasite" lumpen state power.

Marx paid special attention to that *Garde Mobile*, a paramilitary force at first cheered as more "democratic," since it was formed from the poor inner city neighborhoods and could elect some of its own lower officers. In outline it was a reserve, something similar to a u.s. National Guard, only paid as full-time state employees. Militarized poor male youth, then, many from the same neighborhoods that had just thrown up barricades and overthrown the royal government only months before in February 1848. It had been that working-class anger and will to fight then that had forced the fall of "Citizen King" Louis-Philippe and his dictatorial capitalist monarchy.

In fact, many of the new *Garde Mobile* recruits had been part and parcel of the anti-government street fighting by the Parisian working-class districts earlier that year. Given military arms and eventually their own uniforms, some minor training, officers from the regular army, and a handsome wage to switch sides—but kept at home in the urban neighborhoods where their unit was recruited. It was a combination of manpower officially justified as backups to feed the regular army in case of a major war; but really hanging around the city as enlarged SWAT teams, armed with rifle and bayonet against any working-class uprising.

Marx pointed out that it was recruited not from unemployed peasant boys from the countryside at large, as French national armies customarily did, but from city youth previously active in street fighting. From the very neighborhoods of the combative young proletariat. Starting and pretty much ending with Paris. Using the proles against the proles. Their employment as a strong-handed militia against the workers' street actions they once were part of, quickly made piles of bodies and ruled streets for the government. This use against the barricades of poor working-class rebels was militarily decisive for French capitalism, which previously had been unable to put down the working-class unrest without retreats and concessions. Marx described this changed class situation in *The Class Struggles in France, 1848–1850*:

"The February Revolution had cast the army out of Paris. The National Guard, that is, the bourgeoisie in its different gradations [i.e., was composed originally of only part-time units of "elite" volunteers from the upper classes—editors], constituted the sole power. Alone, however, it did not feel itself a match for the proletariat. Moreover, it was forced gradually and piecemeal to open its ranks and admit armed proletarians, albeit after the most tenacious resistance and after setting up a hundred different obstacles. There consequently remained but one way out: *to play off one part of the proletariat against the other* ...

"And so the Paris proletariat was confronted with an army, drawn from its own midst, of 24,000 young, foolhardy men. It gave cheers for the Mobile Guard on its marches through Paris. It acknowledged it to be its foremost fighters on the barricades. It was regarded as the *proletarian* guard in contradistinction to the bourgeois National Guard. Its error was pardonable."[28]

As Marx underlines, with this new armed insurance policy, the emergency capitalist government started pressing the Parisian workers back, step by step, provoking them to give up completely or do battle. In particular, each month saw new restrictions placed on the unemployed workshops which were the source of state subsistence payments to the jobless. At last, in June 1848, a final decree ordered that all unmarried men were to be denied subsistence aid unless they enlisted in the French army. Marx wrote:

> "The workers were left no choice; they had to starve or let fly. They answered on June 22 with the tremendous insurrection in which the first great battle was fought between the two classes that split modern society. It was a fight for the preservation or annihilation of the *bourgeois* order. The veil that shrouded the republic was torn asunder.

> "It is well known how the workers, with unexampled bravery and ingenuity, without leaders, without a common plan, without means and, for the most part, lacking weapons, held in check for five days the army, the Mobile Guard, the Paris National Guard, and the National Guard that streamed in from the provinces ..."[29]

He continued this harsh story later in his *The Eighteenth Brumaire of Louis Napoleon*:[30]

> "The *bourgeois monarchy* of Louis Philippe can be followed only by a *bourgeois republic*, that is to say, whereas a limited section of the bourgeoisie ruled in the name of the king, the whole of the bourgeoisie will now rule on behalf of the people ... the Paris proletariat replied with the *June Insurrection*, the most colossal event in the history of European civil wars. The bourgeois republic triumphed. On its side stood the aristocracy of finance, the industrial bourgeoisie, the middle class, the petty bourgeoisie, the army, the *lumpenproletariat* organized as the Mobile Guard, the intellectual lights, the clergy and the rural population.

> "On the side of the Paris proletariat stood none but itself. More than three thousand insurgents were butchered after the victory, and fifteen thousand were transported without trial. [Marx was referring to the many anti-capitalist prisoners sent in chains into mostly life-long penal exile, such as to the infamous Devil's Island prison colony—editors]. With this defeat the proletariat passes into the *background* of the

revolutionary stage. It attempts to press forward again on every occasion, as soon as the movement appears to make a fresh start, but with ever decreased expenditure of strength and always slighter results ...

"The more important leaders of the proletariat in the Assembly and in the press successively fall victim to the courts, and ever more equivocal figures come to head it. In part it throws itself into *doctrinaire experiments, exchange banks and workers' associations, hence into a movement which renounces the revolutionizing of the old world by means of the latter's own great combined resources, and seeks, rather, to achieve its salvation behind society's back, in private fashion, within its limited conditions of existence, and hence necessarily suffers shipwreck* ... But at least it succumbs with the honors of the great, world historic struggle; not only France, but all Europe trembles at the June earthquake ..."[31]

We should explore what Marx has been outlining, his active conclusions from that bitter class struggle then that was still warm.

If the traditional *"vagabonds, criminals, prostitutes"*—those residual and always-present social fragments whom

A QUICK SHOT OF HISTORICAL COGNAC

France was the revolutionary center of the whole European struggle then, going deep into the 19th century. Where the embers of the great 1789 French revolution still flared up into deadly street battles. The legacy of the Parisian artisans and handicraft workers in 1789, who first freed all the captives from the dreaded royal prison of the Bastille, and then overthrew the absolutist rule of royalty and aristocracy, still lived on in the minds of skilled workers and laborers alike. With a fanfare of bullets they had kicked off the final transition from the old feudalism to the new bourgeois capitalism. Which is why Marx zeroed in there with his weapon of class analysis.

Tempest-tossed, the post-1789 revolutionary regimes of Robespierre's violently dictatorial Committee of Public Safety and then the larger, more bureaucratic Directory, led only to the contrary rise of Emperor Napoleon Bonaparte and his endless wars to conquer all of Europe. Starting when he was a brilliant young general and ruler for the French Republic in 1797; dramatically escalating when he put an emperor's crown on his own weighty head and started his expansionist super-empire in 1804. Leading his armies across the Germanic states into Russia, into Spain and Italy, even into Egypt.

His bold imprint in state modernizing was shown in everything from mass technological innovations like instituting canned food for his armies; to a new uniform secular code of law for his subjects; to bringing Pope Pius VII back to France as the ultimate trophy prisoner. Only with his second and final defeat and imprisonment in 1815, was that French "revolutionary" empire which had creatively disrupted all the maps of Europe, finally stilled.

After that, a chaotic succession of French regimes from Bourbon royalty to more bourgeois governments shakily came and went. Including the compromise "bourgeois monarchy" of Louis-Philippe, "the King of the French." An adaptable "man of his times," the young Louis-Philippe had become part of a liberal aristocrats' group which supported the 1789 Revolution, while desperately trying to moderate it. Even being a lieutenant-general in the army of the new republican regime, before splitting from it and going into exile.

Louis-Philippe had become Duke of Orleans after his father's execution on the revolutionary guillotine, but had spent the long Napoleonic years mostly in England. After the French royal house was restored by King Louis XVIII in 1814, with Napoleon's first defeat and capture, Louis-Philippe rushed to support it. Eventually, when Charles X was forced from the throne by popular unrest in 1831, Louis Philippe became the "Citizen King" of a very limited constitutional monarchy, in which the aristocracy shared the government only with the wealthiest upper bourgeoisie of financiers and industrialists. To increasing strains and increasing repression, the "Citizen King" and his wealthiest allies held state power until February 1848. In the historical distance, it is easy to see Louis-Philippe's awkward monarchy as an only makeshift state, in the difficult transition from feudalism to industrial capitalism.

During those transitional decades, if some political stability had been bought for whatever French ruling classes by the mass distribution of small farm holdings to peasant men, by 1846 France as well as all of Europe was facing mass uncertainty and rebellion.

Enormous wealth had poured into Europe by the violent looting of colonial empires such as France's—which had conquered territories in the Middle East and Africa, in the Caribbean islands such as Haiti as well as elsewhere in the Americas, and far across the Pacific. Industrialization and new slavery-based commodities and the constant increase in world commerce had long eclipsed feudal agricultural classes, and empowered the bourgeoisie. But not only had most capitalists as well as the attendant classes of middle-class tradesmen still been kept away from power, but the post-feudal working class had seen none of those gains.

The tearing distortion between new classes and the still under reconstruction state and society only grew larger. A Europe-wide economic depression, with fallen crop prices, large-scale unemployment and urban misery, became a final destabilizing factor which precipitated the Europe-wide revolts of 1848.

Another much smaller constant in Paris was the opportunistic political career of one Louis Bonaparte, a distant but very ambitious alleged younger relative of the great Napoleon. Who had spent wildly to publicize himself as a "noble" celebrity of high society, as if he were the first Kardashian. Fixated on seizing state power by armed force in that very unstable nation, Bonaparte was miraculously the first elected president of the Second French Republic. Even before which, in 1836 he had launched an unsuccessful coup for state power from Strasbourg. That failure didn't stop him from trying again in 1840, proclaiming himself "emperor" and attempting to gather the army around him in Boulogne. That, too, failed.

When he couldn't get reelected again as president, he unleashed his third and finally successful *coup d' etat* in 1852, with the help of rented army generals, declaring France and its rich colonies his own empire as the new Emperor Napoleon III. Holding power in a tin-pot monarchy for French capitalism, with its toddler growing pains, whose warring capitalist factions froze unable to form a regime themselves. Until Bonaparte's capture at the rout of Sedan, in his ill-prepared army's disastrous defeat in the 1870 Franco-Prussian War. Which marked the rise of the new greater Germanic state, as France's replacement as continental Europe's leading power.

It was in his denouciation of Louis Bonaparte's coup that Marx wrote one of his most famous descriptions of the lumpen: *"Alongside decayed roués with dubious means of subsistence and of dubious origin, alongside ruined and adventurous off-shoots of the bourgeoisie, were vagabonds, discharged soldiers, discharged jailbirds, escaped galley slaves, swindlers, mountebanks, lazzaroni, pickpockets, tricksters, gamblers, pimps, brothel keepers, porters, literati, organ-grinders, rag-pickers, knife grinders, tinkers, beggars—in short, the whole indefinite, disintegrated mass, thrown hither and thither, which the French term la boheme ..."*

While a dramatic recitation of supposed underworld street characters and professions, it is usually forgotten that Marx in framing his "laundry list" of lumpen was trying to paste this disreputable collection onto Bonaparte's face, as his sordid followers and coup conspirators. Maybe reasonable in its intent, but practically speaking not likely to be on-target. What use to a clandestine seizure of a major national state would rag-pickers, pickpockets, beggars, or escaped galley slaves be, for example?

It was probably very different lumpen who most aided Louis Bonaparte: using his powers as French President, he rearranged his army so that the generals most loyal to the republic were coincidentally sent to distant commands, while generals he had heavily bribed to support him personally were elevated and put in command of forces near Paris, to enforce his coup. For all that cunning, in the end Bonaparte became only a historical footnote, remembered not as any illustrious successor to Napoleon but as one of the most meteoric of upstart adventurers in Western history.

Marx in his *Capital* specifically termed, *"the lumpen-proletariat proper"*—were of no use to the regime against the working class in that revolutionary crisis, that doesn't mean that the lumpen contained no possibilities of help for the French rulers then. This is where it gets more interesting.[32]

The ruling classes could and did reach down into the lowest levels of the largely unemployed, poor youth of the working class districts, who had been streaming into Paris from the peasant countryside. Many of those children being surplus in their farming villages, trying to find a better life or at least survival as urban workers. Numbers of them had already been bloodied as fighters from their neighborhoods against the hated municipal police and army holding up King Louis-Philippe's dictatorial regime, only a few months earlier. Marx is explicit that this is a split in the lower working class itself, as when he writes that the capitalists aimed *"to play off one part of the proletariat against the other."* And that most of all the Parisian workers recognized the *Garde Mobile* recruits as *"drawn from its own midst."*

Marx's analysis about that special repressive force for early French capitalism in crisis is important. Both because its sharp class analysis has made a lasting imprint on radical thinking; and because in its fabric are folds and patterns that aren't unfamiliar to our own time.

The capitalist Provisional Government, which took over ruling France in February 1848, had an unusual governmental problem: It was in one most important way "powerless," having no armed force of its own to police or coerce society or even to defend itself. Paris, France's million-person capital and economic center, was embroiled in sharp-edged conflict then, but no disbanded police or demoralized soldiers patrolled the streets and buildings.

At first only the militant workers and their allies held the city. Alexis de Tocqueville, the aristocratic democrat whose travels through and sympathetic writings about euro-settler America brought him lasting literary fame, was also involved in French politics most of his life. Tocqueville being at one time a member of the National Assembly, and at another Louis Bonaparte's foreign minister during his last run as president (Tocqueville resigned rather than go along with Bonaparte's coup). Tocqueville was struck by one important detail as he crossed the city:

> *"Throughout this day* [of February 25, 1848] *in Paris I never saw one of the former agents of authority: not a*

*soldier, not a gendarme, or a police-
man; even the National Guard had
vanished. The people alone bore arms,
guarded public buildings, watched,
commanded and punished; it was an
extraordinary and terrible thing to
see the whole of this huge city, full of
so many riches, or rather the whole of
this great nation, in the sole hands of
those who owned nothing."[33]*

**The radicalized proletariat in Paris
was significant opposition.** Out of the
300,000 workers living then in the capital, over 100,000 had turned out in mass
protest marches supporting the struggle.
The armed rebellion of June 23rd of 1848,
was estimated then as high as 40,000 to
50,000 workers. Although there was little
coordination or planning by the poorly
armed militants, whose shouted slogan
was "Liberty or Death." Rapidly over 1,000
barricades were thrown up to fortify
working-class neighborhoods, with the
insurgents initially holding about half of
Paris by area, including some key streets
in the city center. Soon enough, though,
within days full of stubborn defense of
their districts, the disorganized insurgents were defeated piecemeal, neighborhood by neighborhood, by government
forces superior at the point of attack in
arms and concentration. Still, the workers' rebellion was a major challenge to
capitalism.[34]

The new French capitalist state in
embryo must have been in serious panic
in the early months of its shaky rule, without any armed men to give it substance
against the restlessness of the working
class.

Even still, the lower class origins of
its new militia of desperation, teenagers
often literally in rags, made the wealthier
classes fearful that they were only arm-
ing unreliable street proletarians. When
these *Garde Mobile* turned out to be the
vanguard fighters in defense of the establishment—actually *leading* the more
uncertain regular army troops and those
fearful bourgeois National Guard volunteers—astonishment mixed with political relief in the better neighborhoods.
The *Garde* teens' enthusiastic savaging
of workers with their sharp bayonets and
rifle butts was applauded, as were the
mass killings of surrendered workers.

A day when the turn in the situation was fully revealed was April 16th
of 1848, when a rebel workers' march
headed towards the undefended Hotel
de Ville, the headquarters of the besieged
Provisional Government. The spectre
of an armed workers takeover, whether
intended or not, shimmered as an alarm
sounded by the regime. Four battalions of the finally uniformed and armed
Garde Mobile were rushed to intercept

them. Breaking up the march into smaller clumps at bayonet point, the youth of the *Garde* led the regime's other supporters in shouts of *"Down with the communists!"* Momentum lost, pushed around by the eager teenage militiamen, the workers left in defeat. That was a turning point. After that, the *Garde* was called out at least once a week and sometimes daily, to put down not only localized violent outbreaks but labor strikes and other anti-capitalist actions.[35]

There was actually little disagreement over the facts of what those young, rag-tag militiamen were like in early 1848. Conservative Louis Garnier-Pages, one leader in the Provisional Government and at one time acting Paris mayor, said of them:

> *The constituent elements of the Mobile Guard were essentially revolutionary. Drawn from the barricades, they bore the mark of their origins: they had the intrepid quality, but also the turbulence and fickleness of the people.*

Radical Marc Caussidiere, who had marched in and taken over the empty police headquarters after the February Revolution, and formed a small, stopgap "people's police" of militants, followed those poor enlistees with no little bitterness: *"The Mobile Guardsmen who issued from the barricades of February turned their arms against the barricades of June and stained the working-class quarters with the blood of their families."*

The first major French account of these events was by the noted liberal writer, "Daniel Stern," who in a multi-volume 1862 work still consulted by historians, *History of the 1848 Revolution*, was eye-witness for readers and judge of history both:

> "Recruited, as we have seen, on the marrows of the barricades, the Mobile Guard was composed, nearly in its entirety, of the turbulent swarm that had previously been thought beyond all discussion, of those children, the vagabonds of alleys and street corners, who are called 'urchins of Paris'. The rest were a mix of men of all conditions ... At the time of which I am speaking, most of them were still in rags and tatters, many lacking shirts and shoes ...

> "The courage of the children of the Mobile Guard in this first and terrible test cannot even be imagined by those who were not there to witness it. The sound of the gunshots, the whistling of the bullets seemed to them a new game which brought them joy. The smoke, the smell of

powder excited them. They charged at a run, climbed over crumbling paving stones, clung to every scrap of cover with a marvelous agility. Once launched, no order could hold them back. It required only this transport of youth and this mad thirst for glory … If the Mobile Guard had passed over to the insurrection, as was feared, it is virtually certain victory would have passed over with it."[36]

Marx's analysis of the lumpen in the 1848 revolution & counter-revolution was ground-breaking radical theory at that time. Reporting in as the historical wave broke, on the question of the young capitalist state's strategy of forming new kinds of repressive paramilitaries out of the commonly available scrap materials of lumpen elements from the margins. To cap their defeat, a new type of "empire" restabilized the French state, built around a core of lumpen leadership. Discarding the fumbling efforts of the politically-active capitalists themselves. Remember that the bourgeoisie were frequently the political allies and even leaders of the working class, in the 18th and 19th century civil wars for more democracy and economic equality against Europe's feudal absolutism. So this new class weapon back then had more than simply tactical implications in the movement.

Early reports are just that, pioneering but not necessarily completely accurate by more developed later understanding. Over a century and a half ago, we should underline. But which served to first draw attention. To read some fundamental code about the far-reaching possibilities of the lumpen, there in the turbulent mix of the early class struggle of the industrial capitalist epoch. We're now going to take apart the densest part of that complex Marx passage.

"Daniel Stern" was the pseudonym of Marie comtesse d'Agoult, one of the most free-spirited bourgeois intellectuals of her times. Leaving her husband for a decade-long relationship with the pianist and composer Franz Liszt, she was an active member of a creative circle of musicians and intellectuals. The composer Frederic Chopin was a close friend, and dedicated one of his works to her. Under her pseudonym, she was well known as the author of romantic novels.

To start with a baseline, then. In the earlier *Communist Manifesto*, remember, the lumpen were described as "that passively rotting mass thrown off by the lowest layers of old society." That was Marx and Engels' first try at explaining the lumpen/proletariat, and it served to *introduce the idea* of these "partial-class" strata but was otherwise inaccurate. **We can mostly forget about all that "passive rotting mass" stuff.**[38] Since in a quick jump forward the lumpen/proletariat, in the electrically charged French class struggle of the 1850s, were immediately seen by Marx as really the reverse—maybe not all so progressive as we might wish, but certainly *animated*, new formed, politically alive, and vibrant with the energy to help decide society's major political struggles. That was a radically different picture.

In contrast to *The Communist Manifesto*'s dismissive words, the emergency x-ray that Marx took of the French class concussion in the mid-1800s, put the lumpen/proletariat right in the epicenter of the crisis. Right on center stage. **For one thing, as openers it was not small in size but relatively large, spilling over its own previously thought boundaries**. Marx admitted in his sharply penned essay, *The Eighteenth Brumaire of Louis Napoleon*:

"To the four million (including children, etc.) officially recognized paupers, vagabonds, criminals, and prostitutes in France must be added five million who hover on the margins of existence ..."

Recognizing the destitute, paupers, at the edges of society, Marx was including a category which comprised both the lumpen and lowest working class mixed together. Orphans and some other destitute children, disabled former workers, the surviving aged, and so on, might have been excluded from the ordinary employed capitalist workforce, but many were still very much part of the working class. Then as now.

But if only half of only that first total of 4 million lumpen plus others on the margins—which included all street criminals, professional gamblers, unemployed mercenaries, counterfeiters, beggars, sex workers and so on—were really lumpen/proletarians, those outcast class strata would have been within the range of 6% or more of the whole French population then of 35 millions. So that is a fairly large number for people completely outside a society's economic production and distribution. But as we shall see, **that was only a start to build on for Marx.**[39]

There were important things that Marx didn't know. Not a surprise for theory, however brilliantly written, but based on limited information now a century or two old. Misunderstandings came in the first place from Marx's seriously exaggerated idea of the success of the *Garde Mobile*'s recruiting efforts on the Paris streets.

Marx tells us several times in his writings then that this *Garde Mobile* in Paris was composed of 24,000 young men, which was close to the "25,000" numbers authorized in its founding directive and generally accepted. But what *wasn't* as publicized by the authorities was that was a considerable inflation of their real strength.

By the time of the critical fighting in the June 1848 Revolution, only 14,918 men had actually been signed up, not any 24,000. Minus those who had been discharged for various reasons, who had deserted, or were reported missing at the critical days, it is estimated that probably no more than 13,000 to 13,500 men at most fought for the new state in the *Garde Mobile* against the working class rebels.[40]

This *Garde Mobile* militia, so brilliantly conceived of in desperation by capitalist authorities, **was far from popular as a class choice** even for unemployed and hungry young workers. Marx tells us that the new recruits received "1 franc 50 centimes a day," but doesn't explain further, as he assumes that his contemporary readers will know what that meant. The bribe was actually considerable. The *Garde Mobile*'s young recruits in Paris received *six times* the pay of a regular infantryman in the French army! That amount was a normal working-class wage for that time. In addition, of course, the recruits got free housing in the barracks, free uniforms and boots, and in the early months free food at their own military mess halls. At a time, we must keep in mind, that the Chamber of Commerce estimated 54.4% unemployment and much homelessness in the Parisian working-class districts.

Yet even those inducements weren't enough to convince most of the young and desperately poor to go to work as enforcers for the state. To be some kind of cops, in other words. Just as in our world the constant propaganda din of "Lethal Weapon" type tv cop dramas, added on top of Hollywood crime movies and politicians' speeches and minority recruiting drives in the community—still cannot convince more than a handful of New Afrikan and Latino kids in New York City to apply for the police academy. i mean, class enemy is class enemy.

Back then in France, even with the *Garde* recruiting boys younger than the official starting age of 16 (there were public references to brave "15" year olds as well as the kind of enlistment document irregularities of underage street kids, we can well imagine) and illegally recruiting foreigners—who alone made up 6% of the *Garde*—**the regime wasn't able to recruit anything close to their new paramilitary's planned strength.**[41]

But Karl M's underestimating how much grassroots resistance there was to the *Garde*'s recruiting, is directly related to problems in the movement's analysis of the lumpen/proletariat in that battle.

Marx was saying what he thought most important about the struggle—however contradictory those out of sync facts might appear to some readers. When he writes that the new capitalist state's teenage militia were recruited from *"one part of the proletariat,"* it doesn't stop him from declaring a few lines later that they "belonged for the most part to the *lumpenproletariat,* which in all big towns forms a mass sharply differentiated from the industrial proletariat ..." So that on the one hand, the *Garde* are said to be recruited from the Parisian proletariat, but on the other hand are said to be despised criminal lumpen who are nothing like workers and completely separate from them. You can see the contradiction pop right up, just in one paragraph. **This kind of reporting was perhaps fine for starters, in early days, but not clear enough for us today. It is too much of a half-finished house.**

While Marx has been accused by modern professors of being inconsistent in his definition of the lumpen, or just using the term impressionistically, willy-nilly, in that passage, that doesn't appear to be the case. He dramatically emails us two separate cellphone photos—both more or less true, but very different—with no explanation of how the lumpen appeared in the picture from one image to the other. Marx, just starting to bring the lumpen/proletariat into our political focus, doesn't explain how the situation morphed from one class reality to a different class reality.

Stormy Karl M was so bent on labeling the repressive *Garde Mobile* as an amoral clan of declassed criminals having nothing to do with "his" decent working people—*"sharply differentiated from the industrial proletariat,"* as he puts it—that he stumbles past the way in which those emerging class realities worked. Which was not like assembling the rigid wooden blocks that kindergartens use, but was all about the sensuous interplay of currents of young people along partly fluid class borders. **Making life choices of who they were, some inconsistently**

or opportunistically trying different things, trying even to change back and forth. You know what i mean.

We can really pick up Marx's own still undeveloped class understanding when he talks about those youth as barely having minds of their own, but only being objects of manipulation: *"... at the youthful age at which the Provisional Government recruited them, thoroughly malleable, as capable of the most heroic deeds and the most exalted sacrifices as of the basest banditry and the foulest corruption."*

The deal is, those youth did really have minds of their own, in a hard and for some even a life-or-death situation. Some made the choice to work for the state, repressing and killing poor working people who were rebelling for just cause. **That *choice* was the moment in which they coalesced in a tangible way, made solid, their partly ambiguous class identity, some becoming lumpen/proletarian**. Most chose otherwise, even those committed to a lumpen life, from what we know (if estimates of roughly 100,000 declassed outcasts in Paris even much earlier were true, it's obvious that most had little to do with helping that weak regime in 1848). So some youths may well have been lumpen street people before joining the *Garde*, but even those who were simply jobless would-be workers *became* lumpen

in choosing the *Garde* and its class role. **Lumpen were not simply gathered by the capitalist state, but more importantly also *created*.**

Marx's first-in theoretical scouting didn't at that time answer a basic question: If poor youth were so "malleable," such apparent clay at the hands of the capitalists, then why did so many of them resist the regime's bribes and inducements in the first place? Why were many of them being so human and risking death and lifelong imprisonment in revolution? The reality is that those lower-class youth in Paris were making choices, not so much of "employment" but as to who they would be. That's what youth is, we all know, that period in which you leave childhood by making life choices, experiencing being both the shaper and the shaped. Trying out choices in the only real way you can, on your own life and its risky future.

The assembling of poor youth who came to make up the new force were *created as lumpen in the instant of their own choices* as much as anything else; when they chose to become uniformed thugs tasked specially to repress rebellious workers. They were *made* as lumpen/proletariat by the dialectic of violent capitalist activity and their own mercenary choice to be the flesh and body of that class-on-class repression.

MARX'S KEY PASSAGE ON THE LUMPEN/PROLETARIAT IN 1848 PARIS REVOLUTION

"There consequently remained but one way out: *to play off one part of the proletariat against the other* … For this purpose the Provisional Government formed 24 battalions of *Mobile Guards*, each a thousand strong, composed of young men from 15 to 20 years. They belonged for the most part to the *lumpenproletariat,* which in all big towns forms a mass sharply differentiated from the industrial proletariat, a recruiting ground for thieves and criminals of all kinds, living on the crumbs of society, people without a definite trade, vagabonds, people without hearth or furniture, unapologetically with no fixed address, varying according to the degree of civilization of the nation to which they belong, but never renouncing their lazzaroni character; at the youthful age at which the Provisional Government recruited them, thoroughly malleable, as capable of the most heroic deeds and the most exalted sacrifices as of the basest banditry and the foulest corruption. The Provisional Government paid them 1 franc 50 centimes a day, that is, it bought them. It gave them their own uniform, that is, it made them outwardly distinct from the blouse-wearing workers. In part it had assigned them officers from the standing army as leaders; in part they themselves elected young sons of the bourgeoisie whose vain boasting about death for the fatherland and devotion to the republic captivated them."[37]

The incompleteness of Marx's theoretical explanation wasn't just some abstract question about class. It directly could lead to misunderstandings, practically affecting how revolutionaries understand the struggle. Not his fault as a ground-breaker, as first-in reconnaissance, for sure, but more on all those who came after him.

From what we can reconstruct, most lumpen rejected helping the new state and its *Garde*, and some number quite probably fought on in the rebellion with their working-class neighbors. We know that even hundreds of young *Garde Mobile* deserted, legally discharged themselves, or simply "disappeared" when push came to shove. Just as we know that when the workers' revolution was finally crushed in June, some 163 *Garde Mobile* soldiers were captured and arrested by the government forces, being caught on the other side with the anti-capitalist fighters. **Lumpen could be on both sides, when it all came down. That should have been a small but real practical signal.** Not just on one side or the other, as a wooden block is only solidly one thing.[42]

What Karl M didn't feel that he had to emphasize, is that the *theoretical* under-development in Paris by not recognizing the lumpen class morphing going on, strategically disarmed the working class movement there. There was a popular illusion that the new militia being poor home boys from the 'hood, surely meant that in the end—after they had finished hustling the sucker capitalist state for new clothes and many meals and even weapons—they would suddenly go over to the side of the rebellion, their real loyalty, at the last hour. Ensuring the working class socialist victory over the old oppressive France.

This was widely believed by the rebels, even their leaders. Rather than be organizing and preparing to subvert and politicize and out-maneuver and battle an even more dangerous new enemy, the movement put its trust in imaginary allies and easy hopes. Which exacted a terrible cost at war's end.

That kind of opportunistic political valium was such an influence that even after the bloody crushing at the bayonets and rifle barrages of the *Garde*, some still maintained that the regime's strong-arm boys had just been about to go over to the revolutionary side (same as if my Mom had had four wheels she would have been a Cadillac). Even Fred Engels himself moaned that the left rebellion had been *"within a hairsbreadth of victory,"* since he believed that the teenagers of the *Garde "needed but a slight impetus to make them go over to their side."* And all that together with a buck fiddy gets you a cup of coffee.[43]

Theory isn't just for intellectuals to make comments from the sidelines about capitalism. It's the practical radar that tells us what our real landscape is, how we have to prepare for battles in storms whose full strength is still building.

💀 💀 💀

When Marx bitingly described the newly self-crowned "emperor" Louis Bonaparte as "chief of the lumpenproletariat," he included not only Bonaparte's criminal footsoldiers and hired applauders of his dummy political conspiracy, the Society of December 10, as lumpen/proletarian, but even Bonaparte's generals and cabinet ministers and officials as well. It was in Marx's stepped-up vision an entire party of lumpen/proletarians leading to an unnatural government headed by lumpen/proletarians. Which he thought of as a "parasite" state.

This has usually been taken to mean primarily that the capitalist state is parasitic in its basic nature, which is of course obviously true. It goes beyond the obvious,

though. **Like a science fiction vision, Marx was raising a redrawn class map for consideration. In which parasitism was a major factor *beyond* the usual class privilege. On the redrawn class map, the lumpen/proletariat were no longer simply those marginal to society.** This has more than a little importance, but Marx and Engels never fully followed it up because they remained preoccupied with the main political arena, featuring the capitalists versus the industrial proletariat clash of the Titans. In which even the massed peasantry and middle classes and other still lesser class strata of the lumpen seemed very secondary factors.

Marx's redrawn class map was really different on this. When he and Engels first started pointing out the lumpen, in *The Communist Manifesto*, they were the scattered disreputable fringe elements of the gutter. Recognizable on the spot by their very ragged and soiled street lives. Without beating a drum about it, Karl M's analysis evolved quite quickly, becoming more defined and more material.

Now the lumpen/proletariat to him were defined *structurally* on this futuristic class map. Whether high or low, respectable or not, everyone who was without a role in capitalist production and distribution was thus out of the

actual class structure, and had therefore fallen or jumped into the lumpen margins. Don't know about you, but to me this took some getting used to.

That meant that even quite large groupings in society were considered lumpen by Marx and Engels. Even masses of people. Or even well-to-do and socially respected elements. In his biting *Eighteenth Brumaire of Louis Napoleon*, Marx shocked readers by insisting that not only Emperor Louis Napoleon was lumpen, but so were the mass of his state officials and the mass of his army: *"... Bonaparte looks in himself as the chief of the lumpenproletariat to which he himself, his entourage, his government and his army belong ..."* Generals and sergeants, tax scribes and provincial governors, imperial aides and ministers, were as far away from the gutter then as you could ask—yet were now cast down into Marx's purgatory as lumpen/proletarian. No wonder that some readers didn't know how to interpret this, while others viewed it as just the cranky Karl M abusing the enemy any way that came to his infuriated mind.

But the record is quite clear about this. Writing in 1887, in his mature intellectual years, Fred Engels was analyzing Germany's aristocratic Junker landowners, going down their class levels until, at the bottom ... *"On the lower fringes of all this clique of nobles, there naturally emerges a numerous parasitic nobility, a noble lumpenproletariat, which lives on debts, dubious gambling, importune begging and political espionage."* So even entire layers of supposedly high-born people could have become actually lumpen, to Marx and Engels' eyes.[44]

In the *Grundrisse*, Marx's private notebooks from the late 1850s, deliberately bringing together in one writing a survey of his economic and philosophical thought, he was quite explicit that social status and even wealth did not determine who was in the lumpen/proletariat or not. And that the number of lumpen in society was far larger than most assumed: *"From whore to pope, there is a mass of such rabble. But the honest and 'working' lumpenproletariat belongs here as well: e.g. the great mob of porters etc. who render service in seaport cities etc."*[45]

(We should add here that in the 18th and 19th century European ports such as London, porters were not considered simply another word for commercial laborers, but a suspect category of semi-criminals. Among the poor circulating around the docks seeking independent hire by the job: carrying a passenger's baggage for them or taking places as extra hands on the spot, unloading cargo alongside regular workers. In their customary big aprons, porters were always said to use their recognized presence on the waterfront to cover for the casual theft that was their real sustenance.)

In *The Eighteenth Brumaire*, Marx uses the term "parasite" over and over, applying it to specific class strata or even large groups of French. His explanations indicate that he used the term purposefully. About Louis Bonaparte's revamped French army, Marx wrote: "The army itself is no longer the flower of peasant youth; it is the swamp-flower of the peasant *lumpenproletariat*. It consists in large measure of *remplacants*, of substitutes, just as the second Bonaparte is himself only a *remplacant*, the substitute for Napoleon. [Here Marx refers to the widespread practice of hiring poor youth as mercenary replacements for drafted farmers, a regular practice soon to also be common for families who could afford it in the u.s. Civil War—editors] It now performs its deeds of valor by hounding the peasants in masses like small antelopes, by doing special police duty ..."[46]

The question of whether there could be an entire capitalist state shaped to the lumpen, and what that might mean, has been rarely considered. He further wrote:

"This executive power with its enormous bureaucratic and military organization, with its vast and ingenious state machinery, with a host of officials numbering half a million, besides an army of another half a million, this appalling parasitic body, which enmeshes the body of French society and chokes all its pores, sprang up in the days of the absolute monarchy, with the decay of the feudal system, which it helped to hasten."

In his mind, Marx made the distinction between a "regular" state which would maintain the ruling class, keep roads open, might sponsor inferior public schools, and so on—contrasted with "parasite" states and sectors which only loot and exploit what is public, violating even their own criminal laws with nonchalance. Was that an ominous foreshadowing of the fascist capitalist states later to come into being—or simply Marx's 1800s innocence about what capitalist "normal" when full-blown would look like?

A few stray professors have tried to explain away Marx's explosive class analysis of that French revolutionary struggle against a new state power. Saying it was merely literary hyperbole. In other words, he didn't really mean it. According to these bookie interpreters, Marx in all those writings was just venting his grumpy self, angrily flinging around the term "lumpenproletariat" as a mighty insult, like colorful bowls of jello flung around the dining room in a political food fight. In general, this doesn't ring the bell.

We *do* have to be reasonable here, since as with many sainted icons, every stray word of Karl's is treated by some like holy relics of Jesus's foreskin. Just as we might tease a friend who took a better school job as "bourgeois"—when a schoolteacher is hardly a capitalist and we expect everyone to know we don't mean it literally—Marx could sometimes use "lumpenproletariat" that slanging way. Like referring to some journalists he didn't like as "lumpenproletarian," which he didn't necessarily think. On the other hand, he

and Engels sometimes called their revolutionary opponent Bakunin a "lumpenproletarian prince," and meant every nasty nuance of it. It's just like hearing someone say, "Christ, we should just shoot that bastard!" You have to know whether he's talking about the owner of the New York Knicks or what.

While some other professors have tried to iron out that record that Marx saw as pretty twisted; saying, for example, that Louis Bonaparte couldn't really have been lumpen since he had once been a financier, a much more substantial class identity. Or so they assume. Intellectual dance moves, yes, but the evidence doesn't support these post-Marxist professors.

It's interesting that professors keep arguing against Marx's class analysis of the lumpen in mid-1800s France (maybe it's a measure of the power of anti-capitalist ideas that current bourgeois intellectuals keep trying to put them down). As an example, Dr. Mark Traugott's study of the working-class rebellion of 1848, *Armies of the Poor*, insists that the young recruits to the *Garde Mobile* could not have been lumpen. Because few guardsmen were known criminals with arrest records or so the government said, and because both the guardsmen and the arrested rebels claimed the exact same backgrounds: of coming from rural families and then being attached as workers to the skilled trades in Paris. So he asserts both warring sides must have had the same working-class identity. As though what one *used* to be determines your present identity. By that silly mental backflip, Bill Gates of Microsoft, worth $80 billion plus and usually called the wealthiest man in the world currently, should be regarded as only middle-class because he came from a physician's family. Even if those old state documents are true and not forged or fiddled with, the fact is that most lumpen are made, are created or chosen, not merely inherited from birth. Duh.

Snarling or not, Karl M obviously meant just what he said about that regime being an actual state of the lumpen/proletariat. Still capitalist but renovated for temporary occupancy by a criminal "lumpen-proletarian prince," as Marx named him. Marx underlined how immediately after Bonaparte seized state power, in an exceptionally widespread day of repression, many financiers and other members of the propertied classes were attacked in their businesses and homes by the army, roughed up and imprisoned or even shot right on the spot, in an orgy of very educational terror and slaughter. Not exactly a show of upper class solidarity there.

As for Louis Bonaparte being a financier not a lumpen, Marx thought that, too, was as fraudulent as his tinfoil imperial crown. Marx didn't consider Bonaparte a real capitalist any more than we consider Bernie Madoff a regular businessman. Since Bonaparte's role as a financier was to take part in various embezzlements and swindles by which politicians and their cronies could simply loot the French treasury. To say that he was a "businessman" or a "financier" seems a bit like calling Rasputin a "government employee."

As Marx said specifically of France at that time: "The finance aristocracy, in its mode of acquisition as well as in its pleasures, is nothing but the *rebirth of*

the lumpenproletariat on the heights of bourgeois society." [his emphasis] Because that particular class, at that historical moment, was not centered in business loans or financing construction and other such usual activities, but only lightly veiled criminal activity. Thefts of public funds, using the state for robbery, graft, swindles, and big and small fraudulent ventures. Like in the pro-Western stage prop "government" in Afghanistan at this very moment. Where explicit criminal activity isn't a byproduct of government, but criminal activity *is* the government.

What Louis Bonaparte was personally, was a lumpen adventurer and seeker of over-the-top personal power, at a time when French society was a gambling casino that had been thrown open in disarray by feuding owners and managers. By the deadlock of the industrial capitalists wrestling with the finance capitalists, while the old feudalistic agricultural estates were pushing their backward interests, as at the same time the young urban proletariat was trying to lead the middle classes into violent democratic rebellions. **No one was strong enough to hold the state.**

In Marx's analysis, this "bonapartism" rescued a capitalism in violent dysfunction, unable by the temporarily irreconcilable splits in power to take

the helm of its own state. Many radicals believe that "bonapartism" foreshadows and partly explains in theory the rise of European fascism in the 1920s–1930s. We should recognize that, since the u.s. empire doesn't appear too far from that situation itself. So for a small fee, an emperor's cut of the loot, Louis Bonaparte and his mercenary cohort did the dirty work of ruling someone else's messed-up society for them.

Karl M was, by the way, explicit, in saying several times that Bonaparte's improvised regime was detached from the feudal or bourgeois ruling class hand that usually controlled the state. He wrote in *The Eighteenth Brumaire*: "Only under the second Bonaparte does the state seem to have made itself **completely independent.** As against civil society, the state machinery has consolidated its position so thoroughly that … an adventurer blows in from abroad, raised on a shield by a drunken soldiery …"[47] (our emphasis)

To initially identify this new variant of a capitalist state of the lumpen, in class terms, as Marx did, was a critical first step towards understanding. But it wasn't such a complete understanding itself, wasn't the final analysis—that would be an even more difficult task. Marx tried various complicated class explanations of Bonaparte's base, and personally

i find them more confusing than enlightening. Perhaps it's because *The Eighteenth Brumaire* was never written as one revolutionary essay, but as a handful of different newspaper articles that were later stitched somewhat hastily together.

One thing Karl M does underline, was that as ersatz emperor Louis strained to be all things to all classes. He promised the rented army which brought his dictatorship to state power that he would restore their military to its shining heights under the great Napoleon, as his main priority—only to lead an underweight army to its greatest defeat in French history. He insisted on wearing the crown of an emperor, but claimed to be a "democratic" imperial dictator (a forerunner perhaps of Putin's Great Russian stalinate). In a strange plebiscite affirming his violent *coup d'etat*, Bonaparte won a large majority of male voters (the Provisional Government had earlier bought support by installing universal manhood suffrage in France, a first in Europe). You know, Trump's election wasn't the first time, really.

Taking it to the extreme even more shamelessly than today's Don De Trump, King of the Whites, Louis Bonaparte actually claimed to be the first "socialist" emperor!—who could bypass the need for those messy and uncertain revolutions by using his imperial powers to simply "inaugurate social reform by his decrees," as anarcho-socialist pioneer Pierre-Joseph Proudhon happily predicted. This act amazingly convinced some number of people, notably including Proudhon, who said: "I will forgive him his coup d'etat and will give him the credit for having made Socialism a certainty and a reality."[48]

Karl M himself tried to view that setback with optimism. In the famous paraphrase of Shakespeare's line, "Well grubbed, old mole" from *Hamlet*, Marx in *The Eighteenth Brumaire* tried the hopeful analysis that Bonaparte's lumpen coup had only further undermined French capitalism. Hypothesizing that with the capitalists knocked out of the political ring, the working class would soon finish the fight by knocking out the supposedly far weaker lumpen "executive." Good try, Karl, but that didn't work out so well. By the way, the Third International tried a variant of that line after the Nazis grabbed power in 1930s Germany, the infamous, "After them, *us!*" line, as though Hitler's historic mission had only been to weaken capitalist Germany enough for Communist conquest. Which was only "Whistling while walking past the graveyard," as we used to say.

What solidified Louis Bonaparte's regime, was that his rule was widely and correctly recognized as violently hostile to capitalist parties and politicians, but protective of the overall capitalist system and culture itself. Marx quotes London's *The Economist* as praising Bonaparte's leadership in 1851: "The President is the guardian of order, and is now recognized as such by every Stock Exchange of Europe."

The political "improvised explosive device" in Marx's backpack was the idea that the lumpen/proletariat could sometimes be much greater than marginal players, could even take state power into their own hands.

More than minor disturbances or hired actors in criminal coups—instead, in extraordinary situations the lumpen could be very large, a mass force themselves at the very center of the political struggle, if only temporarily. Could even take state power themselves. Not fear the government, but *be* the government.

Marx's posing of this is more preliminary, outlines not always filled in. Like, his phrase "parasite" for a type of state is evocative but not really explained yet. Aren't all states today parasites? How does a lumpen state differ from a violently disruptive capitalist state? It doesn't mean that he was wrong, just that this theory about "bonapartism" left many theoretical areas only barely opened, and for later revolutionaries to fill in or cross out.

Just because you are marginal to production and distribution, doesn't necessarily mean that you are always marginal to state power. If you can be large enough and organizable enough to take over the 19th century French state, no less, and run it for its dysfunctional capitalist owners, then why not entire movements and nations and continental regions in other times and places? (Remember, that was a time when the industrial proletariat itself in European nations was small, like 5% of the population or similar, and yet was shaking the governments in their capitals).

So in several brilliant years, years of concentrated analysis, Karl Marx first tested using his theory of dialectical and historical materialism in a "live" mass struggle, in close to real-time. The results were startling. Quickly discarding the estimation of the lumpen/proletariat he and Engels had just penned in the famous *Communist Manifesto*, Marx x-rayed the role played by lumpen in the French revolutionary crisis as *pivotal*. Now he saw the lumpen not so much as passive ragged outcasts on the margins of society, but as an infectious class vector capable of taking over the state itself and its mass instruments, such as the military. Of lumpen rulers and lumpen army divisions unrestrained by any leashes held by civil class society. This was perhaps brilliantly prophetic, and in any case was a bold futurism which radical movements have had heavy static rebroadcasting.

10. the class in hiding

One of the reasons that you might not notice the lumpen in action more often, is that they are a class in hiding. This need for camouflage is actually one of their characteristics. The German philosopher Bernard Groethuysen once said: *"I find it hard to understand why the bourgeois dislikes to be called by his name; kings have been called kings, priests priests, and knights knights; but the bourgeois likes to keep his incognito."* Same goes for the lumpen, who as culturally made creatures of the capitalist epoch, are in this regard just like their bigger brother, the bourgeoisie at the very top of society as they are at the bottom.[19]

In the lumpen/proletariat's case, being divorced from a class role in production and distribution, they are naked of identity. And need to always be borrowing their neighbor's to cover that up. So we find the lumpen/proletariat as street hustlers and civil rights leaders, as imams and politicians, if not as often as being policemen and armed robbers. In nationalistic movements as well as being nation-erasing warlords and terrorists. Just as Louis Napoleon once threw on the jumbled costumes, first of modernizing social reformer, and then of the restorer of faux royal grandeur. Having no regular class ideology, in politics the lumpen find it convenient to use ideologies and causes even as temporary uniforms, sometimes changing them like clothing.

As an example: At the heart of the International Brigades of Communists and sympathizers fighting in the 1930s Spanish Civil War against the fascists, were the German "reds" of the Ernst Thalmann battalion. Who were famed for being the bravest of the brave, exiles fighting with no country to retreat to. Always had wondered how that had come about, since Hitler had most hard core leftists in concentration camps or drafted into his army or factories—not let run loose to go fight against his side in Spain.

Then, an older comrade who had served in Spain and was a member then of the Spanish Communist Party, told me that although it wasn't talked about in public, the German men of the Thalmann battalion were mostly street fighting veterans of the Nazi "Brownshirts." Yes, he said, former fascist storm troopers who had gone into exile. Who deeply hated Hitler for betraying their own crazy faction in the bloodbath of "the night of the long knives" inside the Nazi Party, and were carrying on their blood feud to the bitter end. Far right zip to far left in the political spectrum in one step. Made sense to them.[50]

It is convenient for some of the lumpen/proletariat politically to wear the robes of a religious holy mission—or the macho uniform of some militaristic campaign of national salvation. Urgent larger causes help justify the extreme violence and extraordinary chaos which parts of the lumpen/proletariat can create in their adventures. As well as help gather the many followers and allies from other classes that they need to bulk out their ranks and become fully operational. Just biz as usual.

11. the iron force-feeding funnel of the cash nexus

By the time those trouble-making boys Marx and Bakunin and Engels entered the scene, there had been a newly created English working class which had been violently cut down to fit, mutilated in daily life to be crammed inside the bloody tin can of the capitalistic system. These were people who previously had one foot in the semi-feudal past of "rights" of the commoner, of being paid in kind, sharing in what was being made out of nature and labor. Inevitably, much of their protracted class war with the then-new industrial capitalism took the form of forced mass criminalization.

We are brain-washed today to think of the slow, inexorable transition from feudalism to capitalism as being one of increasing "democracy"—as though in past European history ordinary people had no rights. If anything, the reverse was equally true. It was just different.

What made the intense class war in that change inevitable were the system-wide ruptures going on at the workplaces of society. There was a world of meaning in Marx's terse reference, *"into the discipline necessary for the wage system."* For the cash nexus of the new capitalist wage system which we ourselves grow up in

This entire analysis of the evolving struggles of 18th century British workers draws from Peter Linebaugh's illuminating investigation of London's working-class executions in the 1700s, and the exploitation of that post-feudal working class, as detailed in his classic, *The London Hanged*. It goes almost without saying that this subject for him as for all of us was first shaped by E.P. Thompson's ground-breaking work in *The Making of the English Working Class*.

without a second thought today, required a prolonged, hundred-year bloody hacking and cutting away at the social economics of people's daily lives.

Semi-feudal class relations of the 17th and 18th centuries in Europe were not yet fully cash relations and were not necessarily centered on an abstract wage. The urban artisan and small businessman in the feudal period—the *"burgher"* or *"bourgeois"*—the self-employed, middle-class city dweller who was the lineal ancestor of today's ruling bourgeoisie, didn't really pay the apprentices who were his little semi-skilled labor force. He put them up and shared his home and his table with them, feeding them and teaching them as well. It was a relationship in which they directly *shared* the fruits or the poverty of his trade, however unevenly. Just as the feudal lord and tenant each directly took a *share* in what had been grown on lands owned and tenanted respectively by their families together for generations, however unfairly.

That had also, we have to note, made possible in fugitive places the survival of matriarchal economics, which sustained pockets of independent women. Such as the household communes of the free Beguine women, principally in Belgium, the Netherlands, Germany and France from the 13th to the 17th centuries.

Thus the early European working class was accustomed to working not so much for a wage per hour but for a *sharing* of the material bounty of the enterprise. Which was only *natural*, however un-natural modern capitalism has made it today.

Although each craft or trade had its own slang for the unpaid *share* of materials that each worker expected to take home in addition to any pittance of a cash wage, as a whole such takings from the employers were often known in Britain then by terms like "cabbage" or more formally as the polite term "perquisite" (which still lives on today in our familiar term, "perk"—though ironically enough, today's "perk" usually refers to extra privileges for higher end corporate executives and the capitalist affluent). The term "cabbage" itself most specifically started as slang for the leftover ends and remnants of cloth from the tailoring trade. This was an age when clothes were still made by hand in many small artisan shops by many thousands of multi-national tailors and seamstresses, not mass produced in large factories.

Taking home a bundle of scraps or too old goods or refuse—usually to barter "blood for blood," or without cash, for some prepared food or used clothes or other necessities in one of the large street markets—was the "perquisite" of the cook or maid, the tailor or apprentice, the sailor or the laborer unloading and moving the cargo. Pubs and brothels were also common places where the "overweight," "sweepings," "gifts," "flow," "vails," "samples," "castings," "drainage," "wastage" (just some of the terms for shared materials taken licitly or illicitly by the workers involved) could be sold.

This trade in materials and objects, taken individually and collectively as a rightful little share by British workers, was an underground economy of the laboring poor, a vast trade altogether, involving directly or indirectly much of a city's population during the 18th century. Such takings by custom, directly sharing in the river of goods, made up the bulk of the real earnings of British workers then, at the false dawn just before industrial capitalism.

In the household of a well-established or even titled family, such "vails" made the official cash wages of household employees look like the nothing they were. "Vails" in kind were widespread and important, where each class of household servant was entitled to a specific type of leftover or scrap—from butlers taking candle stubs and empty liquor bottles,

and cooks taking fat and bones, to maids as well as the other servants taking worn uniforms and stable gear, old linens and old clothing.[51]

British seamen of that age, for example, were in effect vagabonds almost by definition, and their sailing ships were the most numerous "factories" in the colonial economy. That great merchant fleet was critical, since what value would Britain's colonial empire have without the large assemblage of cargo ships to carry the

sugar and flax and rum and tobacco and coffee and dyes and cotton and iron and spices and tea and lumber and grains and other loot back to England.

Together with the longshoremen or "lumpers" who unloaded cargoes and afterwards readied the ships, the lightermen whose small river boats ferried the boxes and barrels of cargo from anchored ships in to the docks, and so on, those who worked in shipping accounted for "perhaps a third of the adult labour force of London" or more—the great city's largest single industry.[52]

By tradition, merchant seamen then had the right to each carry free a small amount of their own goods onboard to profit by, which "Privilledge" had been set at no more than 5% of the ship's tonnage in the 17th century. By 1772, for instance, the personal free total allowed all the seamen on any one British merchant ship was capped at 25 tons total outbound and 15 tons for the return leg back to Britain. A sailor carrying some personal rum picked up might earn only 2 or 3 pounds sterling wages on the whole Jamaica round-trip, but sell his little barrel of rum for 10 to 20 pounds sterling back in London.[53]

And the cargo, especially if it were physically convenient and anonymously profitable in nature, such as hogsheads or large barrels of sugar, was also partially shared by all as a matter of right. While the authorities and merchants made great fuss over the "plunderage" by lightermen and longshoremen, the question was only a matter of how much. A hogshead of sugar delivered was allowed, for example, to be 10–14 pounds underweight from its original plantation weight, for "sampling." Some sugar was considered unavoidably spilled in official sampling, which was taken in "sweepings" by the workers.

One ship owner explained to a Parliamentary investigating committee that the longshoremen or "lumpers" were paid so little, that they considered that "they had a right to take sugar." To which the Member of Parliament said, *"They all helped themselves to make up for short wages? ... Therefore, this, which used to be called plunderage, was at least in a considerable degree, a mode of paying wages?"* The ship owner answered, "It certainly was an understood thing." Again and again, it can be seen how payment in kind was primary to British workers back then, not their formal but far too scanty cash wages.[54]

It was understood in the printing trades, for instance, that a pressman by agreed upon custom could keep one unpaid for copy of any book that they had printed. A custom quietly claimed even today by pressmen. In 1796, a printer who was indicted for theft of a book, was freed by the jury, which found: *"a practice prevails ... among compositors and pressmen of retaining a copy of every book they work upon."* In trade after trade, this principle of *sharing* the products of labor as a right, in an underground wage system, was to different degrees acknowledged as established custom in the Great Britain of the 18th century.[55]

This had resulted in real income that was far too high for the ruling classes' tastes, in some cases being almost sufficient to survive upon. In many cases not, which is why so many butchers and injured soldiers and weavers and house servants and so on were forced by the threat of starvation and homelessness into thieving and robbing and conveying and sex work and counterfeiting and the like. Counterfeiting, by the way, was considered a high crime fit for torture by the Crown, but this was a view not shared by commoners. After all, to craft a metal coin and "wash" it with a coat of silver was a real job—and the practical utility of a good home-made coin was almost as much as one from the haughty Royal Mint. So counterfeiting among the poor was like parking in the wrong space or making a tongue-in-cheek tax deduction would be to us: technically a "crime" but not really.

It was commonly claimed by the owning classes that under this spontaneous system of underground wages paid largely in "perquisites" aggressively taken, that the working classes lived like spoiled kings. When examined, of course, that was a poison drink of capitalist exaggerated propaganda.

SAILING SHIPS DISSOLVED BY WORKERS INTO ALE & FURNITURE & SHOES

The thousands of workers in the six Royal Navy dockyards during the 18th century, for example, where the wooden sailing ships were constructed, were the next thing to unpaid labor. Waged, yes, but not actually paid. It was common for the sparse cash wages to be months or even years late in arrears, and at best their paydays were officially only twice a year! They and their families survived only by the aid of the so-called "chips," which are thought to have provided maybe between a third and a half of their real income.

"Chips" were scrap pieces of wood from the shipbuilding, supposedly the cut-off odds and ends leftovers. By traditional right, each dockyard worker was entitled to take some of these wood "chips"—always under three feet long—under his arm when he went home. How often, how much, was part of the continual back and forth struggle between bosses and workers.

Crowds of women who claimed to be family members started appearing, too, to go over the worksites, in order to glean and carry out wood "chips" and "sweepings" too small for the men to bother carrying. So new regulations were posted de facto admitting their rights, too, but limiting them to only certain days, and so on.

Those wood "chips" and "sweepings" became for over a century a strange but logical type of currency or native trade goods in dockyard areas. Not only were "chips" a major source of fuel for home fireplaces and stoves, but building-materials dealers, pubs and other merchants took them in trade or bought them at the usual discount for resale. All as part of the underground economy of the working class not yet completely chained to capitalism.

The intellectual planner Samuel Bentham, who had been the organizer of Russian Prince Potemkin's shipyard, became Royal Inspector-General of Naval Works in 1795. Bentham took rented dwellings by Portsmouth Yard gate, solely to spy and discover how much timber was lost to the working class as "chips." To his

surprise, he found that the dimensions of the "chips" completely dictated the physical shape of workers' housing in the neighborhood: "Stairs were just under three feet wide; doors, shutters, cupboards, and so forth were formed of wood in pieces just under three feet long."

The diversion of timber into "chips" was somewhat masked by its ambivalent existence in the shadow of official cash wages. However, eventually this practice grew so large that it was an inescapable factor in naval economics. Experienced shipwrights believed that only a sixth of the timber entering Deptford Yard left it in ships. A Yeoman at Deptford Yard estimated that sixty per cent of the timber they had ordered for building a 74-gun ship of the line, went right back out the gate as "chips."[56]

IT'S ONLY A CRIME IF THEY MAKE IT ONE

As a side note, should point out that such natural customs arising from socialized production are hardly dead even now. They keep springing spontaneously to life time and again, all over, because there can't be anything more *natural* than us directly sharing even in a small way in the production and distribution itself that we do and make possible. Once when i was working at the great rail yard for "piggy-back" freight containers on Chicago's South Side, found that we all were supposed to honor various long-standing customs which loosely resembled criminal activity, if you wanted to look at it that way. Except that it was unwritten custom that we were entitled to them. Especially, us sharing what the capitalists had staked out as theirs.

Found this out the old fashioned way, by tripping over it myself. Was a really hot, sunny July day, and i was taking a semi-trailer out of its parking slot. Cutting the wheel, i hit the brakes to double-check our arc—and there must have been something wrong with the hitch pin, because the whole damn trailer slid right back off the "fifth wheel." Hitting the asphalt, the relatively fragile aluminum and plywood "reefer" trailer broke its back and crumpled onto the ground, ripping open. What a disaster, i thought jumping out of the cab, and wondered if i should just fire myself down the road before the boss did it himself.

Looking up, though, froze me. It was like the whole yard had gone mad. Trucks and yard vehicles were being stopped where they were, with the guys jumping out and running towards me. Some men were throwing open their own car trunks—getting the portable grills and charcoal they stashed there, i soon found out. Guys who didn't have trucks were trying to negotiate deals with the guys who did to share the capacity of their pickup or van, so there were knots of workers shouting and gesticulating, coming together and breaking up. Everyone moving towards me like a big party. WTF, really!

One of the yard mechanics i knew started laughing at my dazed face. He explained, that according to ICC regs or somebody's regs, any time a raw food cargo "touched the ground" it was instantly contaminated, considered spoiled, and had to be thrown away and the shipper compensated by insurance. So my "reefer" (for refrigerated trailer) load of entire frozen sides of raw meat hung packed tight—was up for grabs! Free steaks and roasts and spareribs, first come first served. All work had stopped, yard bosses disappearing into offices so that they wouldn't have to officially "see" anything.

Custom was that this occasional bounty was ours by right, to be shared by all the yard workers, everyone getting some. Remember one veteran Black worker set up his little grill right there by the open trailer, and started the fire so happily. So it was a long break for lunch early that day. Consoling me over doing the big accident of the month, one older co-worker said not to worry, by custom every so often at least one "reefer" load of meat got accidentally "spoiled" and shared around. With lunchtime barbeques and takeaways for home freezers.

And he reminded everyone, the union contract specifically forbid them from firing or punishing me for a first "accident"—although the boss to save face upstairs, did officially suspend me for a week (only *with* pay as per the contract). So the bottom line was, for accidentally getting everyone at work some yard-cooked barbeque and tons of meat to take home, i got an extra paid vacation that year. On some days you got to love the "class struggle."

Okay, back to work.

12. jane austen goes to school with the lumpen/proletariat

There are many roads to understanding the root process of capitalist criminalization, but one of the most direct is surprisingly the classic women's novelist, Jane Austen. Not only are her novels still read and admired by the literary world, but in a case of life-after-death even today her old stories keep being remade to some success both in renovelization and as Hollywood movies. The amusing junk movie, "Pride and Prejudice and Zombies," was only the latest and most exploitative of these at this writing, literarily speaking.

Austen was born in 1775 in a galaxy far, far away, to a well-connected but far from wealthy middle-class family, in the small rural hamlet of Steventon. Where her father was a local clergyman. With "connections" one of her brothers became a major rural landowner, complete with mansion, and two of the other brothers went away for naval careers in Great Britain's world-spanning colonialist military. Each eventually becoming a gold-braided admiral there. It was in such a top-heavy rural setting, peacefully distanced from the feverish backdrop of world colonial empire, that she set her very popular novels. Around and about young women of upper middle-class families, with their strong ambitions and domestic maneuvers for happiness.

Although she was of the lower layer of the landed gentry, Jane herself was writing at a time and place when women were not expected to be writers, and was published at a time when women were not allowed to be published. Her first novels sat in a drawer for years, because of the censorship. Although eventually becoming popular, her novels had to be published anonymously by "A Lady," and herself unknown in her lifetime. Jane Austen was never dispossessed or homeless, never had to sell her body for sex on the streets, or maim herself tied to a factory machine for nearly all her waking hours. Her family provided a single place for her within their privileged world. But she was no less ruled and bound by patriarchy.

Her plots reflected women's understandings because they pictured "well born" men with less illusions and more comic skepticism than society was used to. She focused on young women having to make difficult and life-altering decisions about imperfect men, given the patriarchal reality that their lifetime "job" as well as future children's lives would be determined by picking the "right" or "wrong" marriage. Like a lottery where losing tickets really make you lose.

Three quarters of Austen's own life was spent in two rural communities in Hampshire, and she loved the green fields and forests of the English countryside. She even told her niece once that nature's scenery was so beautiful that it must be "one of the joys of heaven." Counterbalancing that as a barely mentioned but approaching weather front in her stories, was the increasing threat of the lumpen/proletariat. Menacing even respectable households and dampening the desire of women to travel by horse and carriage to visit friends in other villages or to go to London. It was a surprise, back then, the intrusion of violent highwaymen and bold nighttime thieves both men and women.[57]

These two different things, though, the typical to us "beauty" of England's lush green fields set off by rows of thick hedges, and the discordant dimension of lumpen crime and violent people on the loose, were not unconnected. They were united, as two opposite dialectical elements of the same contradiction. Typically, it is culturally disguised, as in that flimsy horror movie remanufactured from an Austen novel, "Pride and Prejudice and Zombies." Where the invading dead zombies falling beneath the frantic swords of the skinny young white women of the manor, dressed of course in ballroom gowns, stand in symbolically for the "dangerous" proletarians; those that landowner capitalism had exiled from their own living homelands and transformed into something "dead" as outcast subhumans.

That lush and serene countryside didn't actually exist fully yet when Jane Austen was born in the later 18th century. The ruling class movie set was still being cleaned up and re-arranged. The traditional English countryside was for centuries far more uneven and scruffy in appearance than that. Agriculture in each town or hamlet was done in the "open field" system, particularly with several large unfenced fields of different grains, where varying strips of land belonging to different farm families were plowed and worked. Bare and scrubby lands lay between the unevenly shaped farmed strips. With meadows beyond those fields, where hay for Winter livestock fodder was grown.

Inconveniently further away beyond that and along the sides of roads and marshes was the "waste land" or "commons," which was owned by the village and was more haphazard and unkempt and in some spots more bare. Where any and all villagers could bring a few goats or sheep or cows to graze, or gather nuts and berries, pick mushrooms and greens, as well as cut sod for cheap fuel for the fireplace. Fallen branches could be gathered in the "commons" woods, as well as timber cut for repairing any family's fences and buildings.

That old traditional village agriculture was almost entirely family subsistence farming and gathering, growing what they ate, with only some surplus being sold on the local market or not at all in bad years. In the 18th century, as Great Britain evolved in a final rush from the remnants of feudal class relations into a capitalist class structure, this "open field" system of village life was anachronistic and no longer acceptable to the ruling classes. It was too fair.

In frank imitation of the more "efficient" commercial agriculture of the New Afrikan captive en-slaved labor plantations of Virginia and New York and Jamaica, new "Enclosure Acts" in Parliament laid the foundation for fully capitalist landholding and agriculture. Where scattered strips of traditionally-shared farmland amidst "open" or un-owned fields could be consolidated or "enclosed" by landowners into larger, more contiguous areas all neatly fenced off or bordered by big hedgerows to mark exclusive personal ownership and control. When all the "common" and "waste lands" had been added to that and also divided up between large landowners, the increase in wealth from commercial farming soared. Historian E.J. Hobsbawm emphasizes how drastic this change in landholding in many counties was:

"Between 1760 and 1820 about half of Huntingdonshire, Leicester and Northampton, over forty percent of Bedfordshire and Rutland, over a third of Lincolnshire, Oxford and the East Riding of Yorkshire, and a quarter or more of Berkshire, Buckingham, Middlesex, Norfolk, Nottingham, Warwick and Wiltshire were thus enclosed, mainly from open fields ..."[58]

As a vampire in our tv shows yearns for blood, so the landlords of Jane Austen's rural villages acquired an overpowering, almost visceral hunger for more and more land of their own. Imitating the greater culture of their world empire, which always hungered for more and more colonies and alien peoples to imprison or dispossess. And that class bloodlust wasn't so harmless as vampires in fiction.

In her first published novel, *Sense and Sensibility*, Austen pictures the cold and selfish John Dashwood, who has recently come into inherited lands and wealth, as he reneges on his promise at his father's deathbed to provide for his widowed step-mother and sisters. He feebly tries to excuse his tight-fisted theft to his sister, Elinor, by explaining his powerlessness before the all-consuming sensual attraction of Capital, to which they all must bow:

> "'The inclosure of the Norland Common, now carrying on, is a most serious drain. And then I have made a little purchase within this half year; East Kingdom Farm, you must remember the place, where old Gibson used to live. The land was so very desirable to me in every respect, so immediately adjoining my own property, that I felt it my duty to buy it. I could not have answered it to my conscience to let it fall into any other hands. A man must pay for his convenience; and it *has* cost me a vast deal of money.' ...

> "Elinor kept her concern and her censure to herself; and was very thankful that Marianne was not present, to share the provocation."[59]

Many poor rural families already struggling to survive, were pushed off their tiny homesteads by that more "efficient" enclosure, which was the other result of the capitalist remodeling of the English countryside. Many lost their tenancy. Becoming hired laborers by the week or day. Others were no longer able to maintain their few pigs or cow (pigs were thought the most useful of livestock then to many small farmers, since their meat could be easily smoked or pickled or cured to preserve it—and even the leftover bits could be used in sausages).

Often barred even from gathering berries and nuts, or kept from picking up fallen branches in the forests for firewood, or even to fish familiar local streams, more families lost their footing atop narrow household economies and were forced further down in the countryside. Or, increasingly often, forced onto the road to some city in a hard search of bare survival.

Jane Austen's local newspaper, the *Reading Mercury*, reflected the new world order where nothing of Nature was to be shared with the lower classes. In 1772 it published a formal notice that: "Whereas great damage has been done for many years past, to the hedges, lands, and coppices at Popham in the County of Southampton by several idle and disorderly people, by the gathering of mushrooms and nuts, this is to give notice, that whoever is found trespassing thereon for the future will be prosecuted to the utmost extent of the law."[60]

The historian E.J. Hobsbawm admits that for those English "small cultivators" in the 1700s–1800s : "Enclosure might well reduce them to simple wage-labour. More than this: It would transform them and the labourers from upright members of a community, with a distinct set of *rights*, into inferiors dependent on the rich. It was no insignificant change." He then quotes from a rural Suffolk clergyman writing of his villagers in 1844, of their loss of communal rights:

> "They have no village green or common for active sports. Some thirty years ago, I am told, they had a *right* to a playground in a particular field, at certain seasons of the year, and were celebrated for their football; but somehow or other this right has been lost and this field is now under the plough ..."[61]

Desperate men and women without any right to live, the livelihoods they tried out were not always so agreeable a "trade" as farming and gathering.

THE RIGHTS OF THEM

Small wonder that the home-taught radical pamphleteer, Thomas Spence, said in his "Rights of Man" in 1775—the year Jane Austen was born—that the ruling class claim to "own" all of nature as their exclusive property was a false tyranny: *"... no man, more than any other creature, could claim a right to so much as a blade of grass, or a nut or an acorn, a fish or a fowl, or any natural production whatever, though to save his life, without the permission of the pretended proprietor."*

Born poor and died poor, the brash Thomas was always proud that he was the first to put into print the phrase, *"the Rights of Man,"* and that his words had once won over the Duke of Portland's forester, no less; when the rebellious but often hungry Spence was surprised in 1788, while at Haydon Bridge, gathering hazelnuts:

> "While I was in the wood alone by myself a-gathering of nuts, the forester popped through the bushes

upon me, and, asking me what I did there, I replied, 'Gathering nuts.'

"'Gathering nuts!' said he, and 'dare you say so?'

"'Yes', said I, 'why not? Would you question a monkey or squirrel about such a business? And am I to be treated as an inferior to one of these creatures, or have I a less right? But who are you,' continued I, 'that thus take it upon you to interrupt me?'

"'I'll let you know that,' said he, 'when I lay you fast for trespassing here.'

"'Indeed,' answered I, 'but how can I trespass here where no man ever planted or cultivated; for these nuts are the spontaneous gift of Nature, ordained alike for the sustenance of man and beast that choose to gather them, and, therefore, they are common.'

"'I tell you,' said he, 'this wood is not common. It belongs to the Duke of Portland.'

"'Oh! My service to the Duke of Portland', said I. 'Nature knows no more of him than me. Therefore, as in Nature's storehouse, the rule is "first come first served," so the Duke of Portland must look sharp if he wants any nuts.'"

Finishing up, Spence opined that if any war came he was inclined to throw down his musket, for, *Let such as the Duke of Portland, who claim the country, fight for it!"*

We can see how such wit wasn't appreciated by the authorities, who had him in prison awaiting trial for "Treason" and other such political speeding offenses.[62]

Thomas Spence might as well have been speaking for the New Afrikan workers a century later in the u.s. empire, who

discovered after the Civil War that their new capitalist "freedom" did not include the right to share in the bounty of nature as they once did by informal custom even as captive laborers. In 1867, in a typical example, in Marksville, Louisiana, a woman and three of her family were discovered and arrested for trespassing "into a field and picking from the ground a few walnuts."[63]

The time of the "enclosures" (roughly 1750–1850) marked the absolute end of the English peasantry as a feudal class, their wholesale final dispossession and uprooting from rural society; them who had existed since early feudalism as the major population of the countryside. The people still existed, but had gone from hereditary workers attached to a farm to being day laborers or less. For many, no longer in rural hamlets but in different classes in more crowded and perilous environments.

So the green and scenic English countryside which Jane Austen loved, its peaceful distance from the harsh crowded worlds of the most desperate people fighting and scrabbling for survival, was entirely due to the violence of the class "cleansing" it was undergoing, as the less-noticed "other end" of global colonial capitalist empire.

PUTTING ON THE PARTY MASK OF CRIME

Not as a surprise, some of those in Jane Austen's countryside who could no longer raise a chicken for eggs or grow even some rye or barley to eat, felt little remorse at plucking the feathers of the well-to-do. Such highway robbery by armed men became a constant preoccupation among the "better" classes. Jane Austen's cousin, Eliza Hancock, wrote in a letter in 1788 after her safe return from a trip to Blenheim:

> "We returned to Town on Sunday and of all the dreadful storms of Thunder Lightning & Rain I ever remember, I think that we experienced on that aimiable place called Hounslow Heath was the worst, however I believe it saved us from being robbed as we afterwards heard that two Highwaymen were at that very moment in waiting for their Prey & nothing but the violent storm prevented them from stopping us."

There had been violent resistance and protests from the beginning, as soon as the rural workers and small farmers began to lose their rights and class standing with the brutal enclosures taking apart their countryside. In 1759, Jane Austen's uncle, James Leigh Perrot, started enclosing the land by his estate in North Leigh, near Oxford. The local periodical, *Jackson's Oxford Journal*, reported that "... certain ill-disposed Persons did destroy ... the fences and the new-planted Quick-Hedges, upon Norleigh-Heath ..." on his lands. Later, on a new farm elsewhere, Jane's uncle promptly had his hen-house broken into and a number of valuable fowls stolen. This became a new "normal" for class relations between the upper classes and the dispossessed. For what, to paraphrase a later rebel peasant defense attorney, was the vandalism and theft against the great estates compared to the founding of the great estates? Which is the real crime and which not?[64]

By the Summer of 1793, the growing armed robberies had become so numerous not only in London and the great cities but in Jane Austen's remote neighborhood, as to merit a large article in the local newspaper, the *Reading Mercury*. The nearby town of Overton, three miles from the Austen home and where the mail coach to London ran (and where Jane Austen's letters were posted) was at the center. "... many robberies have of late been committed in and about the neighbourhood of Overton, in the county of Southhampton, by a person supposed to be a stranger."

It said that among many other robberies, the Austen family friend, Mrs. Bramton, and a companion had their carriage stopped on the night of June 6th, and the two women robbed of eleven or twelve guineas (the guinea was a royal gold coin then, worth slightly more than the silver one pound sterling coin—and called the "guinea" because much of England's gold had long come in trade from what is now Ghana on the "Guinea coast" of West Africa).[65]

"Respectable" households were so fearful about these incidents because there was no British police force, by our meaning of the term as professional fulltime law enforcement, in the countryside until sometime in the 1830s. Under feudalism there had been little need, as the local feudal lord and his men-at-arms arrested and enforced the rules. With the lord himself as usual judge and jury. In Jane Austen's childhood years, highway robberies and nighttime theft of livestock and goods only grew more common, undeterred by the ineffective single volunteer constable usually appointed by the justice of the peace in each parish.

(By the way, the honorable ineffectiveness of the constable system can be later symbolized by the surprise election by his neighbors of an astonished Karl Marx as Constable of the Vestry of St. Pancras in

London. Marx and Engels were overcome with laughing about it.)[66]

Family manors turned, in that early dawn of the industrial age, to the security of metal guardians. Just as in today's digital age the capitalists turn to ever-present CCTV, of video surveillance recording endlessly in stores and homes and elevators and lobbies and all public spaces. A few years before Jane Austen was born, inventive metalsmiths adapted the simple spring traps used for animals to catch humans on nighttime incursions. Placed in shallow depressions on paths leading to barns and gardens and orchards, loosely covered with leaves and grass, these steel mantraps snapped around the victim's leg, immobilizing and lacerating or breaking it. Also used were spring-guns, where walking into an unobtrusive string stretched low at leg height across a path triggered a shotgun fastened to a nearby tree.

For instance, after his garden of melons and cucumbers was torn up one night in March 1789, the Rev. St. John took an angry advertisement in the Austen family's local newspaper offering a 10 pounds sterling reward for information naming the offender. The advertisement angrily warns: *"Spring guns, thigh snappers, and body squeezers are and will continue to be set in various parts of the said garden and all other premises in the occupation of the said William St. John."* Such menacing notices were not rare then.

Growing up, Jane had been aware of all this. In one of her unpublished teenage romance stories written when she was around 14, her young character Lucy is first met one night lying "in great pain underneath a Citron tree." She had been trying to find a house, and going through a wood *"when I found myself suddenly seized by the leg & on examining the cause of it, found that I was caught in one of the steel traps so common in gentlemen's grounds ... I screamed as you may easily imagine ... but not before one of my legs was entirely broken ..."*[67]

Their answer to all this chaos of resistance, was the state's relentless campaign in the 18th and 19th centuries to wipe out all traces of sharing land and production and to outlaw still further informal wages by workers' direct appropriation of goods, concentrating wages into the narrow force-feeding funnel of the cash nexus. And piling on supervision and workplace "security" and repression. Lots of repression.

It was common for workers to be arrested then for theft, in the centuries-long tear gas haze of social confusion, as the iron cuffs of the capitalist cash nexus system were gradually placed over the customary traditions of sharing nature and social production.

What was previously rights and custom became crimes and violations by the new norms. The London house servant John Franks was arrested for burglary after he had been fired, and had broken into his employer's house on Boxing Day 1779, taking two damaged silver spoons. Boxing Day was when by custom servants received holiday gifts from the home-owners, but Franks' employer absented himself that day. The two damaged silver spoons had been accidentally bent by Franks himself. He had confessed his fault to the mistress of the house, who had taken the two spoons out of use and put them away.

Franks argued that taking the bent spoons was *"my money,"* his *"vails"* of old household goods as per established "right" and custom. Judges often preferred—instead of jailing these criminals against property in the overcrowded old prison ships or "hulks" anchored in the Thames river—to first try and enlist them in army regiments going abroad to colonial wars. Or give them to "pressgangs" as involuntary navy or merchant sailors. The other alternative especially pushed on women inmates, was to bind them over for "transportation," to be forced

indentured servants or field laborers for many years in the euro-settler colonies in the Americas or Australia. But too old and blind to be that useful, in 1780 John Franks was discarded by the inexpensive method of being hanged by the neck from the gallows. For two bent spoons.

This repression was not and never could be directed in any even-handed way, of course. Those considered from subhuman peoples, such as from Wales and Ireland, were more often than not assumed to be guilty if charged. It was also severely aimed against women. Prostitution had recently been made a crime, for example; implicitly since it was the "theft" of the patriarchy's right of all men to use women's bodies for sex free of charge. There was a special barb in that indictment: by law all that was needed to convict a woman of criminal prostitution was the unsupported complaint of one man. So under new British capitalist law, any man could have any woman arrested and convicted as a prostitute just on his word. The results were as we might expect.

With the added twist that sentences were sometimes death by hanging for luckless women for some small crime. The severity was to convince them to take the offered escape of "transportation" to the euro-settler colonies and seven years or more of indentured servitude as a house domestic or field laborer. As the British Empire wanted their labor *and* their reproductive labor having and raising a new population, to anchor its overseas colonies with manageable European subjects. While having if anything a far larger than necessary surplus at home of dispossessed poor. So capitalist "crime" was ever shaped and reshaped again to fit the dictates of ruling class strategy.[68]

Workers fought back with means public and private, over and over, with primitive trade unions and secret associations, with new "criminal" tactics and strikes and pitched battles. In 1768, shipwrights successfully fought a unit of Royal Marines over their customary taking away bundles of "chips." There were even "riots" with crowds of women and men burning the mansions of the wealthy

---

"**After 1688 even the summary conviction of sexual offenders was increasingly called into question.** Throughout the middle ages, the sixteenth century, and the seventeenth [in England], as we have seen, it had been common practice to punish harlots summarily for their evil life. The societies for reformation continued this practice, systematically using so-called general warrants, which empowered constables to round up anyone they suspected. Yet by the early decades of the eighteenth century it had become highly contentious.

"We can see this partly in the rise of popular resistance to the arrest of streetwalkers. The presence in London of ever-larger numbers of soldiers and sailors in the course of the eighteenth century meant that antagonism towards moral policing became increasingly aggressive and commonplace. In 1702 and again in 1709, reforming constables were stabbed to death in public while attempting to detain streetwalkers. In the Spring of 1711, a drive against 'loose women and their male followers' in Covent Garden was foiled when 'the constables were dreadfully maimed, and one mortally wounded, by ruffians aided by 40 soldiers of the guards [*guards* here refers to men of the elite regiments such as the Coldstream Guards, Scots Guards, etc., that traditionally guard Buckingham Palace and other royal residences—editors], who entered into a combination to protect the women'.

"On another occasion in the East End, a crowd of over a thousand seamen mobbed the local magistrates and forcibly released a group of convicted prostitutes being sent to a house of correction."[70]

and looting the aristocracy, put down only by the military. On the night of June 6, 1780, simultaneous with the great assault on Newgate prison, a "negro" woman, Charlotte Gardiner, directed a "mob" who looted and set fire to a wealthy pub owner's house. "Huzza, well done, my boys—knock it down, down with it," she was reported to have shouted, as she herself took two candlesticks from the house. Arrested later, she was tried and refusing to deny her deeds, was hanged until dead.[69]

In London, in Birmingham, and other major cities, the large increase in crime was propelled by the surge of dispossessed taking for survival. A Parliamentary Committee found that from 1776 to 1780 alone, burglaries in London had increased by 800%. In new criminal street culture, anonymous boasting rhymes like from highwaymen became popular, just as thug hip-hop and the *narcocorrido* (or drug ballad) is so today:

"I keep my Horse, I keep my Whore;
I take no Rents; yet am not poor;
I travel all the Land about,
And yet was born to ne'er a Foot."[71]

The historian E.P. Thompson, in his classic *The Making of the English Working Class*, tells us that crime back then was not limited to a survival necessity, but for many men if not women on the street was a better or more profitable way of life, compared to being a worker:

"Taking a deep statistical breath, we can hazard the view that the standard-of-living of the average criminal (but not the prostitute) rose over the period up to the establishment of an effective police force (in the late 1830s), since opportunities for pilfering from warehouses, markets, canal barges, the docks, and railways were multiplying. Probably a good many casual workers supplemented their earnings in this way. The genuine professional criminal or 'traveller' would seem, on his own confession, to have had a splendid standard-of-life; he may be counted an 'optimist'. The standard of the unmarried mother, except in districts such as Lancashire where female employment was abundant, probably fell ..."[72]

MASS CRIME AND
LUMPEN EMERGENCE

The mass presence of crime in the oppressed world, in proletarian "streets," which we all know so well, is not some symptom of imaginary "backwardness" or "lack of family values." It was created and imposed from the very start by capitalism itself, newly minted both as rotten and as particular to capitalism as a corporate bond or a grimy hundred dollar bill. Capitalism also criminalized our traditional rights to share in social production, with every worker a likely criminal. As a new urban proletariat and lumpen/proletariat were made willy-nilly together side-by-side out of the harrowing of the suddenly obsolete and unwanted peasantry.

So the rise of the modern capitalist working class was always bound, at every step, with crime itself as a mass proletarian experience. Imposed by the system itself on us, this was never our choice.

Crime itself—a phenomenon of class society—is so many-layered, a dialectical reality. Not at all simple and straightforward. Which we all know, but usually without fully thinking it over. Like most of us, i have run into or known many criminals in my lifetime. But you know, a real chunk of the criminals i've known have been my bosses. Only their many crimes almost always get covered up or passed over or restamped "legal."

To start with, then, the biggest criminals are always the ruling class, the patriarchal capitalists and their state. Bakunin had pointed this out, in his *Immorality of the State*: "What is permitted to the State is forbidden to the individual. Crime is the necessary condition of the very existence of the State, and it therefore constitutes its exclusive monopoly, from which it follows that the individual who dares commit a crime ... above all, he is guilty against the State in arrogating to himself one of its most precious privileges."[73]

Then too, criminalization itself is always used as repression, to justify their punishments and contort the bodies of the lower classes and peoples. Massachusetts judge Webster Thayer, who was to famously sentence the anarchists Sacco and Vanzetti to death, had also sentenced Bartolomeo Vanzetti to fifteen years in prison for robbery—actually saying, "This man, although he may not have committed the crime attributed to him, is nevertheless morally culpable, because he is the enemy of our existing institutions."

Angela Davis reminds us that in the exact same way, the leading German Nazi constitutional law theorist, Carl Schmitt,

Some groups of colonial peoples or aliens were always singled out first for criminalization and harsh punishment in England then. Such as Welsh, the Irish, Africans, and always the Roma (then as now widely called by the slurslang, "gypsies"). A typical view could be seen in the 1775 letter which Rev. Gilbert White in Selborne wrote to a friend: "We have two gangs or hordes of gypsies which infest the south and west of England, and come round in their circuit two or three times in a year … while other beggars lodge in barns, stables, and cow-houses, these sturdy savages seem to pride themselves in braving the severities of winter, and in living in the open air the whole year around."

The Roma in England back then didn't yet have the wheeled caravans they became known for, and sheltered in simple tent encampments in out-of-the-way spots in the woods. It was most important for them to be even further from the eyes of judges and landlords. For the harassment and attacks against them were only applauded by society. As an example, in August 1797, *The Times* reported of one such police raid: *"On Sunday morning, about five o clock, ten police officers came to Norwood in three hackney coaches, threw down all the gypsey tents, and exposed about thirty men, women and children and carried them to prison, to be dealt with according to the Vagrant Act."* Their offense was *"telling fortunes for foolish young girls and even experienced dames."*[75]

argued that some people should be found guilty of crimes whether they actually did them or not, because those peoples were criminals at birth "by their very essence." We know that armed uniformed thugs of the state practice that same principle as they patrol the oppressed zones of the inner city and encircling bantustans tonight. That such ideological repression is heavily used against the proletariat, against colonized peoples, is the right arm of today's decaying 21st century "zombie" capitalism.[74]

Frederick Engels' classic book, *The Condition of the Working Class in England*, played a role in establishing industrial capitalism's responsibility for the mass degradation of human life. Written in the 1840s, when the exiled young Engels was still in his twenties, it was as controversial and criticized as any dissident's words might be today. And at over a century and a half distant, Engels' viewpoint definitely has aged out in places, and sometimes veers off from what we might think from our lives today.

His criticism of women's presence in the factories, for example, which he flatly states *"dissolves the family utterly,"* only further leads to his displaying a personal horror at their unemployed husbands then having to stay home *"condemned"*— as Engels puts it—to doing unnatural acts for real men like having *"mended his wife's stockings"* and even *"minding"* children. *"Can anyone imagine a more insane state of things,"* the manly Engels cries out. He was getting a bit wound up there. His lofty moral condemnation continues all the wilder:

> "But that is the least of the evil. The moral consequences of the employment of women in factories are even worse. The collecting of persons of both sexes and all ages in a single work-room, the inevitable contact, the crowding into a small space of people, to whom neither mental nor moral education has been given, is not calculated for the favorable development of the female character ...

> "... the consequences are not wanting. A witness in Leicester said that he would rather let his daughter beg than go into a factory; for they are perfect gates of hell; that most of the prostitutes of the town had their employment in the mills to thank for their present situation."[76]

The young Engels, even as a rebel, obviously still had internalized the values and outlook taught by his German bourgeois class, in the patriarchal and class-bound Europe of those times. Right then he was still trying out different ideas about the nature of class society, hit or miss, including about criminals and crime. About which he was in many ways speaking unfiltered there, which was a contribution we often don't think about. That's necessary to get straight. Because although *The Condition of the Working Class in England* was written just before he and Karl got around to fully intuiting the presence of the lumpen/proletariat, Engels did probe the class politics of crime for himself and for his readers:

> "Hence with the extension of the proletariat, crime has increased in England, and the British nation has become the most criminal in the world. From the annual criminal tables of the Home Secretary, it is evident that the increase of crime in England has proceeded with incomprehensible rapidity. The numbers of arrests for *criminal* offenses reached in the years: 1805, 4,065; 1810, 5,146 ... 1841, 27,760; 1842, 31,309 in England and Wales alone. That is to say, they increased seven-fold in thirty-seven years ... So that two districts which include great cities with large proletarian populations, produced one-fourth of the total amount of crime, although their population is far from forming one-fourth of the

whole. Moreover, the criminal tables prove directly that **nearly all crime arises within the proletariat** ... The offenses, as in all civilized countries, are, in the great majority of cases, against property, and have, therefore, arisen from want in some form; for what a man has he does not steal."[77] (our emphasis)

There, Engels was limiting himself to using the same "facts" or half-truths as the ruling class, only from his different political vantage point.

Take for instance the 1830s "Swing Riots"—not "riots" at all but arson attacks against the rural great houses; in the name of the pseudonymous "Captain Swing," but really suspected of being by the proletarian "mob." Engels quotes approvingly from the writing of Liberal Party MP Edward Wakefield. Wakefield's pamphlet on "rural incendiarism" maintained the ruling class position that the new proletariat or dispossessed laboring poor were essentially *all* criminals, a sordid complete class of criminals, by the very nature of their circumstances if nothing else. It was this that explained the threats of the mythic "Captain Swing" and his followers' incendiary deeds in the dead of night, that English politician wrote, his ballpoint dripping with contempt:

"An English agricultural labourer and an English pauper, these words are synonymous. His father was a pauper and his mother's milk contained no nourishment. From his earliest childhood he had bad food, and only half enough to satisfy his hunger, and even yet he undergoes the pangs of unsatisfied hunger almost all the time that he is not asleep. He is half clad, and has not more fire than barely suffices to cook his scanty meal ...

"He must support his family, though he cannot do so, whence comes beggary, deceit of all sorts, ending in fully developed craftiness. If he were so inclined, he yet has not the courage that makes of the more energetic of his class wholesale poachers and smugglers. But he pilfers when the occasion offers, and teaches his children to lie and steal. His abject and submissive demeanour towards his wealthy neighbors shows that they treat him roughly and with suspicion; hence he fears and hates them, but he will never injure them by force. He is depraved through and through, too far gone to possess even the strength of despair."

Engels found this explanation of mass anti-capitalist crime in the countryside so entrancing that he didn't even slow down to deal with Wakefield's own cartoonish slam of England's agricultural workers.

The uber-arrogant Wakefield, said to have been blessed with exceptionally corrupt gifts of political interest and persuasion, was himself widely shunned within the British ruling class and certainly is stamped "USDA choice" *lumpensomething*. His unusual background of having served a three year sentence in Newgate prison himself, even as a young climber in the ruling classes, had led him into being a self-appointed expert on the criminal poor and England's need for more mass euro-settler emigration to its colonies. Frederick Engels sums up the rest of Wakefield's description of the English countryside's lower classes for his reader:

"The author adds that besides this class of agricultural labourers, there is still another, somewhat more energetic and better endowed physically, mentally, and morally; those, namely, who live as wretchedly but were not born to this condition. These he represents as better in their family life, but smugglers and poachers who get into frequent bloody conflicts with the gamekeepers and revenue officers of the coast, become more embittered against society during the prison life which they often endure, and so stand abreast of the first class in their hatred of the property-holders."[78]

There is no doubt that this was also Engels' view of the 1840s rural proletariat in England, since he wrote: *"Down to the present time, this description applies to the greater portion of the agricultural laborers*

About Wakefield's checkered lumpen-aristocrat career as rapist-kidnapper and convict and only a semi-legitimate founding father of New Zealand and Australia— as well as acts such as his infamous kidnapping of and coerced marriage to a 15-year old heiress who didn't even know him—there are many sources. See, for example, *Te Ara—The Encyclopedia of New Zealand*, at www.teara.govt.nz

of England." (He then follows in his book with an energetic defense of the morality of poaching and smuggling.) Putting aside that British MP's class prejudices and insults, there is still the picture of the early agricultural proletariat as having little respect, on a daily basis, for ruling class laws or property. While beyond that, there can be seen people who have left "work" behind them altogether, and with boldness went at seizing their livelihood by being professionals at poaching, thieving, and smuggling. Or in a word, remaking property boundaries to their desires—just as the capitalists did first.

What we see in that early attempt at summarizing the difficult lives at the bottom of the new rural class structure, was the beginnings of class differentiation. Although Engels wasn't using the concept of the lumpen/proletariat yet, observers were starting to recognize the lumpen as different people; as some being in the proletariat but yet not in it, as being an emerging element classwise by themselves.

Out of that dispossessed working class in which breaking property laws was simply a normal form of grassroots custom and survival: A veiled emergence of those outside lawful life altogether, who accepted exchanging violence with lawmen, along with the inevitable—prison time or even the hangman's rope. Who might mingle among laborers they had grown up with, but who had given up laboring for "wholesale" professional crime. No longer workers or anyone's employees in any sense, they were said to be smarter, more risk-taking and violent, even physically stronger, thus having more macho status or at least more notoriety. (We might question how factual or accurate that 19th century English criminal gentleman and that early German communist were about the alleged superior ability and even physique of these new lumpen outlaws, versus the run-of-the-mill working class—or was that just another case of guys' admiring cross-class "bromance"?)

Fred Engels closes in on a significant understanding, though: that such law-breaking and violence against English property and lawmen themselves was *"the first stage of resistance to our social order, the direct rebellion of the individual by the perpetuation of crime."*[79]

This exact same observation in their own times and places was also scribed by Mao Z back in old China, as well as by the influential anti-colonial revolutionary Frantz Fanon in the 1950s, then by 1960s New Afrikan theorists here (often quoting Fanon) such as George Jackson and the Black Panther Party. And as Atiba Shana reminded us time and again about boys on the street: revolutionaries always have to search in the juvie, in prisons, and in the midst of the lawless for their own, because for colonially oppressed young men, *"The first rebellion is always crime."*

What do we know overall about the social weight of the lumpen back then, in the England of the 1700s–1800s, at the start of industrial capitalism? The British historian E.P. Thompson tried his best to get a factual handle, a census of some kind or even good estimates on the lumpen, in that system transition. But as he says early on, available reports from back then are untrustworthy: "Such facts as are available were often presented in sensational form, and marshaled for pejorative purposes."

He goes on to note that "one of the most industrious investigators, Patrick Colquhoun" found that there were at the end of the 18th century in England "50,000 harlots, more than 5,000 publicans, and 10,000 thieves in the metropolis alone [i.e. London]; his more extended estimates of the criminal classes, taking in receivers of stolen property, coiners, gamblers, lottery agents, cheating shopkeepers, riverside scroungers, and colorful characters like Mudlarks, Scufflehunters, Bludgeon Men, Morocco Men, Flash Coachmen, Grubbers, Bear Baiters and Strolling Minstrels totals (with the former groups) 115,000 out of a metropolitan population of less than one million."* Or one out of every ten persons.

"His estimate of the same classes, for the whole country,—and including one million in receipt of parish relief—totals 1,320,716. But these estimates lump together indiscriminately gypsies, vagrants, unemployed, and pedlars and the grand-parents of Mayhew's street

* Although carrying somewhat exotic names as in much street slang, those were just common and well-known informal street trades of that time. "Mudlarks" were those who searched at low tide in the riverbank mud and flats for stray bits of cargo. "Scufflehunters" were the lowest class of dock laborers, also called "Bob Tails" after their wide work aprons, wandering from pier to pier, seeking spot cargo handling jobs from which they could supposedly look to steal small amounts of goods. "Bludgeon Men" were just as they sound, strong-arms for hire to bash a few heads or get rid of someone. "Flash Coachmen" were carriage drivers who specialized in serving thieves, prostitutes, receivers, and other criminals. And so on.

sellers; while his prostitutes turn out, on closer inspection, to be 'lewd and immoral women', including 'the prodigious number among the lower classes who cohabit together without marriage' (and this at a time when divorce for the poor was an absolute impossibility)."[80]

Many who were on early English poor relief, with its strictness and demand for the innocent "worthy poor," for instance, were hardly lumpen. Most parishes banned "foreigners"—which were the destitute from a different English church parish—and demanded that they must return "home" to where they were already known. Many on poor relief were in the category of "decayed householders," dwellers in the parish who due to old age, illness or disability, could no longer support themselves. Ditto the classic widows and orphans. Instead of the 16% of the English population as a whole that Patrick Colquhoun's count might have suggested, the number of actual lumpen/proletarians at that time & place was certainly much less; but if the true number of lumpen in London in 1800 were placed at less than half his estimate, a 5% or 6%, that would not be out of the question.

E.J. Hobsbawm's historian colleague and sometimes collaborator, George Rudé, in his study of European popular protests and rebellions in the 18th century, also considers this Patrick Colquhoun's estimates. He believed them meaningful and that together with corresponding French data on poor relief in Paris in the 1770s–1790s, he estimated that it would be safe to place such declassed elements at about 100,000–120,000 in London and Paris each. He recognizes but excludes from that number the industrial proletariat at the known factories in Paris, for example, saying: "But, in both cities, there was also an equally large, but 'submerged', group of poor, destitute, beggars, homeless, vagrants, part-employed, seamstresses and homeworkers, criminals, prostitutes and *lumpen*-proletarians (Marx's later term), whom the more respectable workers ... thoroughly despised and rejected."[81]

Now they were searching out a real portion of the people, not just a trace sifting.

GENDER DIFERENCE IN "THE CRIMINAL CLASSES"

And what of women, of gender-class and the lumpen/proletariat? You'll have noticed back a few pages when E.P. Thompson said that in the late 1700s and early 1800s, the standard of living for criminals actually rose compared to workers—except *but not the prostitute.* Or when he said that at the same time, except in the factory-district of Lancashire, *"the standard of the unmarried mother ... probably fell."* Just as the income of male highwaymen and thieves and counterfeiters and other such was going up. That is the same as saying flatly that lumpen men in general were better off in that historical moment but proletarian and lumpen single women were worse off. What is "class" then?[82]

One explanation would be that the young lumpen class strata in England, at the start of industrial Creation, was not in itself gender balanced. As Butch Lee points out, the patriarchy has always misrepresented society as paired up in couples two-by-two, male & female, as the respectable animals going onto Noah's Ark. This shouldn't be a shock to anyone. Uneven genders in social classes aren't unknown. On the one hand, there were certainly many women among the vagabonds and street criminals then & there. Maybe not 50,000 prostitutes alone in London in the 1790s, as the social investigator Patrick Colquhoun concluded, but the number was not small—and "street" women didn't confine themselves just to selling their bodies for sex or just to one kind of crime. Survival itself was hard and dirty work for untold masses of women and children there.

There were highwaywomen if lesser in number than highwaymen, just as women thugs and thieves as well as male. According, for example, to the *Public Advertiser*, on July 21, 1784, one "Farmer

E.P. Thompson, early right in the text of that landmark 1963 work, *The Making of the English Working Class*, calls attention to the political need for more historical knowledge of the less "respectable," those outcasts living by taking, by violence and the river of crimes:

"Those who have wished to emphasize the sober constitutional ancestry of the working class movement have sometimes minimized its more robust and rowdy features. All that we can do is bear the warning in mind. We need more studies of the social attitudes of criminals, of soldiers and sailors, of tavern life; and we should look at the evidence, not with a moralizing eye ('Christ's poor' were not always pretty), but with an eye for Brechtian values—the fatalism, the irony in the face of Establishment homilies, the tenacity of self-preservation."[86]

Jackson" was "set upon" while traveling from market after selling livestock in Kent, "by several Men and Women, who pulled him off his horse, and robbed him of Twelve Guineas and some Silver. The Women were for murdering him, that he might tell no Tales, but one of the Men said, it was Crime enough to rob him. They then turned his Horse loose and made off."[83]

The well-known Mary Cut-and-Come-Again was officially hanged for stealing an apron worth 6 pence, but really had been executed for being a "Queen of the blackguards." Mary had gotten her cant name for her high skill at swiftly cutting open people's pockets as they passed in the streets so that she could take their valuables. A bold and bitter enemy of the ruling class and its state, so completely was she known by her cant name, that the authorities had no idea of her "legal" moniker. At her trial they even had to bargain for the knowledge of her birth name, "Mary White," in return for concessions so she would be more comfortable (such as being held but without being chained up).

Still, the number of women hanged in London was small compared to men. In the long period of 1703–1772, there were only 92 women hanged compared to 1,150 men. Even given the court's preference for transporting women who had been first sentenced to hanging, the imbalance may

also be rooted in the fact that many key criminal trades were largely male. In fact, the historian Peter Linebaugh says: "A statistical analysis of all London indictments ... for the year 1740 shows that the *only* felony for which a greater number of women were indicted than men was the offense of receiving stolen goods. Male thieves frequently formed partnerships with female receivers ... In the eighteenth century marriage was a business partnership." Butch Lee's sarcastic comment is relevant right here: *"Even in the lumpen, the woman usually has the fem role. Although everything is changing, we all know."*[84]

We don't think of the lumpen/proletariat as distinct class strata having an economic "boom" or "bust" like normal classes do, but temporary advantages and disadvantages of cycle and circumstance apply to them as to the whole classes. Devastated, atomic-bombed, post-WWII Occupied Japan, for example, was remembered very fondly by one older euro-american lumpen guy i knew, who was among those who went there to bareback ride the black market, to rob and pimp and do the dope trade with their complete American impunity from arrest by "Jap cops," and who thus found it exceptionally "sweet."

The decline in the standard of living for women sex workers and single working mothers in the early English 1800s as compared to male criminals could be because the closely related lower classes were paired in a gender reversed way: with the lumpen being male-centered and the lower working class being women-centered, although there were many of both gender-classes in each. This is not yet adequately explored or mapped out human geography.

So if there were some less women than men in the lumpen/proletariat "street" trades, there were simultaneously less men than women and children in the proletariat of the new factories. Engels in his survey of the working class in England in the 1840s, tells his reader that shockingly, men and particularly English men were definitely the small *minority* of the active factory workers. In 1839, women and girls were the majority of the 419,560 factory workers in England, while **adult men were "*not one full quarter* of the whole number."** Many of whom weren't English but miserably paid colonial subjects from Ireland. Taking away the higher-paid men's skilled trades in the factories as carpenters, foremen, engineers and so on, Engels wrote that ***"the actual work of the mills is done by women and children." The lower working class, the industrial *proletariat*, was really women and children.**[85]

So at the 19th century birth of the modern industrial proletariat, its active workforce consisted of extremely poorly paid women and children. While men at the same time there appeared to be more successful at least financially, as the parallel core of the emerging lumpen/proletariat.

Although as usual for Marxist academics, Thompson doesn't use the term lumpen/proletariat in that book, his history keeps showing what look like lumpen strata starting to surface, in the hurly-burley of that "mix" of the criminalized workforce of early euro-capitalism. And his language about the lumpen all but labels them. He writes at one point using the phrase "the dangerous classes"— but not telling us that when Marx's writings were officially translated out of his original German into English, the translators' wording for Marx's "lumpenproletariat" in *The Communist Manifesto* was precisely that term, "the dangerous class." Writing about the British political crisis of 1831–1832, Thompson names those most feared by the ruling circles in making revolution as "the criminal classes." We can get it, it's right there.[87]

As a student, Peter Linebaugh of *The London Hanged* had read Thompson and decided to take up his challenge of analyzing how those who had swung at London's 18th century gallows, had been forced to take in order to live. He too does not use the term lumpen/proletariat. He writes quite reasonably that: "Research revealed the difficulty of distinguishing between a 'criminal' population of London and the poor population as a whole." Hard enough to do with mass criminalized classes.

Yet, Linebaugh found in the Europe of the 1700s that there was a "picaresque proletariat" as it became known, or *picaro,* which was part of the larger proletariat. Named after the adventuring poor who became *piquero* or mercenary pikemen in the Spanish empire's armies which temporarily conquered so much of Europe. The *picaro* was defined as a rogue or vagabond. As violent transgressors and takers, guided by individualism and boldness. In other words, a potential lumpen/proletariat in the process of being made. Linebaugh writes:

> "To sum up, we may compare the picaro and the proletarian. Like the picaro, the proletarian has nothing; neither a mess of pottage today nor the lands and tools to work with that he or she may fill his or her bowl tomorrow. **Unlike the picaro, who is defined by shunning work, the proletarian is defined as being a worker.** The scene of action of the picaro is the road, the market, the inn or the tea-garden—places of public exchange. The proletarian in contrast operates in places of private production: beneath decks or in a garret. Like the proletarian, the picaro is held in contempt by those who lord over him or her."[88] [our emphasis]

Again, we can see class differentiation happening, the lumpen starting to emerge from within the proletariat in the raw class turmoil of a newly made capitalism, in which *both* desperate classes were criminalized.

13. in mid-journey …
some notes towards lessons

While the traditional image of the lumpen/proletariat is of scattered outcasts and criminals at the very margins of society, we can now see that this is only an incomplete corner of the picture. The reports we've brought together have been fairly consistent—to the contrary. In 1926, in an example covering one-fourth of the human race, Mao Zedong estimated that the lumpen in Old China were 6% of their population, or some twenty million persons.

From modern evaluations of then contemporary estimates, it is reasonable to weigh the street lumpen in London and Paris in the mid-1800s at no more than 100,000 each or a would-be tenth of those cities' total population. Even if the totals were only half that, it would be a significant minority, especially for those cast out of the regularity of class life in economic production and distribution. And there is every reason to believe that the comparative numbers within capitalist society are even larger now.

We may think that we don't know much about the lumpen, but over many years and many different countries, a large landscape of experience has accumulated. And patterns are definitely forming, pixel by pixel, as we sift this data.

The earliest observations of the lumpen in Europe as distinct class strata by anticapitalist revolutionary thinkers, such as Engels, Bakunin and Marx, were **real insights but also fragmentary and tentative**. We have since then added the lessons of many other peoples and liberation struggles. So we respect the work of early pioneers in radical class theory, but should in no way feel bound to their limitations of time and place. Nor would they have wanted us to be. New knowledge has both validated and called into question various aspects of the old radical theories on lumpen.

As was pretty obvious, Marx's theoretical view of the lumpen was negative, while Bakunin's was pretty positive. And you couldn't convince either of them to change their minds, because each could see plenty of evidence to confirm their viewpoint. While leftists have usually debated this question as one versus the other, actually both were "right" and both were "wrong." They each correctly analyzed what they were looking for, but didn't consider that their own lumpen sample was only one type of strata of a much larger and varied number.

The first key for us to understand this—and the lumpen in general politically—is that they are *not* a class. Everyone, that *Capital*-writing fiend Karl included, kept forgetting this fact in practice. Lumpen aren't like the working class or the assorted middle classes, they aren't one class.

The lumpen are a social category of different class strata or fragments or splinters. They aren't one thing, and certainly not politically. We've learned that the hard way, for sure. What distinguishes the lumpen/proletariat is that they have been cast out of or have left the functioning classes of patriarchal capitalism. Though many of them are among the very poorest, the most desperate, **the step that distinguishes them is that they have fallen out of class. They're "unplugged" socially.** That is, the lumpen/proletariat has no regular role as groupings in "legal" production and distribution, and to survive must often devise immediate if short-lived ways to get their livelihood from others.

In 1848, Marx could discern that underneath the fancy uniforms—"green epaulets"!—of the *Garde Mobile* were lumpen street boys torn from their culture and context. But since the other lumpen weren't wearing Mao caps or even faded old *Bone Thugs-N-Harmony* t-shirts, he couldn't tell that probably many other lumpen poor men and women were active on the opposing side. At that same battle fighting on the *other* side of the barricades, with the workers' revolution. And lots of Paris lumpen surely weren't on either of the warring sides. (If there's an alternative to good vs. evil, our lumpen will find it.) Karl was only really seeing a selected part of the city's lumpen. This is a continual problem with outside observers missing lumpen strata who want to remain as anonymous as possible.

Another basic that is subliminally known but not dealt with cards up on the table, is the gender thing. Is that while the lumpen/proletarian fragments do have both male and female in them, they are not gender balanced at all. Most lumpen subcultures or occupations are predominantly male, often overwhelmingly male, except for full-time sex workers. The standard biblically sanctified paired up M+F gender composition is nowhere in sight hereabouts. Whether it's the chaotic English "swell mob" of the 1700s London street scene, Marx's "laundry list" of the European vagabond "social scum," Mao's rural lumpen in his war-torn 20th century China, or today's heavily-armed criminal occupations—to say nothing of America's postmodern "plantations" of mass incarceration—the actors are heavily majority men and boys. This is a consistent pattern.

The flipside of this mono-gender subculture is an **even more unacknowledged class reality**, that under capitalism the lower working class—the *proletariat* proper—is mostly women and children. That way at the start of industrialization, that way right now in the world. So that often the proletariat and the more desperate lumpen fit together maybe unhappily but readily as shards, family-wise and sometimes gender-wise, to comprise a *favela* or a ghetto, a larger lower class community. **Both "classes" were criminalized at their creation, recall, and live exis-** **tences heavily tinged with crime and being outlawed in various ways both in law and discrimination.** Reminding us again that women sex workers might fit better analytically in the working class rather than in the lumpen. It also means that much of the day-to-day social violence against proletarian women and girls is directly by lumpen men. Particularly when armed male lumpen organizations begin exercising de facto micro-state power over territory.

Mapping the lumpen/proletariat gives us the added bonus of a different angle of triangulation, sometimes discovering unexpected shapes of other classes. Actually, we can't know the proletariat without knowing the lumpen. Never forgetting that society is a class structure, a whole, not just an assembly of separate parts.

As we look deeper into actual mass life, actual class activity, we are finding more and more questions. Like, the counterfeiter in 1750s London, who to the royal treasury was an arch criminal deserving of torture in the Tower of London. And to Marx that counterfeiter was plainly only a lumpen/proletarian, one of the disreputable "scum." But to many working-class Londoners then, the counterfeiter was only an enterprising person plying an illicit but useful trade requiring skill and nerve. Making their own silver coins as the poor neighborhood's equivalent of the snooty royal mint. Just another working person, to many. Just as small smugglers have always been regarded as ordinary workers by many in border areas. Not really criminals at all.

Then why not sex workers as well? Under patriarchy all women as a gender-class are sex workers, after all. Women's primary role in reproducing labor for society is primal production itself. We have to navigate the reality of the class formations capitalism raises up. But at the same time the exploited and oppressed, the outcast and outlawed, have to respect their own need to redefine and remake class for themselves. How else does the class struggle start?

The oh-so sophisticated capitalism of today's Globalization still has the same vicious family traits as the earliest, crudest industrial capitalism. We have many more people than places to put them in the straight capitalist system. That's how the system structures itself to work on us. That's coded in its genes. There's always crowds of folk, in the suburb as well as the favela and inner city, who are forced for survival to make work for themselves out of bounds. If you take the "morality" out of it, it opens the discussion.

Neither Marx nor Bakunin ever got the chance for protracted work with lumpen, large numbers of lumpen, over the whole course of a revolutionary struggle. Maybe that's why it was so much guesswork on their part? It was Mao Z who first made that an ordinary part of anti-capitalist political work and planning, in the first half of the 20th century. Mao Z's line summing up the lumpen for the revolution, became famous among radicals worldwide: *"In every part of the country they have their secret societies ... One of China's most difficult problems is how to handle these people. Brave fighters, but apt to be destructive, they can become a revolutionary force if given proper guidance."*

We know that the lumpen played a key role in the revolutionary process for that big trouble-maker Mao Z. Becoming a major element in China's militant rural struggles in the 1920s–1940s. Even at some times and places being a *majority* of the revolutionary guerrillas that Mao Z coached to overthrow the actually existing capitalism. That isn't a small thing politically.

How Marx thought about the lumpen as class strata changed in an important way. At first he knew them in inherited attitude, as outcasts by semi-feudal rules. But then at a certain point in the early 1850s he started defining them not subjectively but objectively, in a structural way. As all those who were "parasites" because they were divorced from economic production and distribution. This included layers of people even from the upper classes, and contemporary masses of people in some situations serving in a "parasite" state. As he put it so broadly but certainly also colorfully: *"From whore to pope, there is a mass of such rabble ..."*

When you add in the Chinese revolutionary experience of the 1920s–1940s, which eventually defined the "parasitic" lumpen/proletariat as including the mass of regime officials and servants, criminal allies on the streets, the police, jailors, and all the army soldiers on the enemy capitalist side, that was a massive slice of society. All this has major implications for class analysis.

Marx also identified the 1852–1870 French state of Napoleon III **explicitly as a lumpen state, managed and inhabited by them, although fully using the existing capitalism as its operating system.** This was a breakthrough concept, since it opens the door to exploring the class nature of the more extreme varieties of states that keep popping up. Some of which are real problems for the human future. Why should anti-capitalism be less imaginative than science fiction?

So both Marx and Mao Z each reached quite similar analyses of a capitalist state that was deforming deep in crisis, that they were engaged against. In 1850s Europe and almost a century later in Asia, respectively. It's significant that, so far as we know, neither based his findings on any prior generalized theory about the state, but both came to converging understandings independently, piece by piece as they each put together the concrete picture before them.

In both cases, they believed that a capitalist state in severe crisis had become like a criminal organization at its core: with masses of lumpen politicians and officials, lumpen lower-level functionaries and officers, lumpen cops and soldiers. This class concept might help us better break down conflict zones such as neo-colonial Mexico, the Great Russian stalinate, makeshift parasite states like ISIS or Al-Qaeda, or even the shooting gallery of postmodern Chicago.

This stuff needs thinking about and sorting out, particularly since privilege and parasitism are becoming larger and larger characteristics of late capitalism. Which only obscures or confuses the class vision when not factored in.

Here's something really important. There's a characteristic immediacy or urgency in daily life for many lumpen. One of their strengths and one of their weaknesses. Comes out of their specific "non-class" situation. Regular classes in society have well-established paths or routines, which loyally followed are supposed to lead to a successful life under capitalism. Sometimes do, sometimes don't. We all know about this. The middle classes compete to send their young hamsters to elite kiddie schools, then to a Yale or a Stanford or the like, then they get the right internships with the right corporations or the right state agencies. The wheel spins faster and faster in the hamster cage, and—bingo, Bob's your uncle!

With the euro-settler working classes of the metropolis, it's the relative who's the foreman at the small business or maybe the transit repair crew. (i once spent an afternoon by the beach at Coney watching a park department maintenance gang of twelve white guys—one was the foreman, one was a visiting supervisor leaning back against his new dark green city pickup, two were replacing damaged or worn out wooden boards in the boardwalk, and eight were standing around gossiping, joking and watching the two who *were* working. Next year the city said that the community's beloved wooden boardwalk would have to be replaced by concrete and plastic, since wood was too "expensive" to maintain—when euro-settlers do it, "wood" is spelled "w-h-i-t-e," too.)

Thing is, the lumpen have no such safe path or routine in life to follow. **They have to constantly figure out ways to keep their ball up in the air**. Improvise, do things "normal" people aren't willing to do, step off on real risks, even leap into sure failure because you know that you have to do something and maybe out of that crash you find the handhold that leads to something more workable. The one thing that you can't do is just stand around and do nothing, because every day you have to eat something and you have to have shelter of some minimal sort. And it all has to come from somewhere or something you found or did. There's a certain fierce freedom in facing the world bare-handed, alone.

The notion of **having a revolution or any kind of crisis at the grassroots of society without the lumpen—invited or no—is almost laughable**. Try keeping moths away from lights, why don't you, or curious kids away from forbidden music and sex. Any mass festival of discontent or violent political brawl brings some lumpen running. Because society's big disorder is like their order. Containing new possibilities and opportunities. Someone's revolution is someone else's job fair.

124

That kind of restlessness and drive to wherever carries real risks. **Why lumpen go down in flames a lot. But on the other hand, the creativity these brothers and sisters bring to the table can be a big contribution.** We've seen this in the struggle, time and again. Think that both the lumpen and the working class can learn from each other, share things each needs to be better at politically.

Anyway, we've only just opened Pandora's box here. We outlined how these lumpen/proletarian strata were formed in the industrial capitalist epoch—made both in the politics of daily splinter-class life and understood in radical theory. We've not only shown how the lumpen are defined, but how their role in society has been far less marginal than people assumed. In capitalist crisis, in situations of extraordinary state formation, the lumpen/proletariat can even be at the center of political struggles. All this is a foundation, but the intense learning experiences of the 20th century revolutionary movements, of the turbulent 1960s for instance, still have to be uncovered. To say nothing of today's unresolved global capitalist crisis which engulfs country after country, destroying entire societies. When we decided to cut short the writing and print the beginning as this volume, it also meant that a second companion volume had to be coming. **We'll be back.**

addendum /
correspondence: kicking it around

Editor: *One difficulty i keep on having has to do with the idea that the lumpen are solely constituted by their relationship to production, or lack thereof.*

I keep on thinking that people's relationship to the state is a big missing element. The lived form this would take would be what people think of the folks in question, i.e. it would be ideological—in the sense of the social ideologies that glue societies together (maybe cultural is a better term?). And at the heart of this, these people's relationship to the state, and its ideology (largely as defined in its courts and law books), i.e. what the state says about them, and what kind of life and existence it says they should have, if any.

And also how the people in question perceive their own relationship to presently existing state power. I don't see this as just a reflection of their relationship to production, except inasmuch as all ideology is a distorted reflection of material
relationships; i see it as constitutive of who ends up inside and outside of the lumpen, as you use the term. In that sense, ideology as a material force in people's lives. So in my mind, about the lumpen, to adjust what you say: "... it's a certain kind of objective relationship to the regular structure of economic production and distribution, and to the state."*

J: This is interesting, and a good sharing. Think that i focus so tightly on the material basis of this "partial class" or "non-class"— their fall out of structural class roles in production and distribution—because common usage even among radicals is to be so uncertain, so loose and subjective about it all. Where the lumpen are often misdefined as maybe any one of its fragments in a very impressionistic way. Like only the worst amoral criminals, or only the very poorest and dispossessed and rootless. Many people, hearing the confusion, just throw up their hands and avoid the subject altogether. Rather than seeing them as a diverse "partial-class" category of so many different splinters or strata. Many of which may be full-on criminals or persons displaced into vagabondage, or whatever, but all being different kinds sharing in common their free-fall out of class roles in production and distribution.

Certainly the state is heavily involved, as it is in all class questions. From highest to lowest. The popular culture is also heavily involved, coming behind these. Although both these things are not separate from the means of production and distribution. What would the making of an en-slaved New Afrikan proletariat of millions in amerikkka have been, without the u.s. state's genocidal laws and the state-mandated culture of euro-settler race supremacy?

Then again, you have to be mindful, since some progressives race over the cliff's edge here, seeing the state only as some giant robot. It is not simply some behemoth running amok. In general the state isn't separate from the class structure, but an expression of it. Unlike feudal or tribal societies, individual capitalists cannot rule over their society directly as themselves. The state derives its power precisely from its nature as the instrumentality by which the ruling classes operate society. In less common cases the state gets unmoored, floating temporarily out of feuding hands of ruling elites, and very much into lumpen hands. This is warlordism, usually a passing makeshift phase, but as the capitalist system decays and breaks down now it comes quicker and quicker.

... back and forth

Editor: *Relatedly: pre-pinkwashing and the cosmometropolitan world, was being queer something that made one lumpen? There is the vapor residue of something there, and when it condenses (for instance in some queer subcultures), we can see that in those olden days, they resembled some of the criminal secret societies you talk about, more than anything else. Even if the individuals involved worked in productive labor in a factory or office job. I don't think this falls into view except by seeing the state and its laws and its power as an essential reference point in this regard.*

J: That's a sharp example, using the queer community, and a famous one, obviously. Historically, patriarchal capitalism here has always until very recently pictured the queer community as a depraved underworld. The straight fantasy has always been of the gay community as a demi-monde of immoral criminals. When junk filmmaker Oliver Stone did that Hollywood movie on the assassination of JFK, for instance, he even depicted what he said were the actual killers as a perverse cabal of Latin American homosexuals! (Forget about u.s. white right-wing capitalists, apparently.) Wonder who was giving Stone offers he couldn't refuse?

For that matter, the Merriam-Webster online dictionary gives as an example of how the French term demi-monde is used: "a documentary examining the demimonde to which homosexuals were relegated before the start of the gay rights movement." It was all that typical.

Think this example teaches us, we can't do class analysis in a real situation in a cookie-cutter way. It's not that simple because sensuous human life isn't that simple. In the "bad old days" that so many of us have nostalgia for, the gay community was lumpen. Period. It was lumpen because the state had criminalized it as a community, in a serious way. Also, a number of its hardcore members were barred in part or whole from regular jobs or lives—like Black transgender women. Commonly many gays were forced onto lumpen terrain, so often everyone took it as just part of the deal. You're a gay teen guy from a poor working-class background, often

you're tricking for survival in the customary place or meeting your "special friend" in the bar. Traditionally, until at least the 1990s anyway, about half the women in the u.s. army were always lesbians (fact not legend).

In the "bad old days," the gay community with all its big flaws was still criminalized for a good reason. It wasn't just because the power structure was mean-spirited, which is the obvious b.s. they want us to swallow now. The old gay community was subversive against heteronormative capitalism; because it defied the mass regimentation of straight nuclear families owned by men forcing women to endlessly produce/reproduce out of their bodies new workers and soldiers to advance the nation.

This is nothing new as an understanding. What i mean, as an example, there was a small dyke bar on the North Side. But it absolutely wasn't even a general lesbian bar like the old "Volleyball." Just a small dark storefront, really, it was a right-wing bar. Among others, there would be older uniformed service women. That's old-school women cops and correctional guards. Lots of steady eddie alcoholism going down there. But their jukebox also played the "Star Spangled Banner"—and when the national anthem started playing, everyone had to jump to their feet and salute, drunk or not. It was a way of honoring their harsh careers shrugging off disrespect and serving a cruel, indifferent master. But also a certain subversive "fuck you!" to all sides. Their front door was always locked, and no men were ever let in, even though that was against city law. There was an inescapable outlaw element within that old community even while conforming and serving the power.

Yet at the same time, individual gays, for example, were usually members of this class or another class, for real. It was always normal for us to know queer teachers and hospital orderlies and construction contractors and retail clerks and autoworkers. So this was a constant contradiction people lived with—you were middle-class or working-class but your queer community was lumpen. An ambiguous zone of contradiction. Where a gay worker can really be in the working class, but at the same time their other hidden community was always dangerously skirting the gravity well of the lumpen/proletariat. Same with queers in other classes, you know what i mean. So state criminalization means a lot, but so do the long-lived class roles in society's production and distribution.

J: "*Voice off-stage*": *Showed the editor's comments to a comrade who had her own take on this. She immediately started writing rant notes, which i've dropped raw into the mix right here:*

"You can't keep using that old Marxist men's framework. Because thinking of gender is the key. Because **then** you speak for the Other, as Lorde said—Queers, freaks, women, children, the alien. So Marx did important things sure, but he also saw the world through patriarchal lens. The editor's question brings the power of the Other in here. He raises the question of when all queers were lumpen, because patriarchy defined itself as *everything*, the Other as nothing. We were all outsiders, illegal refugees fleeing all our lives across men's territory.

"The biggest sex work by women isn't 'prostitutes,' it's marriage. Whether it's forced marriage—that's the majority in the world—or so-called 'love' marriage. It's still fitting yourself into men's class framework. That's why it's women's job to be attractive and men's job to make money and run things. Everyone knows this. Saw this imam in Bangladesh on tv news, explaining why women couldn't be allowed to show any part of their bodies: *'Women have been made to be respected. Then to be useful to men. That is the main theory in Islam.'* That's what these men's religions are, manuals for managing property.

"i think of women kinda as a class, but even more as a people. Women aren't a different kind of men, no matter how we're forced to wedge ourselves into men's jobs and men's corporations and men's states. Like children aren't just little adults. That's why the Right hates Planned Parenthood more than they hate some Communist Party. It embodies concealed in drag some of the most advanced ideas about womanhood. And folks wonder why they're hysterical about it? To say it another way—If you take the reproduction of labor out of society's production and distribution, you distort all class analysis. That's what's wrong with it."

kicking it ...

Editor: *I can't help but feel that parts of this discussion would be strengthened by referring to "primitive rebels," specifically social banditry and the mafia. Mainly because it is such a standard for Marxist discussion of these people, and therefore much of what you say seems to be running parallel, while greatly deepening and complicating, that more offhand and narrow field of discussion. Plus, premodern forms of organization and revolt seem to persist far more within the lumpen non-class, than in either the proletariat or the bourgeoisie, which I suppose "modernize" their members' ways of doing things far more.*

J: Didn't have the space in these essays to really deal with the "primitive rebels" thing. Particularly since my view is, it's not as straightforward as it's been promoted. Always thought that Robin Hood was pretty sophisticated, myself. Are we really talking underneath it all, about the crooked gaze of Western intellectuals, many "Marxists" definitely included? After all, when we see Greek marble statues and read Sappho's poetry, we don't say, "That's pretty good primitive art," do we? Many people think that Pancho Villa's movement was damn sophisticated, while World War I celebrity General Pershing and his u.s. army that was vainly pursuing Villa's forces all around the countryside were really primitive. Is the whole notion a way for Western intellectuals to avoid the land-mine subjects of anti-colonialism and imperialism's real class structure? Think we have to be careful or maybe extra-careful, how we approach this.

Editor: *... Regarding cops and career soldiers being lumpen. Agree that there is a relationship here. I was at a conference a year ago where this women's group was talking about how their analysis is that the cops target kids in their neighbourhood in two ways, one being criminalization & the other recruitment. Others have also said about Robin Hood types that "policemen, mercenary soldiers are often recruited from the same material as social bandits," and about the Sicilian mafia that "there are no other individual methods of escaping the bondage of virtual serfdom but bullying and outlawry" ...*

But i think calling cops and soldiers lumpen skirts over too much. In terms of the repressive bodies of the state being populated by lumpen, this process, through which the state soaks up large numbers of would-be lumpen, doesn't just put them in disguise, it gives them a different life and politics than those who don't get absorbed in this way could manage. And even then there is a difference, in historical terms, between the current hegemonic state soaking up violent young men into its repressive apparatus, and the big land owners or factory owners of the 19th century hiring similar violent young men to be their (private) enforcers. Different lives are produced by these different relationships to state power ...

Out of the large mass of people who you identify, cut loose from the normal places in society, there is a "last chance" for respectability, for not being lumpen despite being irregular—and that is within the state apparatus (especially its repressive branches). But these people are only lumpen in an inverted sense, they're like the anti-lumpen lumpen, only displaying typically lumpen traits as an example of what you point out, that everything contains both itself and its opposite.

J: It's true that the young dude making his "payday" jacking up people on the street is usually lumpen, as is the cop who chases him. And that young street actor's uncle who is doing yet another tour with his combat support unit in Iraq, too. But they aren't the same kind of lumpen.

The lumpen/proletariat has many, many different kinds of "non-class" shards and strata. They sometimes resemble one another, having similarities—like the stickup boy can shift boundaries and become the cop, and often vice versa—but many other times these lumpen fragments have no relationship to each other. Don't care or are affected if each other gets blown up or not. The sex worker doesn't care whether the cops live or die. The drug hustler could care less if the national army all jump into the ocean. Con artists working the asphalt driveway hustle are indifferent to the fate of on-road burglary teams hitting stopped semi-trucks and trains. There's more diversity in the lumpen "partial-class" than in the whole rest of society put together, it sometimes feels like. Plus, the lumpen/proletariat is much bigger than most people think.

You seem to toy with the idea that having a "respectable" legal role with the state or corporation means that you dodge being lumpen. No, it doesn't, not one bit. "Lumpen/proletariat" isn't another way of saying "criminal." These are very related but distinct and different things. Class role and identity is deeper than legal or illegal, "respectable" or criminal. The gigantic capitalist state contains millions of lumpen of various kinds, mixed in with class everybody else. Just as prostitutes are criminalized sex workers in this patriarchal society, while the straight "girlfriend" and "wife" are perfectly "respectable" and not criminal—but hey, also sex workers themselves of a different kind. It's all in the karma not in the harma.

Also, we always have to resist criminalization itself. We fight its power to make class lines over our bodies. An Eric Garner selling cigarettes out of his pockets is not necessarily the same as someone who sells drugs on the street. To quote a famous text, its seeing these people's lives "only in the form of the object or of contemplation, but not as sensuous human activity, practice, not subjectively."

The late Eric Garner selling "loosies" on the street was not doing lumpen stuff, even though it was technically illegal in a small way just as so many survival activities are. By itself this is the kind of hustling lower working-class folks may do to survive. This is a long established part of the informal economy in the Black Nation and around the world. When we go to the big public health clinic and hospital for our appointments, there are men slowly walking through the rows of seats quietly vending out of their coat pockets and shoulder bag. Selling "loosies" cigarettes and selling candy bars, as well as a guy downstairs in the lobby selling the daily newspapers. The guy selling "legal" packs of cigarettes behind the counter at the corner bodega, where Eric Garner was killed outside, he may be the one that's lumpen/proletarian. If the bodega's main thing is as a front for drug sales. Or he, too, may be working-class—or if he's the working owner he might be lower middle-class of some kind. Let's take things as they come, not get carried away and letting the power identify class over us in an abstract way.

Editor: *Straying a bit from this, when people are "cut loose" from regular classes, they seem to be more prone to attaching their lives to some other center of gravity. It's difficult to stay unattached. Thought of this in your "Marx" text: Why is nation such an important qualifier in regards to the lumpen, to an even greater extent than it is in regards to the regular classes? I think oppressed/oppressor nation is one big part of this, as it is with everything else. But also can't help but feel that there's this element of being unattached making life more open to being reattached in a more full-on way, to something "bigger than yourself." And being useful in a way that the attached and regulated are not?*

endnotes

MESW = *Marx and Engels: Selected Works.* Vol. 1. Foreign Languages Publishing House, 1962. Moscow.

1. Mary Anne Weaver. "The Thread." *New York Times Magazine.* May 5, 2015; Ben Joravsky. "Blue Island." *Chicago Reader.* November 10, 2016.

2. Butch Lee. "'The Evil of Female Loaferism'." In Lee. *Jailbreak Out of History.* Kersplebedeb Publishing, 2015. Montreal. 2nd Edition. Pages 99–168.

3. Jacqueline Jones. *American Work: Four Centuries of Black and White Labor.* W.W. Norton. N.Y., 1998. Pages 192–193.

4. Bryan D. Palmer. "History." In Kelly Fritsch, Clare O'Connor, and A.K. Thompson. Editors. *Keywords For Radicals: The Contested Vocabulary of Late-Capitalist Struggle.* AK Press, 2016. Chico & Edinburgh. Page 194; Raymond Williams. *Keywords. A vocabulary of culture and society.* Fontana Paperbacks, 1983. London. Page 146. Also see: Jairus Banaji. *Theory as History.* Haymarket Books, 2011. Chicago.

5. Manjit Kumar. *Quantum. Einstein, Bohr, and the Great Debate About the Nature of Reality.* W.W. Norton. 2010. Pages 358–359.

6. Karl Marx and Frederick Engels. "Manifesto of the Communist Party." In *Karl Marx and Frederick Engels: Selected Works.* Vol. 1. Foreign Languages Publishing House, 1962. Moscow. *(MESW)* Page 44.

7. H. Draper. "The Concept of the 'Lumpenproletariat' in Marx and Engels." Source: *Economies et Societes.* Vol. 6, No. 12. December 1972. Pages 22–85.

8. Karl Marx. "The Eighteenth Brumaire of Louis Bonaparte." In *MESW.* Pages 294–295.

9. Peter Linebaugh. *The London Hanged. Crime and civil society in the eighteenth century.* Second edition. Verso, 2003. London. Page 297.

10. Michael Bakunin. "Social Revolution & the State." In Commander Josh. Editor. *Bakunin—Better Writer Than Marx.* ARA Photocopy, 2004. Chicago.

11. Arthur Lehning. Editor (*Archives Bakounine*, International Institute of Social History, Amsterdam). *Michael Bakunin. Selected Writings*. Grove Press, 1973. New York. Pages 184–187.

12. Karl Marx. "The Class Struggles in France 1848–1850." In *MESW*. Page 155.

13. Karl Marx. *Capital. A critique of political economy*. Vol. I. Charles H. Kerr, 1921. Chicago. Pages 805–809.

14. The original text of this quotation also had interspliced source citations, which have been editorially removed to avoid unsightly clutter and dust bunnies. Nicholas Thoburn. "Difference in Marx: the lumpenproletariat and the proletariat unnamable." *Economy and Society*. Vol. 31, No. 3, August 2002.

15. Frederick Engels. "Prefatory Note to *The Peasant War in Germany*." In *MESW*. Page 646.

16. Alan Gilbert. *Marx's Politics. Communists and Citizens*. Rutgers University Press, 1981. New Brunswick. Pages 247–249.

17. Karl Marx. "The Class Struggles in France 1848–1850." In *MESW*. Page 155.

18. Touré. *Who's Afraid of Post-Blackness? What It Means To Be Black Now*. Free Press, 2011. New York. Page 214.

19. Edith Thomas. *The Women Incendiaries*. Haymarket Books, 2007. Chicago. Pages 105–107.

20. See, for example: Anne McClintock. ""The Scandal of the Whorearchy: Prostitution in Colonial Nairobi." *Transition 52*. Oxford University Press, 1991. New York; Luise White. *The Comforts of Home*. University of Chicago Press, 1990.

21. Mao Tse-tung. "Analysis of the Classes in Chinese Society." In *Selected Works of Mao Tse-tung*. Vol. 1. Foreign Languages Press, 1965. Peking. Page 19.

22. See Mao's own account of that time in: Edgar Snow. *Red Star Over China*. First Revised and Enlarged Edition. Grove Press, 1968. Pages 163–171; also Stuart R. Schram. "Mao Tse-tung and Secret Societies." In *China Quarterly* No. 27. July–September 1966.

23. Phillip C.C. Huang. "The Jiangxi Period: An Introduction." In *China Research Monographs Number Thirteen. Chinese Communists and Rural Society 1927–1934*. Center for Chinese Studies, University of California at Berkeley. August 1978. Pages 11–13; Agnes Smedley. *The Great Road: The Life and Times of Chu Teh*. Monthly Review, 1972. N.Y. Pages 88–89; Snow. Op cit. Pages 333–334.

24. Mao Tse-tung. "On Correcting Mistaken Ideas in the Party." In *Selected*

Works of Mao Tse-tung. Vol. 1. Page 114; Schram. Op cit.

25. John E. Rue. *Mao Tse-Tung in Opposition 1927–1935.* Hoover Institution, 1966. Stanford. Page 99.

26. Mao Tse-tung. "Report on an Investigation of the Peasant Movement in Hunan." In *Selected Works of Mao Tse-tung.* Volume 1. Peking. 1965. Page 33; Mao Zedong. *Report From Xunwu.* Stanford University Press, 1990. Pages 116 and 122.

27. For all other sources please see the complete version of this chapter in *Mao Z's Revolutionary Laboratory & the Lumpen/Proletariat.*

28. Marx. "The Class Struggles in France 1848–1850." In *MESW.* Pages 154–155.

29. Ibid. Pages 160–161.

30. Incidentally, Marx's essay title, "The Eighteenth Brumaire of Louis Napoleon," was a sarcastic dis unfavorably comparing Louis's December 1851 "imperial" seizure of power to his great relative's—it would be like one of us dissing Donald Trump's "Make America Great Again" slogan by titling a critique of him, "The 1776 of President Don Trump." Marx was using the actual date of the *real* Emperor Napoleon Bonaparte's own imperial *coup d'etat* in 1799. Which happened on the 18th day of the late Autumn month of "Brumaire" (late October into November), in the French Republican post-revolutionary calendar in use back then and there.

31. Marx. "The Class Struggles in France 1848–1850." In *MESW.* Pages 254–255.

32. H. Draper. Op cit.

33. Mark Traugott. *Armies of the Poor: Determinants of Working-Class Participation in the Parisian Insurrection of June 1848.* Transaction Publishers, 2002. New Brunswick. Page 204.

34. Ibid. Pages 27–31.

35. Ibid. Pages 37–38.

36. Ibid. Pages 44, 45, 53, 55.

37. Marx. "The Class Struggles in France 1848–1850." In *MESW.* Page 155.

38. Marx and Engels. "Manifesto of the Communist Party." In *MESW.* Page 44.

39. Karl Marx. "The Eighteenth Brumaire of Louis Napoleon." In David McLellan. Editor. *Karl Marx: Selected Writings.* Oxford University Press, 1977. Pages 300–325.

40. Traugott. Op cit. Page 195.

41. Ibid. Pages 76, 204, 214.

42. Ibid. Page 215.

43. Ibid. Page 51.

44. Draper, op cit.

45. F. Bovenkerk. "The Rehabilitation of the Rabble: How and Why Marx and Engels Wrongly Depicted the Lumpenproletariat as a Reactionary Force." Source: *Netherlands Journal of Social Science*. Vol. 20, No. 1. 1984. Pages 13–41.

46. Karl Marx. *MESW*. Page 339. The words *"chamois"* and *"gendarme"* used by Marx in the last sentence, have been translated for the convenience of readers.

47. McCLellan. Op cit. Page 317.

48. John Bierman. *Napoleon III and his Carnival Empire*. St. Martins Press, 1988. N.Y. Page 95.

49. Franco Moretti. *The Bourgeois: Between Literature and History*. Verso, 2013. London. Page 6.

50. Our esteemed editor insists that this point in the text must be footnoted and a reputable source provided, since it goes so contrary to left history and would be so controversial. The only problem is, really, i don't want to do it. Kind of treasure this as an old war story. These are an important "off the record" part of everyone's culture. When i was a little kid, in the Summer the young guys in my family and their friends would gather in the long dusk on the back porch, after their day at the auto garage or factory. Drinking bottles of beer, smoking cigs whose packs they had rolled up in their white t-shirt sleeves, arms dark with summer tan. Laughing and ribbing each other about young escapades back in what my parents' generation always just called "camp"—that's the Japanese-American concentration camps they had us in—as well as the crazy stuff that happened after that in Italy or somewhere with the all-Jap 442nd regimental combat team in World War II. Old war stories. My kiddie ambition was to grow up to be one of those sexy working-class guys dissing and laughing with each other.

In the movement, "old" Trotskyists and Stalinists (some really aged, like in their 40s even!) would hang out with fresh caught kids like me. Telling us inside dope about union history and famous left personalities and what really happened here and there. All not like the cleaned up versions publicized in left lit. Old war stories. Owe a lot to that grassroots custom, and value it still. So am just going to consider that Spanish Civil War episode (which i got from the horse's mouth, as they put it) an informal old war story, too. You can criticize it as "can't be true" or whatever you want, that's okay. Don't blame the poor editor.

51. Linebaugh. Op cit. Pages 25–251.

52. Ibid. Pages 125–417.

53. Ibid. Pages 127–128.

54. Ibid. Pages 417–418.

55. Ibid. Page 406.

56. Ibid. Pages 371–381.

57. Deidre Le Faye. *Jane Austen's Country Life*. Francis Lincoln, 2014. London. Page 8.

58. Ibid. Pages 9–13; E.J. Hobsbawm. *Industry and Empire. The Making of Modern British Society*. Vol. 2. Random House, 1968. New York. Pages 80–81.

59. Jane Austen. *Sense and Sensibility*. Penguin Classics, 2003. N.Y. Pages 212–213.

60. Le Faye. Op cit. Page 147.

61. Hobsbawm. Op cit. Page 81.

62. Thomas Spence, William Ogilvie, Thomas Paine. *The Pioneers of Land Reform*. University Press of the Pacific, 2001. Honolulu. Page 8; J. Morrison Davidson. *Concerning Four Precursors of Henry George and the Single Tax*. Kennikat Press, 1971. Port Washington & London. Pages 32–33.

63. Jacqueline Jones. *The Dispossessed. America's Underclasses from the Civil War to the Present*. HarperCollins, 1992. Pages 32–33.

64. Le Faye. Op cit. Page 147.

65. Ibid. Pages 137–141.

66. Jonathan Sperber. *Karl Marx: A Nineteenth Century Life*. W.W. Norton, 2013. N.Y. Page 488.

67. Le Faye. Op cit. Pages 141–143.

68. Linebaugh. Op cit. Pages 340–341, 361.

69. Ibid. Pages 349–350, 381.

70. Faramerz Dabhoiwala. *The Origins of Sex: a history of the first sexual revolution*. Oxford University Press, 2012. N.Y. Pages 71–72.

71. Linebaugh. Op cit. Pages 189, 335–336.

72. E.P. Thompson. *The Making of the English Working Class*. Vintage Books, 1966. New York. Page 265.

73. Michael Bakunin. *The Immorality of the State*. Anarchy Archives: http://dwardmac.pitzer.edu/Anarchist_Archives/bakunin/bakuninimmorality.html

74. Joy James. Editor. *The Angela Y. Davis Reader*. Blackwell Publishing, 1998. Madden and Oxford. Page 42.

75. Le Faye. Op cit. Pages 144–146.

76. Frederick Engels. *The Condition of the Working Class in England*. Academy Chicago Publishers, 1994. Pages 172–177.

77. Ibid. Pages 159–160.

78. Ibid. Pages 288–290.

79. Ibid. Page 291.

80. E.P. Thompson. Op cit. Pages 55–56.

81. George Rudé. *Paris and London in the Eighteenth Century. Studies in Popular Protest.* Viking Press, 1971. New York. Pages 50–51.

82. E.P. Thompson. Op cit. Page 265.

83. Le Faye. Op cit. Page 148.

84. Linebaugh. Op cit. Pages 92, 143 & 145.

85. Frederick Engels. *The Condition ...* Op cit. Pages 170–171.

86. E.P. Thompson. Op cit. Page 59.

87. Ibid. Page 813.

88. Linebaugh. Op cit. Pages xxiii & 151.

mao z's revolutionary laboratory
& the lumpen/proletariat

**thoughts on the making
of the lumpen/proletariat**

Please take a seat

Take a seat anywhere, now that we've moved from the auditorium to this small meeting room. So this is probably a smaller study group, since we will be staying focused down into details of how the lumpen/proletariat intersected with the Chinese Revolution of 1920–1949. How their theory and practice evolved off each other. Living daily life in the extreme exercise field of revolutionary war. This concentration on one time and one movement, layer by layer, might be trying, but it's meant **specifically for comrades who need to know in much greater detail how class theory can work out in practice, or not**. Not just in general, or abstractly, but in actual political work. In gritty, often unclear situations that are always changing on us. Like ours is sharply right now, in our own time and place. This is a harder study than most generic left talk about "class." Just saying.

There are two really different things about this paper. The first is that it's a study of something rarely discussed: the theory and practice of the lumpen/proletariat's role in actual large-scale struggle. Starting with, but far from limited to, Mao Z's own "dangerous" theoretical ideas. It is dense going at times, since it's applied class theory made by and for revolutionary activists and militants. While *The "Dangerous Class" and Revolutionary Theory: Thoughts on the Making of the Lumpen/Proletariat* in the first part of this book is like the first semester of a course, think of this as the second semester.

The other more mundane difference is that this paper was first printed in a rare form, what publishers call "doubles" or "do-si-do"— or back to back flipped over in one volume. *Mao Z's Revolutionary Laboratory* and the other *The "Dangerous Class" and Revolutionary Theory* are two very separate papers, very different in tone and how they are situated. But they constitute two perhaps contradictory/complementary sides of one critical work. We strongly recommend that you read *The "Dangerous Class" and Revolutionary Theory* first, to get the making of the revolutionary anti-capitalist theory that was then later seriously taken up and applied in early 20th century China, with a warring cast of millions. Even without selling the Hollywood movie rights, how can we not pick up things from that kind of big experience?

Some comrades have already seriously read about China and its revolutions that were brilliantly successful but also brilliantly catastrophic, falling into our today's "Red capitalism." Some comrades don't in a practical sense know *anything* about that land and its political history. If by coincidence you've already studied up on China, freely skip the following six pages. If not, **you might take a few more minutes to first take in this quick skim for orientation:**

background / crazy-quilt of chinese politics

China is always talked about over here as a "major nation," which is technically true but also a misunderstanding. China has always been one of the main *civilizations* of the human world. Unique, really, since it has long had a greater population than some fully populated continents, while its society goes back millennia, thousands of years, imperial dynasty after dynasty. Long called "the Celestial Kingdom," China was a mysterious land that the barbarian West looked up to for fabulous wealth and knowledge. Much basic technology came from China, such as the compass, rockets and gunpowder, paper and printing, even the yoking of draft animals in farming gave birth to larger-scale European agriculture when that breakthrough filtered out from China centuries ago.

But by the time Mao Zedong was born in 1895, in a peasant village, China had long been in steep decline. Both in the increasing brutality of its distorted class relationships, and its economic and technological backwardness. To the West, China became a synonym for the poorest people in the world. Technology and new ruling class ideas then came from the imperialism of the industrial West. Everyone knew that the Old Society was dying, and needed to be overthrown, so that China could be modernized and its people liberated. The burning question was how? By who?

It's hard to get it, the political life of the Chinese lumpen/proletariat back then, without seeing the context of their chaotic country. Which in the early 20th century was like a complex Marx Brothers night at the opera, only with real blood. Back then the state was a heavy relic, the last of China's imperial dynasties, the Qing Dynasty. Which several centuries before had sent its armies out of Manchuria to capture Beijing, and had then simply installed itself as a new hated alien imperium. Right on top of the age-old ethnic Han layers of imperial bureaucracy and feudal landed gentry and other wealthy people and merchants. It was kind of like if Mexican armies had seized America in a surprise war, but had kept the privileged layers of old u.s. class society intact but underneath its own parasitic occupation.

This top heavy, semi-feudal rule was not only viciously exploitative, but backward and rapidly decaying. Newly industrializing Japan had defeated the "bannermen" of the antiquated Qing military in their war of 1894–95, sending shock waves through Chinese society. While the Western powers and their modern armies had simply seized land for extraterritorial bases and economic takeovers penetrating China any time they wanted. The massive trade in opium forced on the Chinese was only the most notorious chapter in the highly profitable, smash and grab Western home invasion.

Beneath all the politics, was the starkest class situation. The journalist Edgar Snow spent weeks walking through stricken villages in the great Northwest famine in 1929, when millions of peasants were dying. In those days, many Western reporters hid in the comforts of the port cities of Shanghai and Hong Kong, keeping to the safe routine of sending dispatches based on rumors and gossip from the foreign embassies and business community. It was to the credit of a handful of journalists like Snow and the feminist Agnes Smedley (both Americans who could only find work at first reporting for European newspapers) that actual news reports from rural China of civil wars and disasters and great world-changing shifts reached international readers. Snow later recalled:

> "I was twenty-three. I had come to the East looking for 'the glamour of the Orient', searching for adventure. This excursion to Suiyuan had begun as something like that. But here for the first time in my life I came abruptly upon men who were dying because they had nothing to eat. In those hours of nightmare I spent in Suiyuan I saw thousands of men, women, and children starving to death before my eyes …

> "Have you ever seen a man—a good honest man who has worked hard, a 'law-abiding citizen', doing no serious harm to anyone—when he has had no food for more than a month? It is a most agonizing sight. His dying flesh hangs from him in wrinkled folds; you can clearly see every bone in his body; his eyes stare out unseeing; and even if he is a youth of twenty he moves like an ancient crone, dragging himself from spot to spot. If he has been lucky he has long ago sold his wife and daughters. He

has also sold everything he owns—the timber of his house itself, and most of his clothes. Sometimes he has, indeed, even sold the last rag of decency, and he sways there in the scorching sun, his testicles dangling from him like withered olive seeds—the last grim jest to remind you that this was once a man.

"Those were things I myself had seen and would never forget. Millions of people died that way in famine ... But these were not the most shocking things after all. The shocking thing was that in many of those towns there were still rich men, rice hoarders, wheat hoarders, moneylenders and landlords, with armed guards to defend them, while they profiteered enormously. The shocking thing was that in the cities—where officials danced or played with sing-song girls—there were grain and food, and had been for months; that in Peking and Tientsin and elsewhere were thousands of tons of wheat and millet, collected (mostly by contributions from abroad) by the Famine Commission, but which could not be shipped to the starving. Why not? Because in the Northwest there were some militarists who wanted to hold all of their railroad rolling stock and would release none of it towards the east, while in the east there were other Kuomintang generals who would send no rolling stock westward—even to starving people—because they feared it would be seized by their rivals."[1]

As the backward shrinking imperial government controlled less and less, self-made military strongmen rose up away from the capital region. Growing from bandit groups and threadbare mercenary armies, these warlords became de facto temporary political rulers of their disputed areas, coming and going with little stability. This always dissolving and re-conquering patchwork quilt of warlord territories and little semi-feudal territories became the actual governance of much of China.

At the point where Hollywood scripts always call for the appearance of a heroic savior, China produced Dr. Sun Yat-Sen, the first president of the Republic of China and "the founder of modern China." Born at the time right after the u.s. Civil War, Sun became a doctor and a Christian who had been briefly schooled as a youth by missionaries in Hawaii. Somewhat familiar with both the u.s.a. and Europe, he took part in attempted armed uprisings against the Qing rule and the warlords.

Even though these specific insurrections failed, the decayed Qing Imperial state died as Sun formed a new Chinese government in 1911 in Southern China, where the new Nationalist movement had its main base of support. His temporary political "party," the Kuomintang or "national people's party," itself became a chaotic united front for a new style Chinese government to make China modern. With everyone involved from bankers and idealistic students to the criminal secret societies and, of course, the new socialists, like Sun himself. Without armies to support him, however, Dr. Sun soon lost control of his embryonic state and went into exile.

Sun Yat-Sen's weakness had never been his idealism or popular support but rather his group's lack of material power. To correct this, in 1923 he signed a dramatic treaty of alliance with the new Soviet Union. Anti-capitalist Russia became the first power to recognize the new government, and to renounce any colonial claims on China. The treaty promised to support Sun's wobbly anti-colonial government with modern German and Russian armaments, money, plus military and political advisors.

China's new Communist Party was launched in 1920 by a dozen delegates, including the young Mao Z, representing sixty members. It soon joined the Kuomintang at the suggestion of its European Communist International advisors, as its left wing, to counterbalance the capitalists and militarists who saw even bigger opportunities in Sun's energetic new Republic. Peasants were not thought very important, so the Communists were allowed to set up the Kuomintang's Peasant Movement Training Institute in Canton, where militant young peasants were taught not only politics and how to organize, but also received military training. Mao and his brother were students there, and eventually Mao Z became the principal of this school for awhile.

China was still largely disunited and chaotic. There had been different attempts by various forces at forming a nationalist government in the South, and in the North there were three large warlord semi-states. Not to forget class warfare in the countryside. With peasants being slaughtered by landlord-controlled militias, and violent politics pounding daily life. Dr. Sun's answer was the Northern expedition, moving out from the Nationalist movement's base in South China to swallow up all the provincial warlord armies and finally unite the country. Guided by his Russian military advisors, Dr. Sun and his officials had started a modern-style military academy at Whampoa, led by the conservative Christian military officer Chang Kai-shek. At the same time, a mix of old warlord units and new units led by young, more idealistic officers were being rearmed and retrained into a new "Nationalist Army."

All the while, the starve-to-death poverty of the poor peasant majority and the crushing oppression of women as sub-human property made China something like a metaphor for hopelessness in the Western imagination. Remember, as a kid in the 1940s, watching girls jump rope, skipping to a certain popular American children's street rhyme as they saw me coming over:

> *"Chink-a, chink-a, Chinaman*
> *Sitting on a fence*
> *Trying to make a dollar*
> *Outta 99 cents!"*

And it was Malcolm, it was X himself, in the 1960s who reminded us how we all used to repeat the old customary American saying for when something was totally hopeless: *"Not a Chinaman's chance."* Then he would pause, and raising his voice to quote Mao Z: "But no one says that anymore, because *'China has stood up'.*"

THEORY STUFF

Our anti-capitalist theory has been so outdated, that despite our good intentions it's more like slogans than maps. This is confusing, but usually on a pragmatic level, at least, subconsciously understood. Most evident in class theory. While radical thinking about the lumpen lies around disassembled, in bits and pieces, at best.

Even postmodern society is fought over continually by classes, no matter how disguised their identity and moves. In real life these classes are much more complex and diverse than they once appeared in the early days of Europe's 19th century industrial capitalism. That's why real-time theory about classes is such a practical need for us.

Our goal is direct, to improve our ability to identify the broken-up class terrain that we are moving across, so that our step is more sure. The lumpen are so critical as a subject to us today because they are at the violent edge of tumultuous change, in every society worldwide.

What's so important for us about theory here, is that theories are *generalizations* that draw on more than one example or one practice, but are a systemic overview from many sources, explaining an entire area of reality.

Our *small personal knowledge or even the community knowledge we personally share in*, however detailed, isn't enough for an overall strategy, or even for a depth of tactical preparedness. For that we need a *much larger view, a map of a larger scope*, as it were, taking in the experiences of many, many other attempts and situations even of both sides in the struggle.

Revolutionary theory gives us those larger *generalizations* based on many experiences and many struggles, over a wide range of space and time. To help us tentatively plan out our work, to tentatively grasp the larger reality we struggle in. We say "tentative" because theory, however useful and necessary, is only a foreshadowing of practice, of actual struggle in the real world. It derives its sharpness and energy borrowing from practice. Theory learns from our real life struggle, in other words. And the highest level of theory is not grand generalizations, but where it reaches upward and narrows toward the specific, and merges with our practice in *"the concrete analysis of the concrete situation."*

One practical note to all theory, is that simply having it doesn't guarantee you anything. Nada, zip, as they say. Like reading a moving book of poetry doesn't make you yourself a poet or an insightful person. Just like having a med school education doesn't guarantee the researcher that their newest trial drug will work. Most times, no, in fact. Theory is an important and irreplaceable aid, but actually carrying out revolutionary resistance against the grain of the harsh world is a higher level of understanding than that.

There are real consequences to being without functional theory. Without such a general theoretical framework, we don't learn well from practice, for instance. We don't do well at building organizations. Or in critiquing our own attempts at confronting capitalism. Nor do we teach well at all. To take one nearby example, without functioning theory, the movement passively drifts and has permitted social democratic cheerleaders of the capitalist state, like Loic Wacquant or John Hagedorn, to dominate the discussion about the lumpen/proletarian street organizations here. To do their white supremacist distortions and undermining of the most oppressed street youth in urban society.

Revolutionary theory is way too large a subject for one discussion. But we can step through the bare-bones outline chalked on the pavement, kind of like a modern dance notation, demonstrating one important part—guiding class analysis of the lumpen/proletariat.

1. theory mao tossed to us

We know the Chinese Revolution of 1921–1949 was one of the great events that shaped the modern world, signaling the armed breakout of the capitalist periphery and its colonized peoples. Its most singular leader, Mao Zedong, became famous as the political-military theorist of that mass journey of hundreds of millions to overturn known society. While his bold example affected rebels then everywhere, in critical ways we still don't realize what was within that mass experience.

For example, the incomplete, partial ideas that European anti-capitalist intellectuals had discovered in the 19th century about the *"dangerous class"* of the lumpen/proletariat, were much more fully worked out in the Chinese experience; proven or disproven in a deeper practice. Because China's revolution held the practical experience of millions of lumpen across several continuous generations of political struggle. Just to tell you, we're probably going to remind you of this several times, since to lose sight of this point is to become to some degree confused about the weight of different theory. Mao Z's theoretical writings are far from the whole of it, being only a doorway to this large room of revolutionary knowledge.

Note: The standard spelling in translations of Marx and Engels' writings is the familiar "lumpenproletariat," or sometimes with a hyphen, "lumpen-proletariat." i prefer and use here "lumpen/proletariat," because it conveys the essential ambiguity of this "non-class." In grammar a slash can join two related things or link two opposites, or both (such as "black/white," "on/off," or "interrogation/torture"). And i say simply "lumpen" most often because in daily usage most of us use that instead of the fuller term, that's maybe problematic on the tongue and mind.

Like a hand grenade of ideas thrown from the distance into our skirmishes, when Mao's iconic writings on the Chinese Revolution from the 1920s–30s were finally translated and widely disseminated here in the 1950s–60s, revolutionary theory on the lumpen/proletariat underwent a major shift. We still haven't come to grips with the confusion of that change, even though the blast zone is far behind us on the highway now.

While appearing to follow the form of Marx & Engels' class analysis of the stormy petrel of the lumpen/proletariat, Mao's theoretical take represented a big remodeling job. From when Marx & Engels started it all by calling the lumpen "that passively rotting mass." Mao's innovation was a sharper turn, in fact, than i personally could hold on to or understand back then. Mao Z first explained China's lumpen—generally known in his society back then by variants of the term *youmin* or "floating people"—as different from all other classes, in his analysis of peasant society in 1926:

"The *yu-min* consist of peasants who have lost all opportunity of employment as a result of oppression and exploitation by the imperialists, the militarists and the landlords, or as a result of floods and droughts. They can be divided into soldiers, bandits, robbers, beggars, and prostitutes. These five categories of people have different names, and they enjoy a somewhat different status in society. But they are all human beings, and they all have five senses and four limbs, and are therefore one. They each have a different way of making a living: the soldier fights, the bandit robs, the thief steals, the beggar begs and the prostitute seduces. But to the extent that they must all earn their livelihood and cook rice to eat, they are one.

"They lead the most precarious existence of any human being. They have secret organizations in various places: for instance, the Triad Society in Fukien and Kwangtung; the Ko-lao-hui in Hunan, Hupei, Kweichow and Szechuan; the Big Sword Society in Anhwei, Hunan, and Shantung; the Society of Morality in Chilhli and the three north-eastern provinces; the Green Gang in Shanghai and elsewhere. These serve as their mutual aid societies in the political and economic struggle. To find a place for this group of people is the greatest and most difficult problem faced by China. China has two problems: poverty and unemployment. Hence, if the problem of unemployment can be solved, half of China's problems will be solved. The number of *yu-min* in China is fearfully large; it is roughly more than twenty millions. These people are capable of fighting very bravely, and if properly led can become a revolutionary force."[2]

Shortly thereafter that same year, in his better-known *Analysis of the Classes in Chinese Society*, his key theoretical summary was cast in the final form that became so memorable later for many of us: "*Brave fighters but apt to be destructive, they can become a revolutionary force if given proper guidance.*"[3]

Mao Z's terse last line summing up the lumpen became well known among many 1960s–70s revs in the u.s. back then. Most notably by the Black Panthers, who quoted it frequently because they were led by lumpen and aimed at organizing lumpen. When white students tried following their breakthrough, the idea reverberated far beyond the much smaller ranks of those leftists who called themselves Maoists. It seemed so basic, it didn't occur to would-be revolutionaries like myself that it wasn't anywhere as simple as it seemed, and that in fact i didn't fully understand it.

Mao Z's starting analysis accepted the lumpen as ordinary people, not as primarily "dangerous" or exotic. Our guy wasn't afraid of them. Humanizing them in his analysis, Mao was painting there with broad brushstrokes, in optimistic colors, of the lumpen as victims shaped by poverty and oppression—thus as potential revolutionary tinder. This concise, seemingly easy to understand explanation of Mao's was a pretty radical change of class understanding for Marxists. It reflected new understanding of realities by new thinkers out in the capitalist periphery.

Mao Z had known of the lumpen's involvement in rebellion against the powers that be *all* his political life, literally from childhood. When very young, he had loved "Robin Hood" type stories of lone poor heroes fighting evil and corruptly powerful men. This wasn't some unheard of thing to him. As a child, one of the most exciting events for him and his schoolmates was a dispute between a rich landlord and some men who turned out to be members of the lumpen secret Elder Brother Society. The landlord easily prevailed in the corrupt courtroom, having bought himself a favorable verdict, but the secret society men refused to give in.

They rebelled against the local government, retreating to a fort they had built on a nearby mountain. Finally, after some fighting, imperial Qing troops arrived and overcame them. The rebel leader, a man named P'ang the Millstone Maker, fled but was captured and executed as a public example. Only the authorities guessed wrong at what kind of example that was.[4]

In his teenage student years, Mao moved for schooling "to Changsha, the great city, the capital of the province" of Hunan. That's where he read his first newspaper and learned about the new revolutionary movement, writing and posting his first political poster on the school wall. With a friend, he cut off his pigtail to show his rejection of the Manchu imperial society. There he witnessed the 1911 Revolution that eventually overthrew the

---

One of the big things i didn't really understand then, was that the lumpen weren't and aren't one "class." Keep repeating that here, sorry, because i know from personal experience it takes time or repeated blows on the head to sink in. Like every other comrade, for convenience sake i talk about "the lumpen," but technically that term doesn't mean they are one class. The lumpen/proletariat are more like a class category made up of disparate elements. They are shards or splinters, bits socially "unplugged" from the class structure of production and distribution. Fallen out of many different classes into unique different social strata and fragments. That's maybe implied in Mao's five categories of lumpen soldiers, bandits, beggars, robbers, and prostitutes, but isn't clear in reading his theory. But if you get into the details later, that understanding infused his own practice.

Even his language betrayed his focus on not the lumpen as a whole, but on some lumpen fragments and not the others. Taking the lumpen as disparate elements not one class or a single strata. He calls them "Brave fighters," because his primary political focus was to find fighting men as reinforcements for the war in the countryside. In other words, mostly politically recruiting male soldiers-for-hire and bandits. Rifle-bearers. As we can see in the more detailed view in other sections, the party in the countryside was also hungry for men who survived by their wits and were used to manipulating people, such as some professional criminals, con-men and gamblers.

158

Qing dynasty. Saw spontaneous working-class street actions alongside planned military attacks led by the lumpen secret societies that had allied with the democratic rebel, Dr. Sun Yat-sen. Mao still recalled years later:

> "On the following day, a *tutu* government was organized. [*tutu* was a military governorship—editors]. Two prominent members of the Ke Lao Hui [the Elder Brother Society—editors] were made *tutu* and vice-*tutu*. These were Chiao Ta-feng and Chen Tso-hsing respectively ... The new *tutu* and vice-*tutu* did not last long. They were not bad men. And had some revolutionary intentions. But they were poor and represented the interests of the oppressed. The landlords and merchants were dissatisfied with them. Not many days later, when I went to call on a friend, I saw their corpses lying in the street."[5]

So from his childhood, Mao Z was familiar with the organizations behind armed revolts against the wealthy and their government being the secret lumpen societies, before there even were any socialist or anarchist groups.

Just to warn you in advance. It isn't that Mao didn't know what he was doing with the lumpen, practically speaking.

However young in years Mao was back when he started laying down this line of theory, he was also already experienced, a brilliant practitioner at the art of actually making revolution. With a feel for classes like a professional gambler does for his familiar deck of cards. You'll maybe recall, though, that a card shark has no need to inform you about what moves he's making. And like that, Mao's theory should have come with a few consumer tags: *"Some assembly required"* and *"Read instructions before using."*

The other thing that many of us didn't grasp, is that Mao's words weren't just another theory. Not because he was any smarter, but because his theory was colored and molded by the larger revolutionary experiences of both lumpen and poor peasants. These ideas had been made in the intense furnace of oppressed people's experience, up to and including all-out revolutionary war, year after year. Understanding which carried that much more than personal weight to it.

Even so, there's an important point we have to keep our mind on: Whatever Mao Z's terse theoretical flashlight may have been in 1926, it couldn't be the theory summing up the groundbreaking experience of his lumpen/proletariat. *Because it came before most of that experience.*

In 1926, to lay it out on the table, even the forming of the Red Army was still a year away. The Chinese Communists then were still a big city party of workers and intellectuals, not peasants much less rural lumpen. The vast civil war which would transform rural Chinese society was only on the verge of starting, had not even begun much less completed itself. So in the 1960s–1970s, there was the mistaken assumption without thinking about it, that Mao's classic line on the lumpen was something really definitive. It simply couldn't be.

But what our guy Mao Z knew even then, subtly coloring those first words in 1926 when he called them a potential "revolutionary force," was that the lumpen played a key role in the revolutionary process. They weren't just bit players or minor actors on the large stage of overturning society. The lumpen in China were major wildcards in the mass revolutionary struggle that actually took place. Whether that fits anyone's theory or not. Their lived politics were far more real than all that.

"THE VAGABOND ARMY"

Over and over, in the struggle in those early years, Mao ran into and found common cause with lumpen/proletarian fighters. Retreating after the disastrous, ambitious 1927 Autumn Harvest Uprising during the first year of the open civil war, the small core of a thousand revolutionary soldiers led by Mao took shelter upon the Chingkangshan mountain range. This was a large, elevated and remote plateau with only five easily-defended paths up its mountainous slopes, a traditional refuge for bandits and other fugitives. They were only a tenth of the forces that the Autumn Harvest Uprising had started with, and Mao Z had been disavowed by the Central Committee and stripped of his party leadership positions. Not that it had made much difference to those revolutionaries resting and regaining strength in the mountains. They were being schooled in learning how to survive as guerrillas 101.

The "red" survivors ran into two bandit chiefs who were said to be Triad secret criminal society members—Wang Tso and Yuan Wen-t'sai—with their little armies. Both of them former bandits turned army unit commanders of the new modern capitalist national army, turned back to bandit leaders. Their bands quickly became "red" and joined Mao's small

army on the mountain, which increased then from one to three "regiments" (later, after Mao's main force left the area, they were rumored to have reverted to being bandits, and in any case both chiefs were killed in the constant fighting, as so many were).[6]

Starting the next Spring of 1928, other "red" forces began converging with Mao's, as the new Red Army began to take shape. General Chu Teh (*Zhu De* in the new translation system) became the commander-in-chief of the rapidly growing central Red Army, with Mao Z as the chief political officer. In a historic partnership that shifted the center of gravity of the entire revolutionary leadership to the distant solar system of mass guerrilla war in the countryside. Chu Teh was then the more famous, as a mercenary general, and the force was often called "the Chu-Mao army" in the Chinese newspapers and by the public. With many tens of thousands of soldiers.

A career military officer, Chu Teh had won battlefield promotion in difficult circumstances to general, and was a star in Chinese military circles. Eventually, after the 1911 overthrow of the Qing dynasty, holding powerful government offices that came with a high income from the customary bribes and graft, Chu Teh soon had a mansion, a harem with several wives as well as concubines, and a heavy opium habit. Before he conquered his long-time addictions to put everything else away and become a revolutionary. It's no surprise that Chu Teh was also covertly a senior member of the Elder Brother secret society, a tie he freely admitted actively sustaining in his Communist guerrilla years.[7]

The Elder Brothers were the dominant lumpen secret society in the key Yangtze valley region. Many members came to hold responsible positions in the local revolutionary movement and the insurgent military. Another famous Elder Brother general was Ho Lung (*He Long* in the new translation system), who, in fact, was said to hold the highest rank in the secret society of "Double-headed Dragon." Like Chu Teh, Ho Lung was a legendary figure

in China, and had been famous as a successful warlord figure before joining the revolution.

Edgar Snow, the American journalist who first reached Yenan in 1936 and came away with the first and only oral history of Mao's life, said of Ho Lung that he: "led an even more remarkable life than the largely hearsay account ... may suggest ... he organized armed peasant insurrections at least a decade before Mao Tse-tung tried it. His reputation as a 'bandit' was well earned. A youth of sixteen, with no schooling and an empty belly, he tried to kill a government officer, then gathered a band of outlaws in the mountains. By the time he was twenty-one his 19,000 followers held eight counties. Rebels in three provinces united around him, calling themselves a Peasant Army. They became so formidable that government forces were obliged to grant them amnesty and monetary rewards to disband."

Red Army commander Chiang-lin, who had been a labor organizer in the great 1922 seamen's strike in Hong Kong and took part in 1925 in the first revolutionary delegation to meet with General Ho Lung as a possible ally, told stories about Ho as a legend:

> "it is said of Ho Lung that he established a soviet district in Hunan with only one knife. This was early in 1928.

Ho Lung was hiding in a village, plotting with members of the Ke Lao Hui, when some Kuomintang tax collectors arrived. Leading a few villagers, he attacked the tax collectors and killed them with his own knife, and then disarmed the tax collectors' guard. From this adventure he got enough revolvers and rifles to arm his first peasants' army."[8]

The radical journalist Agnes Smedley's first person account of meeting him in embattled rural China is still a vivid picture: "Talking in this way, we reached Ho Lung's village headquarters. As we approached, a tall man with a black mustache and wearing a tall fur hat that accentuated his height came out of the building and waved. Ting Ling shouted: 'Comrade Ho Lung, we have come!'

> "'Shades of the Taiping rebels!' I exclaimed to myself, for Ho Lung looked not Chinese, but like some old print of a mustachioed folk-tale Mongol or Central Asiatic. He was a man in his middle forties, but he walked with the lithe grace of a panther. As he drew near I saw that his dress seemed so strange and vari-colored because it was made up of the remnants of many uniforms. His jacket was of faded gray and his trousers black, the latter fitting so

tightly that he appeared to be made up for some medieval drama. Above his blue cloth Chinese shoes white socks showed, and from his ankle to the knee was a splash of green—puttees wrapped tightly in a long leaf-like pattern. Something seemed missing from his uniform—oh yes, a blazing sash and a curved scimitar!

"This was Ho Lung of fame and fable. A poor peasant of central China, he had been described as a local militarist, and even as a bandit .... After the split in the nationalist forces, he had become commander of the powerful Second Red Army. This ever increasing force held large areas to the north and west of Hankow and had for years fought death to a standstill. He was illiterate and his army had not been so well trained politically as other Red armies ...

"Even his elder sister, a big-footed woman almost as tall as himself who had been a laborer on the estate of a landlord, commanded a unit of his troops. In the '30s, at the age of forty-eight, she died with a gun in her hands while leading her troops in battle."*

Interviewing him about his origins, Agnes Smedley wrote: *"During the warlord years, Ho, a poor and illiterate peasant, seemed to have gained the idea that since almost everyone had become a warlord he might as well become one himself."*

"Famous" certainly described Ho Lung. In an age when China's rural population didn't have sports stars and actresses on tv or gossip magazines, much less the internet, scandalous celebs were in short supply. So spectacular outlaws like Ho Lung helped fill that gap. As a teenage bandit and warlord and then as a revolutionary "bandit chief," he had the kind of fame where little boys played at being him and respectable businessmen literally fled towns when rumors placed his army nearby.[9]

In those first years of the Red Army, when the whole democratic movement was reeling on the defensive, retreating under constant attack, forced under that

---

* Ho Ying, Ho Lung's older sister, was one of the only two women fighters known to command a regular Red Army unit of men. She was killed in combat in Hupeh.

The commonly used expression in China back then, "big-footed woman," meant a woman whose parents had decided not to prepare her while still young to be a sex object. Instead of compressive binding of her young foot bones into a tiny, high arch, her feet were left normal sized and flat to be more useful for physical laboring. Many non-Han ethnic minorities, such as the Hakka, also often did not follow such torturous practices.

great repressive pressure to transform into an illegal mass movement of undergrounds and partisan organizers and rebel militias and soldiers by the many thousands—or perish—the lumpen/proletariat were the indispensible social base for the revolutionaries. Not simply some useful people, but temporarily the key strata, maybe not according to anyone's political doctrine but in the actual real time situation.

At the party's 1929 Gutian conference, two years after the Red Army's founding, **Mao Z's report on their political-military situation bluntly said that their military's "roving banditism" and other such political problems had their root in the reality that** *"the lumpen-proletariat constitute the majority in the Red Army."* (While in those years of rebuilding after the Autumn Harvest uprising, Mao also had reported that *"the soldiers of peasant or working class origin in the Fourth Army in the Border Region constitute an extreme minority."*)

Lumpen/proletarian soldiers were the definite *majority* of the many thousands of revolutionary fighters under his leadership in the early years. Although neither Mao Z nor the rest of the party leadership were eager to broadcast this heretical or scandalous situation in what their enemy derisively called "the vagabond army."

PEASANT CHINA THROWS MILLIONS INTO THE GAME

This significant revolutionary role for the lumpen was only normal, we should say, in the context of China then. Since the same surprising class configuration had been responsible for the much larger mass movement that the new revolution drew its lifeblood from.

It seems that everywhere Mao looked in those early days of the 20th century in rural China, the lumpen/proletariat were involved when battles against the rulers broke out. That this was true of the most important mass movement in China's history—the peasant movement which became the popular base of anti-capitalist guerrilla war and eventual revolution—only throws more fuel onto our theoretical camp fire.[10]

A giant peasant rebellion in the form of militant Peasant Associations had broken out in 1926 across Southern China, where the progressive and radical political currents were strongest. Centered in the expansive rural countryside of Hunan Province and contiguous areas, comprising at least 4.5 million peasants and growing rapidly.

Loosening the gentry and landlords' brutal chokehold on village life and politics, often by spontaneous mass violence, their tactics ranged from militant village street protests all the way to storming the guarded compounds of the landlords. And even starting the redistribution of food and farmlands.

In reporting on the new rebellion in the countryside, Mao Z *didn't* place the Communist Party at the center of events, because they weren't. Particularly since the party's central leadership and their Kuomintang military allies were basically opposed to any peasant rebellion at all. Mao told his biographer: "By the Spring of 1927 the peasant movement in Hupeh, Kiangsi, and Fukien, and especially in Hunan, had developed a startling militancy, despite the lukewarm attitude of the Communist party to it, and the definite alarm of the Kuomintang. High officials and army commanders began to demand its suppression, describing the Peasants Union as a 'vagabond union,' and its actions and demands as excessive."[11]

Although the relatively small numbers of Communist cadres in the countryside then would try to hold village meetings and inspire the peasants to start local branches of the associations, before quickly moving on as they usually had to. Instead of the Communist Party, Mao Z placed as the key instigators a new grouping of the most oppressed themselves—which he referred to as the *"utterly destitute."*

This was difficult to pin down on the surface, because the party was reporting from the countryside through a filter. Bluntly, closeting the lumpen as much as possible. Because the major role of the lumpen in the revolution was so counter to established Marxist class views, both Mao Zedong and the party itself worked to lessen the flashy guest appearances of their lumpen/proletariat on late-night tv talk shows. Remember, this was a time when Mao Z himself was being heavily attacked personally within the party for even recognizing the radical potential of lumpen outlaws. Party leader Li Li-san specifically criticized him for the big-time error of *"guerrillaism infected by the viewpoint of the lumpenproletariat."* (In hindsight, amusing words, don't you think?)[12]

In Mao's 1927 *Report on an Investigation of the Peasant Movement in Hunan*, referring to surveys which showed the overall make-up of the movement, Mao mentions one in Changsha county, which counted the poor peasants as 70% of the Peasant Associations' membership. Which Mao thought was true overall. Mao then added a significant point, that **there was a sub-category of the very most poor, the "utterly destitute," which itself accounted for an additional**

20% of the peasant movement's total members.

Even more, Mao goes on to say that almost all the grassroots leadership at the local level were poor peasants and especially these very poorest. In fact, according to Mao, in one of the best-surveyed areas with mature peasant organizations, it was shown that "... of the officials in the township associations in Hengshan County **the utterly destitute comprise 50 per cent ...**" There's no question that this newly identified social strata he named, *"the utterly destitute,"* played a key leadership role in the militant movement, apparently far beyond their size in the population. But who were they?

In fact, the *"utterly destitute"* were our old friends the rural lumpen/proletariat all over again. The Communist Party central committee editorial group supervising the later republishing of Mao's writings admitted that by the *"utterly destitute,"* Mao specifically meant two groups put together: the "rural *lumpen*-proletariat" and the "rural proletariat." The second was only a tiny fig leaf. What was really happening was that the rural lumpen themselves were playing a big grassroots leadership role in the rural uprising that would transform all China. A good day, for outcasts and outlaws.

Mao was in no sense an anarchist then, unlike earlier in his student days, when his roommates were anarchists and his first revolutionary study group was based on anarchist ideas. Still, it isn't hard to notice that in Mao's rural class analysis, the militant cutting edge of "utterly destitute" lumpen/proletarians and desperate wandering laborers is a lot closer to Mikhail Bakunin's anarchist class vision of lumpen "destitute proletarians" than it was to Marx and Engels' "scum of all classes." Hiding under familiar Marxist forms of discourse, Mao's political recognition about the lumpen in his time and place was actually a profound change.

Both working with the Communist Party and working without the party in many places, the lumpen/proletariat—using their underground outlaw organizations such as the Elder Brothers and the Red Spears—were helping start and lead this massive countryside rebellion. No wonder Mao was dancing around with his words pretty carefully, since this was like big time heresy, like something totally impossible or totally outrageous according to previous Marxist views.

2. imaginary "proletariats" & rural class differentiation

Time out! We have to hit the "pause" button a moment, while we go back and look much more closely at this whole question of the "rural proletariat." Because the Chinese Communist Party in those years kept stressing its importance. Even our big guy had to give ritual bows to it in his reports and writings. Everyone "red" kept saying its name. Although, basically, it barely existed in the real world. Yeah, funny, that. We're going to haul out the big class microscope now.

It's strange that to measure the lumpen/proletariat's full political weight, we would *first* have to consider another even much smaller and much less significant class in the Old China countryside. Talking about what the Chinese Communist Party in the 1920s and early 1930s spotlighted as the "rural proletariat." So the obvious first question is, why?

Well, this isn't about social statistics, really, it's about the problems of revolutionary leadership. Which is why this small matter gets blown up so big as a subject.

The top leaders of China's Communist Party back then—many of them Moscow-trained intellectuals—had the compulsive bad habit of inventing "proletarian" class forces in their strategies which had no material existence except on planet Dogma alongside Flash Gordon and his foe Emperor Ming the Merciless. i mean, pure 1920s science-fiction exercises in wish-fulfillment. Even Mao Z had to make ritual references in reports to this supposedly important agricultural "proletariat."

One big reason harassed Mao Z was so determined to keep doing rural social investigations was to help establish what the class reality really was (and perhaps bring the party HQ back down to factual ground). Don't misunderstand this: it's easy to be amazed by these kind of gross misjudgements long after the fact, but always hard for any new generation of revolutionaries to work out what social forces to base root change of society on. Look at all the ex-college student radicals here in the u.s. empire, who in the turbulent 1960s went into the factories and blue-collar communities to hopefully organize masses of revolutionary white workers for the base of a "New Left." Until they actually lived that class terrain, they didn't know how unrealistic that strategy was.

You might think the problem was just out of touch intellectuals, but it's not that simple. Those young Chinese intellectuals at the party center almost a century ago were among the most aware young rebels in China, and had real educations, too. The puzzle wasn't so easy to figure. Old China was in the last days of an outmoded and dying imperium. Everybody knew that. And for almost a century Old China had been riven by rebellions and civil wars.

The great Tai-ping Rebellion of the 1850s–1860s, led by a civil servant who thought himself to be the younger brother of Jesus Christ reborn on earth, took the city of Nanjing and set up a large neo-Christian state in Central China which lasted for fifteen years. Millions joined in this rebellion against the Imperial society. Farmland was held in common by the peasants there, while the equality of men and women and the abolition of footbinding were declared as Christian doctrine turned into rebel law.

Failed rebellions of all kinds were easy to come by then, but no one had found the key social understanding to succeed. To build a new society on the old. That in 1917 the Russian Bolsheviks had just replaced the Czarist empire with a new socialist state impressed many young dissidents. The Bolshevik program of making working class revolution using urban factory cells and mass councils even in a heavily backward, still mostly peasant society, was taken up by socialists as a model road for a new China. But to do this, the young revolutionaries had to find proletarian classes and strata to build on.

When Mao Z in his 1927 report on the new peasant movement, invented the potent class category of the **"utterly destitute"** as leading the mass uprising, he was mixing together under a new name the *rural lumpen/proletariat* and *rural proletariat* (as the Central Committee editors of his *Selected Works* specifically admitted). One possible aim was to cover up the embarrassingly large role of the lumpen in the peasant struggle. Using a confused exaggeration about the size and role of hired rural farm laborers. That was an often misunderstood class splinter which the party back then tried to talk up in its propaganda about the countryside, strictly for its own ideological agenda of always trying to find a "proletariat" to build on. Well intended, yes, but not particularly accurate in terms of class analysis it turned out.

Mao originally wrote in his *Report on an Investigation of the Peasant Movement in Hunan*, that these "utterly destitute ... are the completely dispossessed, that is, people who have neither land nor money, are without any means of livelihood, and are forced to leave home and *become mercenaries or hired laborers or wandering beggars.*" (our emphasis) While he carefully avoided the use of the term lumpen/proletariat for obvious tactical reasons, this was who he was pointing to. Particularly given the large numerical difference between the lumpen and the rural laborers—the first being some five or ten times as large or more than the second.[13]

Peasants in China then by definition had some owned or rented farmland to support themselves on even if only partially, and had some implements such as a plow or a draft animal to farm with even if rented or borrowed. In varying degrees that materially established their class segment differences from poor peasants to middle peasants to rich peasants. Both land and farm implements were precious and hard to come by in the Chinese countryside of the 1920s, where millions starving literally to death was an ordinary happening.

The rural proletariat, in contrast, were initially defined as bare agricultural laborers, without any cash or material property or means of support save their bodily strength. Wage work in that hungry peasant countryside was extremely scarce and very poorly paid, since few farmers could afford to hire outside labor.

While the rural proletariat was a class that the urban Communist intellectuals initially put great hopes on, this semi-class was thinly scattered across the land and were only a very small and discontinuous part of the rural population, often economic refugees without stable residences. Largely unable to act cooperatively even with each other, they were greatly outnumbered in the revolutionary countryside by the lumpen/proletariat, in embarrassing contradiction to the party's borrowed left preconceptions.

Published statements that the rural proletariat might be 10% of the Chinese countryside in the 1920s–30s were largely hopeful guesstimates, based on what was later discovered to be faulty data. Even later, a 1951 census of Jiangxi province found that in areas not yet land reformed—under post-Revolutionary conditions that were relatively prosperous and unusually favorable to the presence of hired laborers—only 3.7% of the rural population were hired agricultural laborers. Pre-Revolution, the survival rate of rural wage laborers was certainly less, probably much less.

When Mao Z led the temporary "red" local government in 1930 to do a social investigation in Xunwu, they found that rural hired laborers in Xunwu village were so few as to be non-existent, and that class doesn't even appear in Mao's class breakdown there at all. For the whole of Xunwu county, the revolutionary social investigation found that rural wage laborers both permanent and temporary made up *only three-tenths of one percent of the population* there.

Most dispossessed men across rural China could not physically survive as simple hired farm workers in that deadly hostile class environment. Rural proletarians were also a non-self-reproducing class then, in that they were almost all single men with only a few families scattered amongst them. Romance and "love" were seldom factors, as legally and traditionally all women in the Old Society were property. Just as captive New Afrikans in the old u.s. colonial empire had been. **All Chinese women then could be used in any way, exploited, or even sold as the men in their family wanted.** And their marriages were plain economic contracts.

Since rural proletarian men had almost no prospect of obtaining land on any terms or a home to live in—which made them *less* than peasants—village families refused to consider them as marriage prospects. Which is why in one village social investigation, Mao referred to those hired laborer men as *"the most miserable class."* So new members of the class usually came falling in from above as failed peasants.

As a class splinter they might not have even come to any particular political notice, except that the urban intellectual leadership of the Communist Party back then was desperately searching for a way forward that didn't feature the "ignorant" peasant masses they so looked down upon. One theoretical formulation was to demand that in the countryside, party organizers and soldiers build around the rural proletariat, who were grasped at as the next best thing to the urban classes that the party leadership so yearned for. They demanded that agricultural hired workers be formed into unions, be put forward as Peasant Association leaders, and so on. The only problem with this ingenious scheme was that it was based on faulty class analysis and lack of detailed information. For this "proletarian" class that they assumed or hoped would exist was mostly a leftist political fiction.

We can imagine Mao and Chu Teh and their comrades tearing their hair out reading fantasy off-target documents on strategy from far away party headquarters in Shanghai. Mao's reports back were like an antibiotic trying to combat a brain infection, a stream of key facts reassembling a stark picture of the real situation. *Knowing this, we can see why Mao thought that social investigation was such a constant practical need in revolutionary work.* In his 1930 social investigation of Xingguo County's Yongfeng district, Mao found that the rural proletariat barely existed in any numbers and played little if any political role. Out of the 8,800 people in the district, there were only the equivalent of fifteen full-time agricultural laborers hired each year. In the revolutionary governing of the district and its member villages, not

one rural proletarian sat on any committee (although one Red Guard local militia squad had a hired laborer as a captain).

Nor was it simply the case of one or two unrepresentative local situations. When the lack of results became clear, party leaders turned to a wider net in pursuing the same fantasy class strategy. The 1931 Party Congress mandated a push to form new revolutionary unions in the Soviet areas, with rural agricultural proletarians included in with the larger numbers of coolies, industrial workers, and all other wage laborers. Special party branches of only workers were to be set up, to provide better leadership to the struggle.

Mao Z's report to the Second Party Congress of Soviet Deputies in January 1934, however, exposed the underlying contradiction: In all of the Soviet areas, with a population of approximately nine millions, the entire worker class category including factory workers, railroad and other transport workers, miners of all kinds, coolies, handicraft makers in wage employment by an artisan or small manufacturer, as well as the skinniest category, agricultural proletarians, all together comprised less than 3% of the population. Village agricultural proletarians all by themselves were simply not present enough as a class to have any weight on the political scales: They existed barely but had no social or political impact or even relationships. In Marx's analytical terms, they barely existed as a class "of themselves" but not as a class "for themselves."

By the way, for a later generation in the countryside, such as in the 1940s–50s, some from peasant families were often considered "workers" or "semi-proletariat" by the Communist Party if they had left for a handful of years when young for wage labor in the new oil fields, coal mines, or factories in other larger towns, before returning home again to farm. This was actually a completely new and different kind of rural proletariat, a strata that was part of peasant families but had modern industrial experience, often including union activity. Using the same name as the earlier semi-vagabond splinter of farm wage laborers but being a completely different class.[14]

3. add theory & bring to boil

Those early Chinese struggles are still important to constructing useful revolutionary theory, because of their unique place in the capitalist system's history. That was the first time modern revolutionary forces had systematically brought the lumpen into the movement on a mass scale. Over protracted time.

Since the lumpen there were already openly tagged and recognized as "floating people" in old Chinese class culture, we get a much fuller and more detailed picture than we can in today's Western societies where they are so often masked. Hidden under artificial identities as in our 21st century imperial metropolis. That Mao could even give the approximate size of the lumpen/proletariat in China then as "twenty millions" or 6% of the population, gives us the kind of information we aren't close to having about the u.s. empire or the u.k., even though these are the most studied, most data-mined and constantly under surveillance mass societies that have ever existed.

In China's revolutionary crisis, part of the lumpen were drawn as if by magnetism to the armed struggle against the corrupt, semi-feudal capitalism state and its wealthy classes. Many bound themselves to the struggle for their lifetimes, playing a key role. So is this typical, revolutionary politics we can expect to see from lumpen social fragments at the bottom in our own societies and everywhere now? No, absolutely not.

Pay attention to theory, re-check the chemical formula again *before* you mix all the ingredients.

Mao's China is usually analyzed in splendid isolation, as a "non-Western" unique situation. But, look again, it had its strange doppelganger moving in synchronous orbit with it all the way on the other side of the world. This is rarely brought into view, but it's getting into the lumpen/proletariat in terms of class roles that pushes open this window for us.

Just as old Imperial China was dying, a paralyzed society that was constantly producing large numbers of dispossessed and dislocated from its unsuccessful social structure and self-destructive wars, so, too, was imperial Germany. Like a different image of the same underneath all its modern technology and industry.

Mao Z and others of their generation had personally witnessed, after all, the final 1911 dissolution of the very last dynasty of an Imperial China that had endured many centuries. The Second Reich, the strong-armed German empire of Kaiser Wilhelm II, which had grown out of the Prussian kingdom famously led first by 18th century Frederick the Great and then by 19th century "Iron Chancellor" Bismarck, shocked the world by being overthrown into chaos amidst its stunning defeat in World War I.

But Germany had been so similar by being at the opposite end of time from old Imperial China. Only fifty years old as a nation, the young German Second Reich was too immature structurally, too semi-feudal still, to survive the bitter, winner-take-all economic and military competition of the major imperialist powers any longer. Just as the Qing dynasty empire although "great," was structurally too anachronistic and outmoded to compete in a world turned ravenously capitalist.

The fall of both doomed empires had produced great numbers of lumpen/proletariat in their growing class confusion.

Here it's useful to apply oppressor & oppressed nation theory. This concept for understanding one aspect of capitalism, holds that the high imperialist period (end of 19th century to at least three-quarters through the 20th century) was characterized by the ownership of the entire world by the various imperialist powers through colonialism and neo-colonialism. No longer would there be independent countries or autonomous indigenous areas. World capitalism as a system was asymmetrical, though, fitted together by contrasting oppressor nations and oppressed nations, colonizer and colonized. Which had opposite economic roles, opposite class structures, and opposite mass cultures and politics. Stunning conceptual tool, this theory, to be sure.

So while many of the lumpen/proletariat in China were often "instinctively" against the wealthy and the oppressors, and for the leftist politics of fighting for the poor, the mass of lumpen in the German would-be empire were on the far right during the "temporary nation" of the 1918–1933 Weimar Republic. And beyond, as events proved. The Chinese revolution towards state socialism happened simultaneously as the far right German revolution towards the new radical fascist society. Saying this is only the roughest of guides politically. Used here just to show how we can't automatically extrapolate the experience in one society to extend in a linear fashion into another. There's a lot more physics involved.

We've pointed to only the few most readily visible points of Mao's theory and his generation's experience with the lumpen/proletariat in their revolutionary crisis. Only had a quick glimpse of it, really. That lumpen mass experience in China is like a huge workshop room, filled with machinery and processes going full-speed, which we can only take theory from if we go into it and break it down. That's a much bigger task.

4. a mass laboratory of revolutionary crisis

Some of us in the 1960s got thrown by the fact that Mao Zedong was like a demi-god then, a many-armed Shiva or benevolent Buddha of radicalism in those days. Seemingly ever-present, influencing everyone's cultural scene. Like, Mao Z was being praised by Malcolm X from the pulpit in the mosque, while being crabbed at in rock song by John Lennon. When Huey Newton and Bobby Seale went over to San Francisco to buy copies of the vest-pocket edition of Mao's plastic-covered "little red book" for 50 cents—and then hawked them back in Berkeley at the university campus for one buck, to raise money to buy their embryonic Panther party its first shotgun—it was just another tiny example of how Mao's writings had infiltrated personal political life in all directions.

So there i was tripped up by assumptions i unthinkingly made about Mao's theory. My own mess up, but we were fresh caught and unschooled. The big mistake was getting pulled off-course by the prevailing euro-centrism of the left political atmosphere. Not seeing that the most important thing wasn't Mao's words themselves necessarily, but what had given them such resonance: the world's largest single mass experience to date of the revolutionary vs. reactionary practice of the lumpen/proletariat. That went unexplored, particularly since most Asian-Americans, to say nothing of the white left, knew next to nothing about China's revolution—or revolution in general. We were only beginners.

There was practice in the Chinese Revolution touching on and illuminating many questions we have about the lumpen and politics. To tune in to those radio waves, we need to go back and examine why Mao Z was forming theory that way then. Then jump ahead, to the incomplete extent that we can, and pencil in possible theoretical lessons on the lumpen/proletariat from this protracted revolutionary war which drew in one-fourth of the world's population. Not exactly your small scientific sample, come to think of it. This can be so useful for us here because their thoughts and practice on this are like a lens, through which we can capture distant and usually undisclosed class politics played out in suddenly visible struggle.

To do that, however, we have to refocus and go to work with tools and lunch pail. Going to go through more basic Chinese class anatomy and armed politics right here than most of us would ever do just for the fun of it. Yeah, more prep work for student cooks, in other words. Because our current confusion about the lumpen comes from the fact that earlier revs only glanced at the label without opening that lead-lined box.

When Mao wrote so defiantly from the center of the mass peasant rebellion in Hunan province, early in 1926–1927, he and his entire movement were on the edge of a political cataclysm, about to be possibly wiped out. It was that revolutionary crisis that was a great political laboratory, in which the self-activity of first many thousands and then millions of people tested every class theory and strategy. Everything was paid for in blood and risk, tested in people's lives.

Because right then, the modernizing Nationalist united front that Dr. Sun Yat-sen—"the father of modern China"—had put together to revolutionize China as a reborn society, was coming totally apart after his 1925 death. That broad alliance for a "democratic" Western-style nation was impossible anyway, defying even magnetism and gravity, probably, temporarily holding together everyone from local industrialists and imperialist powers such as Japan and Great Britain, to Chinese sweatshop workers in San Francisco, big Chinese merchants and ambitious militarist officers, to say nothing of communists, socialists and anarchists.

That very Spring 1927, would begin the times of great violent repression, of bloody anti-Communist hunts by the new Nationalist regime of Generalissimo

Chiang Kai-shek, of mass executions of hundreds of thousands and many years of bitter civil war. In that deepening crisis, at times the very survival of the Communist Party and the peasant mass uprising itself was doubtful.

In that first five year period when the civil war began, when survival itself was often in question, the most critical and now most often over-looked factor was the coming together and *merging* of a substantial part of the rural lumpen/proletariat with the young anti-capitalist insurgency.

5. social investigation
finds lumpen / proletariat

One of the advanced work traits that our young friend Mao Z kept in his toolbox were social investigations. These weren't surprising exactly, being a part of revolutionary work ever since Karl Marx first tried it out in a modest way, in his "workers inquiry" questionnaires. But they are seldom used. Complete class analysis sometimes as detailed as person by person of the social and economic structure of a given area or workplace, these surveys could be smaller but still a scientific investigation. In other words, a heck of a lot of work (having done surveys and small-scale social investigation of one neighborhood street, can verify that it's a lot of work). Mao Z thought that they were invaluable to revs, though, big-time useful, practically speaking.

So thugs and gamblers and sex workers and many of the other lumpen/proletariat, bump into us on the sidelines in Mao Zedong's major social investigation into Chinese rural society of 1930, *Report From Xunwu* (his seven earlier county social investigations into rural society were lost when the comrades he had left the manuscripts with at those perilous times were killed by the rightists, including five Hunan studies he had left with his martyred first wife, Yang Kaihui). This study involved many local people interviewing everyone, while going through stacks of government and business documents. Making a detailed inventory of knowledge about the economic and social composition and activities of the 2,700 inhabitants of that typical Southeastern China rural town.[15]

The immediate political setting for that investigation was significant, too. Mao, back then a movement specialist in peasant organizing, had been urgently summoned in May 1930 to a Communist Party leadership conference in Shanghai. He decided to quietly refuse. Mao had been bothered for a long time by his party's imitate-the-russian–revolution-and-obey-moscow's-orders robotic mindset.[16]

Their revolution in China was projected to be in the big urban centers, based on the industrial working class. For the previous three years, however, they had been largely driven out of the cities by their former allies, the capitalists and their right-wing nationalist warlord generals. Many, many thousands of idealistic people from anarchist labor organizers to young feminist students had been slaughtered in counter-revolutionary repressions. Now the party was reduced to attempting rural revolutions but under the same old strategy: to establish temporary bases in the countryside, but only so they could turn around and re-attack the capitalist big cities. Although the movement still had hundreds of thousands of supporters and thousands in armed units scattered throughout China, losing everything and being wiped out was very possible at that moment.

Instead of going to that big party leadership meeting, Mao went in the opposite direction socially. He went "down" to the rural area of Xunwu county, where three major provinces met and the Red Army he helped lead had recently seized power. He wanted to work on new theory, to reground the revolutionary movement on a firmer footing. That month, May 1930, he worked on two projects close to his heart. The first was a short paper on the importance of social investigation and critical thinking to revolutionary work. This paper, *The Work of Investigation*, first plainly stated one of the basics of Mao's practice: "If you face some problems but have not made investigations, then stop before you make any pronouncements on these problems." (this influential paper is better known in its published final version's title, *Oppose Book Worship*).

Mao's second and much larger project was a social investigation of Xunwu village, a town whose economy was based on growing and trading agricultural products along with skilled handicrafts.* Where he hoped to make up for his lack of knowledge about the rich peasantry and about the detailed mechanics of rural commerce. This doesn't make juicy political reading for the most part. His work group explicitly didn't focus on either the rural proletariat or the lumpen/proletariat, because their main concern was playing catch-up on the dry details of the

---

* Like in the u.s.a., in China then sometimes a village or city would be located within a larger county—and both might have the same name, as in Xunwu village and Xunwu county.

rural economy the revolutionaries had just taken over. Always, though, Mao had an underlying concern to unearth what basic class politics would aid or hinder the revolutionary struggle.[17]

The findings of that two-week investigation of the newly seized town were surprising when it came to the lumpen/proletariat. Mao categorized women sex workers in this one study separately from the usually male categories of lumpen/proletarians, which the report called "loafers" as was common then in his society (in his writings, Mao made it clear that he considered prostitutes not in a legitimate trade, both victims of oppression and part of the lumpen/proletariat). The "loafers" in his report were a steadily non-employed grouping of men who survived by running gambling, smuggling, doing extortion of various kinds, and acting as "running dogs" for the rich landowners. In other words, male thieves and thugs, drug sellers and gangsters.

Lumpen/proletarians other than sex workers were fully 10% of the town's population, and prostitutes and their dependents were another 6%. While a 60% majority of Xunwu city's population were peasants, the number of all lumpen/proletarians, men and women, was much larger than the number of various artisans or handicraft workers, such as blacksmiths

and jewelry makers and horse and carriage drivers, etc. (10% of the population combined). Prostitutes were larger as a sector of the population than either government workers or merchants, and were twice as numerous as landlords.[18]

As a side note, maybe Mao's separating women sex workers from the other primarily male lumpen was unconsciously motivated by a certain recognition. These two groups existed completely separately from each other, not interwoven or mutually needed by each other as members of one class usually are. In fact, if all the male lumpen had vanished overnight, those village prostitutes would hardly have been affected at all.

Although legal, Mao notes that prostitutes were among the "nine low classes" as set down long-ago for society by the Qing dynasty. They were specifically grouped at the bottom of any respectability with opera singers, barbers, back massagers, pedicurists, chimney sweeps, those who sang folk songs to accompany tealeaf picking, county government clerks, and most instrumental musicians. So to understand that women sex workers in that major society in world terms were "trash" just like opera singers and local government clerical workers, puts a somewhat different spin on things. The seemingly arbitrary nature of who is respectable and who is not in any class society is always interesting when viewed from the far outside, no?[19]

Just as with talking about the characteristics of small landlords or the salt trade, Mao got very specific about the sex workers: "There are 30 to 40 brothels in this town of 2,700 people. The best known among the hard-bitten lot of prostitutes, young and old, are Chang Jiao, Yue E, Zhong Simei, Xie Sanmei, Huang Chaokun, Wu Xiu, Run Feng, Da Guanlan, Xiao Guanlan, Zhao E, Lai Zhao, Yu Shu, Wu Feng, and Yi E ..." (Whatever happened to them, in Mao's writing their names got penned into history, and i'm not going to deny them this).[20]

Sex workers were a small but real part of the non-peasant population in the town, and there was no discussion of them in the report as playing a reactionary political role or opposing the liberation movement. Or helping it, for that matter. Perhaps since the Communists were well known for eliminating prostitution wherever they took over. Although, since their trade depended heavily on the leisure activity of men with spare cash, many sex workers tended to relocate quickly when the Communist forces attacked an area. The revolution did ban much sex work in Xunwu, as elsewhere.

We should break in a moment and clarify: The Communists did ban brothels and explicit fulltime prostitution. They did *not* ban all sex work, which included economic marriages, paid "girlfriends" with a few regular "boyfriends"—what were considered immature "bad habits"—paying family debts with sex, etc.

Following party policy, the new Soviet government in the county treated prostitutes and the other "floating people" not as criminals, but as part of "the People," only who had been forced by oppression into "improper" livelihoods. Despite some village opposition, there was a real push by sex workers and other lumpen to share in land distribution and thus become in part or in whole peasants. The report says:

"The peasants in Xunwu City received the least land during distribution. Every person got land yielding 1 dan 8 dou [of grain—editors]. This is the smallest amount of all the districts in the county. There were fewer peasants than in other districts, yet many loafers and prostitutes who did not farm also asked to share in land redistribution, thus reducing the amount of each share. Those prostitutes who had lovers ran away with them; those who did not have lovers asked to share in the land redistribution. They said, 'There's no business; we will starve to death if we don't get our share of redistributed land.' People criticized them for not being able to farm. They replied, 'We can learn how to farm.' In fact, they are farming in the fields already.

"Most of the loafers and prostitutes have received some land. Among the loafers, some have the ability to farm, whereas others have sons or a small bit of capital. Some prostitutes have husbands or sons. Those with a number of family members are even more earnest in asking for redistributed land. Without it, they may have created a disturbance. Under these circumstances, the government distributed some land to them. Those inveterate loafers and prostitutes who absolutely had no ability to farm still have not been given any land. In the suburban district, 60 percent of the loafers received land; the remaining 40 percent had no knowledge of farming."[21]

Mao's report shows no enthusiasm for recruiting these "hard-bitten" women into the Revolution, or even much apparent interest. What happened to women sex workers who had no farming experience or other immediate way of making an alternate livelihood, the report doesn't bother saying.

Whatever short-comings the party had when it came to women, we have to remember that its takeover revolutionized the real situation of women in the peasant countryside. Previously, the term "peasant" basically meant only men, and in most of Old China women were not allowed to even do farming. Even the rebel Peasant Associations were male-only. The revolution established as a basic right, not only of women's ownership of farmland but the right to farm themselves. That's why Mao Z and those local Xunwu "reds" had so much discussion about whether women had or had not the ability or knowledge to farm on their own. Along with this, in many villages women gained the right for the first time to have names, to be called in public by their own names and not only "so-and-so's wife" or "so-and-so's daughter," as the ancillary possession of a man. This was an epochal change, and for women it shook the earth.

The lumpen/proletariat as a whole might have only been 6% of the total Chinese population by Mao's 1920s estimation, but it's understandable that in any particular pocket within the countryside such as Xunwu village, they were 16% of its residents. A real part of the population and far from marginal. Mao Zedong noted that "one great defect" in the report is that there is "no analysis of middle peasants, hired hands, and loafers." This might not be quite as accidental as he implies, for reasons we'll run into later on.

While most of China's lumpen/proletariat were in the countryside, to fill in the picture of such class splinters we should also touch on the large numbers of "floating people" in the major cities. The great international port city of Shanghai was generally estimated in this period as having at least 100,000 women sex workers, or one out of every thirteen women in the city. While the first and second class prostitutes in the major Shanghai brothels were only counted in the few thousands, the large majority of women sex workers were not only "pheasants" or streetwalkers, but also women who held jobs as tour guides, masseuses, street vendors of newspapers and cigarettes, itinerant menders of sailors' clothing, taxi dancers, waitresses in theaters, and so on. Some jobs for women required sexual services as well. Although Shanghai was the main industrial city in China then, the number of women sex workers outnumbered the number of women workers in the textile mills, for instance.

The varied reasons and ways that women there became sex workers is significant. While the Western anti-slave trade propaganda of the Christian missionaries always emphasized the violent abduction or sale of women into the trade, several Shanghai surveys done around the time of Liberation suggest that was a minority experience.

In one survey of 500 sex workers, only 4% said that they had been tricked into it. While 13% said that they had entered into it because of their voluntary "affinity for the work." The survey researchers wrote that "they were brought up in such an environment and liked this type of life." Another Communist city government survey found that 9% of the 501 women sex workers interviewed had been kidnapped and 11% had been sold into the brothels by their fathers or husbands. Economic necessity due to unemployment, bankruptcy or divorce were the main reasons given for coming into the life.[22]

6. mao's xunwu social investigation built on work with lumpen

Previously we discussed the important time in 1930, when Mao rejected the urgent orders from party headquarters and headed instead to the rural county and village of Xunwu, at the meeting point of three provinces in South China, to do theoretical work and conduct social investigation. Mao's close collaborator there was a local comrade named Gu Bo, who was twelve years Mao's junior and had grown up to lead the revolutionary movement in the area. His close participation helped realize Mao's social investigation.

Critically, Gu Bo had personally survived and guided the battered remnants of their local party network around the savage "White Terror" of anti-communist repression by warlord soldiers in 1927–28. Stitching together the scattered fugitive survivors of that right-wing offensive, forming a Xunwu Military Committee of young would-be guerrillas, and eventually in a few years seizing armed control of the county. Enough initiatives of that kind were taking place around there that Mao and his regular Red Army forces could temporarily advance into that whole larger area and rebase themselves.[23]

Starting in the Spring of 1927, Generalissimo Chiang Kai-shek, his conservative allies and his international capitalist backers, believed that they were finally close enough to seizing supreme power in China for themselves. So that they could break up the broad, nation-building united front that Sun Yat-sen had forged for a modernized and democratic China. Finally dispensing with all the troublesome communists and anarchist labor organizers and feminists and rural village militants. A great violent repression campaign began, at first slaughtering hundreds of thousands of leftists and other democratic-minded people, with the eventual death toll in the millions. Mass executions and even public mass tortures took place in city after city. Sometimes whole villages were left empty, a settlement of only dead bodies and burned out shacks.

It is seldom understood here that General Chiang Kai-shek's Western-backed repression in 1927 against China's revolutionary and democratic people of all kinds, was easily far more severe and bloody than what the Nazis did against leftists and progressives after they took power in Germany. Despite the u.s. left's eurocentric assumptions, the actual physical repression against socialists and anarchists by Hitler was less savage, less murderous, less broad, than what took place in China then. Easiest understood by what they did to women accused as "reds."

Women were not a large part of the Communist Party and were kept out of the leadership, of course, but their early feminism had deeply upset rightists. So they were special targets not only for death squad executions, but sometimes for prolonged spectacles of torture precisely like the infamous lynchings of New Afrikans in the u.s. South. In most cities and villages *every* woman with short hair the rightist soldiers saw was to be killed, that being taken as a sure sign that they were involved in Peasant Associations or had democratic sympathies.

In Hubei, one revolutionary report said that Nationalist Commander Xia Douyin's soldiers putting down the peasant movement "cut open the breasts of the women comrades, pierced their bodies perpendicularly with iron wires, and paraded them naked through the streets." Before they were ritually executed. In some cases, these ritual exorcisms of out of control women drew large crowds of men to watch and add their jeers and shouting to the public spectacle. In Changsha, in front of the Teachers Association building, three revolutionary women ages fourteen, sixteen, and twenty-four were beheaded after being stripped for public display.[24]

In the Xunwu county village of Datian, where Gu Bo grew up, so many were repressed by the right-wing Nationalist soldiers and mercenary thugs that after the communists retook the area, there was plenty of unclaimed farm land for anyone who could cultivate it. A rare situation in "land hungry" rural China. Mao's 1930 social investigation reported that in Datian village *"nearly a hundred able-bodied men and dozens of elderly people and children were slaughtered. Some thirty people became Red Guards or went to other counties to participate in revolutionary work. The population of the township was reduced from 800 to 600, and much land was left uncultivated."*[25]

One of the reasons that Gu Bo and his Xunwu comrades managed to survive is that as the situation there moved towards a capitalist armed crackdown in the late 1920s, he negotiated an *alliance* between the Communist Party and the local secret criminal society. That group, the Three Points Society, was the local affiliate of the large Triads, one of the traditional secret undergrounds of China.

The Triads, Big Sword Society, Society of Elder Brothers, Red Spears and other Chinese lumpen/proletarian secret societies were significantly different from our Western stereotype of a criminal association. Having started in the past as mutual aid societies of outcast men, most were not closed bodies but were open to other displaced ex-peasants and ex-workers turned "floating people." They also had a nationalistic hatred of the then ruling feudal imperial Manchu power structure and its allies, the gentry of wealthy rural landowners.

Gu Bo's alliance with those lumpen was specifically military, and as the outcast society had secret followers and allies and contacts all over the county, they gave the radical fugitives a new toehold in organizing underground revolutionary Peasant Associations and armed cells. Not a small kind of help to those on the run for their lives.[26]

What Gu Bo did in Xunwu, was only the logic of the situation, and was happening all over the country. Because the lumpen/proletarians and their secret organizations had been there on the scene *first*, existing outside the law generations before any ideological leftists had even appeared. They were the underground network of the experienced survivors and outlaws of various kinds that the badly damaged and diminished revolutionaries needed to turn to. When you're forced out to sea with your life at stake, you turn to sailors not real estate agents. And maybe turn to pirates best of all.

In China at that time, *millions* of lumpen were completely involved in sharply changing politics, fighting it out tooth and nail. On all sides, it turned out. It was a unique, real-life testing grounds for the outcast and outlaw "non-class." In a huge political laboratory teeming with mass activity, where classes of peasants, landlords and merchants, intellectuals, capitalists and imperial court officials, foreign states, artisans and workers, criminals and the organized lumpen/proletariat as well, tried out class programs and strategies and larger politics. As seemingly endless civil warfare was going on, inexorably pulling everyone in a rising tempo into its bloody grinding maw. That's the complex reality that breaking open and investigating Mao's theories partially decodes. And Mao Z was right there, fully alive as a young rev in that sensual human reality, and probably having a great dangerous time and smiling like a Cheshire Cat.

Mao Z isn't the central character on the stage for us, though, the lumpen/proletariat as volatile "non-class" fragments are.

7. what happened in xingguo county

We've spoken about Mao and the local comrade Gu Bo leading a social investigation of classes in rural Xunwu county in Southern Jiangxi province in 1930, after the Red Army retook the area from mercenary "White" armies. Just a little distance north of there in Xingguo county, still within Southern Jiangxi province, the revolutionaries faced equally grave challenges which they met with an even closer relationship with the lumpen/proletariat. Just saying it's an example that tells us a lot.

The "White Terror" repression from the right-wing militarists of the Kuomintang kicked off there in March 1927. In the nearby city of Ganzhou, where party organizing had started numerous unions with some 16,000 members in the previous months, a March 12, 1927, memorial meeting marking the second anniversary of Dr. Sun Yat-sen's death had been called by the Nationalist militarists and right-wing officials. Chen Xiang-zhih, chief Communist Party organizer and leader of the Ganzhou Labor Union, had been invited to take part. As he arrived, he was ambushed and shot down. Arrests and attacks on other Communists and militants started immediately. Within weeks, the headquarters of the Ganzhou Labor Union was burned down, its committees banned, and Communists forced to flee that and other cities for their lives.

To understand why the movement was seemingly so confused, so unable to defend itself, we need a bit of background. Now we are going to go deeper into this same situation we introduced earlier. **By early 1927, Mao's Communist Party was choking on an urgent inner debate.** It was then a new primarily urban party of 58,000 Communists, composed largely of intellectuals and workers the party had gained in their trade union organizing in the cities. Fully 22% were intellectuals while 58% were industrial workers. Only 5% of the party in that Spring were peasants, and those rural lives and activity did not have any political priority according to party doctrine narrowly concerned with mass legal politics in the major cities.[27]

Yet, a giant peasant rebellion had broken out across Hunan province countryside and contiguous regions, as the anti-warlord united front army of the Nationalist "northern expedition" moved slowly through South China. This changed everything, including the party itself. The gentry and landlords' brutal hold on village politics was shaken and loosened.

Still, the dominant Communist Party leadership thinking by early 1927 was that whatever "backward" peasants did was only foam on the waves, excessive disruption having no real political worth and not being decisive like organizing urban workers would supposedly be. Even worse, it was held by the "red" leadership that to ever strategically reposition toward the countryside would depoliticize and then eventually dead-end the party, without the superior class consciousness of its familiar urban life.

The party's central leadership in Shanghai, which was opposed to Mao's emerging political viewpoint, made no secret of their unhappiness not only with the great peasant uprising, but even with the subsequent recruitment of thousands of peasants every month into the Communist Party. Political Bureau leader Li Li-san said in a report to the party's Sixth Congress, in October 1928, that these peasant rebellions threatened the party:

> "As a result of the particular development of the struggle in the countryside during the past year, and the fact that peasants now constitute 70 to 80 percent of our party membership, the *peasant mentality* is now reflected in our party ... The Communist Party acknowledges that the peasantry is an ally of the revolution. At the same time, recognizes that the peasantry is petty-bourgeois and cannot have correct ideas regarding socialism, that *its conservatism* is particularly strong, and that it lacks organizational ability ... it may lead to a complete destruction of the revolution and of the Party."[28]

To argue against such doomed politics, Mao Z himself had spent a month in Hunan, the province that was then the center of the rural struggle in South China, and where the militant village Peasant Associations had rapidly gained at least 4.5 million members by early estimates. The countryside had been thrown into the chaos of long-suppressed change. The Peasant Associations were demanding major rent reductions on the farmland from the rich landowners, where rents of 50% or more of the annual crop were customary.

Peasants also demanded an end to the customary "favors," in which peasant men had to "help" the wealthy by doing unpaid labor rebuilding their dikes and cleaning irrigation ditches and repairing sheds and other tasks on the landlord's own plot. While tenant women sometimes had to do unpaid domestic labor in the landlord's house, cleaning and washing and cooking. An end to all abusive privileges held over them was a universal peasant demand.

In the most politically advanced villages, the Peasant Associations had begun dividing up and equally redistributing the land. While in some, their "Peasant Self-Defense Army" used old rifles seized from the corrupt local government "Home Guard" militia to temporarily become the armed power. **The Communist Party leaders back in the urban center were alarmed, and declared as political policy that the peasant movement had gone "too far."** Many association militants had been arrested even by local reformist authorities allied to the party, and even by "red" officials themselves. While at other places peasant "riots" had broken through the authoritarian order and violently attacked landlord compounds. So Mao sent to the party his famed March 1927 *Report on an Investigation of the Peasant Movement in Hunan,* which was throwing down politics. His gun was loaded with the challenge to his big city party and its followers, to change or perish:

> *"All talk directed against the peasant movement must be speedily set right. All the wrong measures taken by the revolutionary authorities concerning the peasant movement must be speedily changed."*

That the party was then urban-centered and largely opposed to the peasant rebellion breaking out, explains why the revolutionaries had no infrastructure in the countryside when they needed to re-center themselves there as a matter of survival. Mao Z was still being criticized for the supposed error of grassroots peasant organizing! Which party leaders put down with the fancy, pseudo-Marxist name, *"localism of peasant consciousness."*[29]

There had only been very roughly 1,200 Communists by one informed estimate in all of Jiangxi province before the Spring 1927 wave of repression started, with maybe 200 of them in the less "red" south end of the province. This number had suddenly dwindled with the mass killings (most arrested radicals, democrats, feminists and militants at that time were only briefly questioned for a few minutes, and then executed right there in the street or nearby fields) as well as the widespread loss of contact in dispersal.[30]

Surviving party cells and individual party members had to flee into the endless countryside, away from the urban centers of the crackdown. There, many survived by joining the criminalized underground life for wanted men, which was a class terrain of the lumpen/proletariat.

At that time the local Three Dots Society was a typical Chinese secret society, linked to the Triads in adjacent Guangdong province. While the contemporary organized crime syndicates we are most familiar with today are like miniature lumpen capitalist armies, tightly organized into a single dictatorial command structure, the Chinese secret societies were composed of free-acting individuals. Each having to come up with answers sometimes every day on how to survive. Some smuggled salt on porters' backs from the next province, evading the salt tax charged by the authorities. Others traded in opium. Some ran gambling games or profited in them. Others were thieves. Or bandits holding up travelers on the roads. Many men with no other choices became rented rifle-bearers, i.e. soldiers, which in the China of that day was among the lowest of the low, a mercenary occupation only serving clashing evil men and having a short life expectancy far from home.

In the secret society each person pledged themselves to the society's principles, swore to render aid to another member in need, and in turn was able to request assistance themselves. Just having the knowledge of a locality's hideouts and safe routes, as well as those local residents willing to hide or assist illegal activity, was important. In extraordinary moments, the secret society's senior members could call on all to voluntarily come together in some major cause.

Some communists on the run in Xingguo county were able to find refuge in the Three Dots Society. Perhaps because they had already quietly been members before becoming communists. Or by knowing a Three Dots member who would put them up for membership, and then swear the oaths that bound them to the secret society and vice versa. Other communists followed them, soon gaining influential posts within the local secret order.

By the next year, in the Spring of 1928, the Communist party organization in Xingguo county decided to take an innovative step, **formally absorbing the entire**

Three Dots membership and secret structure into the party itself. A few traditional lumpen veterans in the Three Dots objected and had to be killed, but the transition into one organization went relatively smoothly or so it seemed. What the new party branch knew beyond how to survive underground was apparently too little, though, and the party branch's work had to be politically reformed several times by periodic Red Army mentors in the next several years. Including none other than Mao Z himself. In its carefully migratory marches, the young Red Army regulars periodically visited as many of the revolutionary strongholds in the South as they could. Not only resting and recruiting, but acting as teachers for the local party branches and peasant organizations, trying to strengthen the political awakening and organizing going on. There were a few major bumps in the road, of course, which we will look at later.[31]

Even several years later, in 1930 Mao's report to the central committee on Xingguo county's new Red government and party showed the heavy balance of the lumpen/proletariat's involvement. Of the eighteen persons who operated the new government in Yongfeng district in Xingguo, for instance, eight had been professional gamblers and one a former Daoist priest turned guerrilla commander.[*] Within those eighteen, the most influential district leadership such as both the current and former chairmen, Mao further reported, were lumpen/proletarians, along with one poor intellectual.[32]

The revolution complete with its own professional gamblers in Xingguo county in 1927–1930, seems like a far out case, although we should underline Mao's words that in the existing mass peasant movement then almost *half* the local grassroots leadership came from varied rural lumpen/proletariat.

---

[*] While Daoists priests may sound kind of interestingly "New Age" to hip Americans now, back in 1920s–30s China, leftists regarded them as part of the not too respectable fringe of hustlers, like spirit mediums and diviners and magicians, who conned the superstitious poor and gullible. In other words, lumpen at best if not outright criminal.

Background: The Soviet houseguests in China's politics

To understand the pivotal turning of 1927, and how everything changed politically in only a few months, we also have to stir into the mix, the big role of the Russian Bolsheviks and the Communist International (widely called the *Comintern*) in both mainstream Chinese politics and inside Mao Z's political food truck in particular.

This is a window on a whole extra, much more intimate layer of politics which Mao had to zig zag his way through. Because the unofficial world of Communism and its factions were real powers with rock-hard reality in his own life. Easy to run into and get bruised up, or even crash one's trip.

In those days, the Communist International united (in theory) all Communists worldwide into a single transnational body. Like one giant international disciplined party, with different national faces; all guided by the single command center in Moscow of experienced Communist leaders and cadre. Starting with supervising hundreds of thousands of largely inexperienced Communists in dozens of different countries. All over the world, the famous "CI reps" or Communist International representatives, showed up sent by Moscow headquarters to observe and report, or even to give strong suggestions. In important revolutionary situations such as 1920s Germany, the CI hadn't hesitated to take over and sit behind the steering wheel of a national party. In 1920s China, the CI headquarters in Moscow could and did replace Chinese party leaders and policies it felt were incorrect.

At that moment in 1927 China, Mao was in the top CCP (Chinese Communist Party) leadership. Sitting not only on the Central Committee but on the even more select Politburo, which led ongoing strategy and organization. Recognized as a leading peasant organizer and someone with real but ordinary experience in rebellions and warfare, Mao Z's strategic views were still in the minority in the party leadership factions. Half out of step with Moscow as well, which wielded unusually heavy weight for foreigners because of the tight Russian Soviet-Sun Yat-sen alliance.

Dr. Sun Yat-sen's coalition in South China had proclaimed the new Republic of China in 1912, but without armies or finances the unformed government had many supporters but little actual power compared to the warlords and the backward but wealthy classes with the Western imperialists behind them.

That started changing in 1923, when Sun Yat-sen negotiated a Soviet treaty giving his would-be state its first diplomatic recognition and material aid. Soviet advisors including a general, a trickle of funds, and modern German and Russian light arms soon began appearing. So Moscow was a power not only inside the world of the left, but as its own strong-armed self within mainstream Chinese politics, too. This was far from simply an intellectual presence.

One of Dr. Sun Yat-sen's chief political advisors in the early 1920s was the Soviet representative Mikhail Borodin, while dozens of "CI reps" acted as advisors in political, diplomatic, military and economic affairs inside both the Chinese Communist Party and the Kuomintang government itself.

"Li Teh" (Otto Braun), a German Communist World War I veteran sent as an advisor by the CI, was famously among the static positional warfare advocates within the party leadership, blamed for the major defeat and loss of the large "Soviet" rural areas it had governed in 1934. That ruling faction favored the European-style warfare of massed armies with fixed front lines, defending and attacking in major united thrusts. Rather than the innovative style of warfare based on guerrilla experience and the precepts of the classic martial theorist Sun Tzu, which the "Chu-Mao army" had developed.

The old party leadership was suspicious of the Central Red Army's new ideas. It wasn't that they were out to lunch, or that Otto Braun's conventional WWI trench warfare experience was nothing. It's that in the violent cauldron of the protracted mass war in the remote Chinese countryside, only those actually trying to survive by new and different warfare could keep up with the steep learning curve. In revolutionary terms, those anonymous fighters were the most advanced in the world. In their fluid style, position and territory were freely abandoned and retaken, while even large armies with tens of thousands of troops split apart and came back together in constant movements to gain tactical advantages in times and places unexpected to the enemy.

The critical 1935 Tsunyi conference while marching in retreat, that confirmed Mao's political leadership of the party after that crushing defeat, also demoted "Li Teh" to only being the advisor he was ranked as, under Mao. He still accompanied Mao and the Red Army for years through the entire Long March and into the guerrilla refuge of remote Yenan, where they rebuilt and re-grew. After years as the sole Soviet rep, long needing dental care and even having difficulty finding Chinese shoes in his big European size, he was recalled to Moscow in 1939. Leaving Yenan in a small airplane that landed for him at a roughly improvised airstrip in that remote guerrilla stronghold.

The earlier Chinese Communist Party leadership had officially rejected Mao Z's "Report" on the militant peasant movement, but still had to change policy when the Communist International intervened to order more support for that historic peasant outbreak. And bend it even more as the mass public radical & democratic presence in China's big cities was increasingly violently purged by rightist soldiers and police loyal to the warlords and Gen. Chiang Kai-shek's new capitalist regime. Still, Mao was not thought of as completely trustworthy in leadership Communist circles, as he appeared "weaker" on working-class politics than the more orthodox and urban-centered leaders such as Qu Qiu-bai and Li Li-san.

Pragmatically, Mao had to be careful to sound at least basically orthodox in a Marxist sense about the lumpen/proletariat, or risk falling politically to accusations of being anti-working class or anti-Leninist or anti-something. For the same reasons, Mao's deepening relationship with the militant lumpen/proletariat had to be covered for or defended as only practical expediency.

8. picking up the thread in xingguo county

One of the useful things about the experience of the revolutionary struggle in Southern Jiangxi Province's rural Xingguo county, is that it wasn't like a Hollywood movie or some slick heroic propaganda. Things down there were a lot more gritty, even though the home team did win in the end.

One of the things we pick up right away there was the reverse side of the coin. Which was the also large numbers of lumpen/proletarians fighting on the other side. Like, fighting with the army divisions of the new Kuomintang imperialist-backed regime. For instance, if the Elder Brother Society was increasingly mobilized as part of the revolutionary forces in the large and critical Yangtze valley region, then the Green Gang in Shanghai on its own coastal territory was committed to working with Generalisimo Chiang Kai-shek's Nationalist state in rooting out and killing Communists and anarchists and trade unionists and other democrats within its reach.

Upset that the Communists and the Peasant Associations weren't all wiped out in his 1927 bloodbath and were rebuilding rapidly, Generalissimo Chiang Kai-shek ordered gigantic encirclement campaigns to finally wipe out the "Red bandits." Where larger and larger armies of his would attack the Soviet areas from different fronts, supposedly trapping and crushing the Red fighters and their supporters. The First Encirclement Campaign in 1930 brought 100,000 Nationalist army troops against barely 40,000 Red Army fighters, but with superior strategy and tactics the "reds" decimated the Nationalist armies and forced their surviving units to flee.

By the time of Chiang Kai-shek's Fifth Encirclement Campaign in 1933–34, his rightist regime had mobilized a gigantic offensive force of almost one million mercenary soldiers to invade and "exterminate" the Red base areas (though over half of his mercenaries came from the regional and local warlord forces). That didn't even include the many city police and village landlord "Home Guards" and other private thugs acting as death squads against any dissidents locally. This unprecedented nationwide mobilization of criminal lumpen men by the rightists threatened to unbalance the whole structure of society. As entire villages were "eliminated" and only the most backward elements in society were encouraged.

The look-alike struggle carried out between revolutionary lumpen versus rightist lumpen wasn't only outside the revolution, obviously, but inside their popular formations as well. To examine the actual results in mass struggle of the new Mao Z line of bringing major parts of the lumpen into the revolution, going back to Southern Jiangxi Province, to Xingguo county, gives us an extraordinary balance sheet. **The political accounting in results pro and con can be detailed there. Confronting the possibly worst aspects as well as the best, to back and forth sift out lessons from it.**

One reason that the surviving Communist fugitives in Southern Jiangxi province's Xingguo county managed to gain the hidden life raft of the criminal Three Dots Society, was that they had reached an alliance with the bandit leader Duang Qi-feng. A known martial arts master from a poor background, Duang Qi-feng with his nine brothers led an influential bandit gang in the area. What was problematic was that his Three Dots Society gang had apparently just been on the other side. Had been said to have just finished taking part in the "White" repression for pay, leading the assault on the CCP headquarters and executing of dissidents in the city of Ganzhou earlier in 1927. Not certain if they were sharing these little business details with their new Communist allies.[33]

Nevertheless, this awkward combination of hardluck forces was immediately successful at turning the tables. Their small victories, such as overrunning a wealthy landlord's compound and redistributing his grain and property for themselves and others, attracted other small bandit bands to join them. Success led to more success in a certain practical logic. Other surviving revolutionary cells in nearby areas similarly grew by absorbing lumpen bandits and military deserters in survival actions against the feudal-capitalist elite.

While simultaneously, loose party cadres on the run, unable to think of any better way to apply the party HQ's new "uprisings" line, were attempting poor peasant uprisings in scattered villages. Whether winning or losing (and mostly they lost, of course) these peasant outbreaks only led each time to more and more recruits leaving home for the guerrillas. Nothing like losing an uprising to make you want to get the hell out of Dodge, and then why not join the growing guerrillas hiding out in the countryside?

While the newborn guerrilla insurgency at the grassroots was skilled at staying alive and striking hard at the rich, their politics too often remained at a "roving bandit" level. Seizing wealthy households and opium convoys was prioritized, not using guerrilla power to create a space in which to organize a base for the politics of change. Although to be sure the second happened as well, just not as it should have. In April 1928, the growing guerrilla forces managed to attack and temporarily hold the county seat in Xingguo, but other than parade some gentry around town as temporary captives, chant a few slogans, and extort "loans" from all the merchants, the revolutionaries with a town temporarily in their hands found few other political tasks to do.

When the "Chu-Mao army" visited the next year on the mobile force's regular sweep through the region, Mao Z was unhappy with them and kept nagging the new-found Xingguo revolutionaries to focus not on better loot but on mass organizing. Setting up Peasant Associations, lightly-armed local revolutionary militia, secret revolutionary government committees on the village and district levels; in other words, enlisting poor peasants into action groups of their own. Simplifying Marxist-Leninist politics a little bit, he left his newer comrades with very basic instructions: *"You must chant every day 'rally mass support, rally mass support ...' the way a monk repeats 'amida Buddha, amida Buddha ...'"* Whatever, it all seemed to work, with local guerrillas and peasant land seizures both climbing.

In November–December of 1930, though, something like the worst head-on political highway car crash happened: an internal armed revolt in the Central Soviet Area of cadre and soldiers against *"the party emperor"* Mao and the leadership of the "Chu-Mao army." It all seemed to start with a security campaign. For some time the CCP leadership had been worried about infiltrators from Chiang Kai-shek's intelligence. Attention came to focus on the "Anti-Bolshevik Corps" or ABC, which was a shadowy, mysterious conspiracy of infiltrators and saboteurs personally sworn to Gen. Chiang Kai-shek himself. Party security had already known them from actions like an operation with forged documents, issued over the name of well-known Lin Wenlin, the commander of the Jiangxi Second Independent Regiment of the Red Army. These documents purported to identify rightist agents as supposed special Communist organizers, to lure unwary students into joining a fake "red" cell, to identify young subversives for the government.

When Mao Z, in agreement with the other factions of the CCP leadership, started a broad anti-ABC enemy agent sweep inside the Red Army, they initially detained over 4,000 persons. A surprisingly large number, although apparently most were simply questioned and released after short political re-education courses.[34]

That triggered an armed mutiny, by other officers and soldiers who had served with the suspects. Initially involved were one battalion of the 20th Army, led by its political commissar. They killed a hundred other Communists and Red soldiers in attacking the headquarters at the Dongguo base area, capturing the town of Futian (*Fut-i'en* or *Fu T'ien* in the old translation system) and releasing detainees. Their entire Red division—the 20th army under General Liu Teh-ch'ao—sheltered the mutiny and moved out of the area, working for a while on its own. While the mutineers issued public claims to be the "new" Soviet center, and called for other party and Red Army units to break away from Mao and join them.

This became world news. As Mao Z said a few years later: *"Fu T'ien being near Kian, then the heart of the soviet districts, the events produced a sensation, and to many it must have seemed that the fate of the revolution depended on the outcome of this struggle."*

Although the 20th army and all the mutineers eventually surrendered after a stand-off of some months, a severe purge of former Xingguo county comrades in the army and party was only the center of a wider purge. It was a major internal rupture in the Dongguo base area, coming just as the entire Soviet area was bracing itself for a brute-force "First Encirclement Campaign" offensive by the much larger "White" capitalist armies.

Red Army security decided at the time that the whole "Futian Incident" had been sabotage created by a network of enemy "Anti-Bolshevik Corps" agents who had gotten in through that same Three Dots Society in Xingguo county. The head of the deep anti-communist penetration of party and army was finally revealed by interrogations to be our old friend Duan Qi-feng, the former martial artist, bandit chief, and secret society leader who had gotten himself promoted to chief of staff (i.e. second in command) of a Red Army unit.

The casualties weren't pretty, in any estimation. Mao in his public statements always blamed the mutiny on out-of-bounds factional opponents with the "Li Li-san line." At that time, recall, the Red "Chu-Mao army" leaders were a minority in the top leadership, and party leader Li Li-san's clear orders to abandon the peasantry and move the guerrilla army against the big cities in a win-or-lose-it-all gamble, were being ignored by the defiant "Chu-Mao" military command. In seeming violation of the party's rules of democratic centralism and top-down leadership. So some officers, troops and cadre in the Soviet area had reason to argue for overturning Mao Z's Red Army leadership, which could be considered illegitimate to the more obedient or factional.

Facing armed mutiny, party leaders in the Soviet area had decided to remove any possible traitors or agents right then, even if it meant surgically cutting widely around the boundaries of the tumor. In January 1931, the newly formed Central Bureau for the Soviet Areas sent a fellow Jiangxi native revolutionary veteran named Zen Bingchun to go stay with the outcast 20th army in protracted discussions, to persuade them to return to Soviet authority. Bingchun was not only a familiar veteran, but a former commander of the 20th army itself and one of the founders of the Dongguo base area. After some months, in July 1931, Zen Bingchun and the 20th army marched back to rejoin the rest of the Red Army, and this all but concluded the "Futian incident."

The "all but concluded" became a more cutting mouthful than many expected, however. Once back and resting, every officer above squad level in the 20th army was arrested, and most were executed. Common soldiers were dispersed as replacements to other units, and the identity of the 20th army was ended. In the widespread investigation and purge, according to an official report, *"over 90 percent of the cadres in the southwestern Jiangxi area were killed, detained, or stopped work."* Of nineteen area cadre studied in one later history, comprising almost all of the founding organizers of the Dongguo Soviet base area itself, twelve were executed as agents, five had died earlier fighting the capitalists, one died from illness, and one survived by moving away and leaving politics altogether.

Zen Bingchun, who had successfully carried out his party mission to convince the 20th army mutineers to return peacefully to Red Army authority, was also then arrested and executed himself. As was Lin Wenlin, the Red regimental commander. Our old lumpen friend Duan Qi-feng, from the Three Dots Society in Xingguo county,

Jiangxi province, escaped custody and became a bandit again, but was captured once more, interrogated and finally executed in 1933.

Within months the whole situation resolved itself, at least on the surface. The "Chu-Mao" army's leadership won acclaim for crushing Chiang Kai-shek's "First Encirclement Campaign," even though badly outnumbered and outgunned. Meanwhile, Party secretary Li Li-san had also recklessly challenged Stalin's authority over the Communist International, and was quickly removed from leadership and called to Moscow for many years of less than voluntary "re-education."

Mao Z characterized that armed mutiny to his first and only authorized biographer, the American reporter Edgar Snow, following the lead of party central at that time: as out-of-bounds factionalism by supporters of the Li Li-san adventurist political-military line. As he said to the journalist:

> "... There was, however, a critical period in the army before 'Lilisanism' was definitely buried. Part of the Third Corps favored following out Li's line, and demanded the separation of the Third Corps from the rest of the army. P'eng Teh-huai fought vigorously against this

tendency, however, and succeeded in maintaining the unity of the forces under his command and their loyalty to the high command. But the Twentieth Army, led by Liu Teh-ch'ao, rose in open revolt, arrested the chairman of the Kiangsi Soviet, arrested many officers and officials, and attacked us politically, on the basis of the Li Li-san line.

> "This occurred at Fu T'ien and is known as the Fu T'ien Incident ... . However, the revolt was quickly suppressed, due to the loyalty of the Third Army, to the general solidarity of the Party and the Red troops, and to the support of the peasantry. Liu Teh'ch-ao was arrested, and other rebels disarmed and liquidated. Our line was reaffimed, 'Lilisanism' was definitely suppressed, and as a result the soviet movement subsequently scored great gains."

Before we move on there's something i need to add: some readers will doubtlessly be horrified by at first the fratricidal fighting and then the internal policing. Certainly understand that. Even at the time of the "Futian Incident," Mao Z was condemned by some party critics as exploiting the mutiny to ignite a general purge, aimed at eliminating the Li Li-san supporters within the army and rural soviet government. At first using an obvious pretext, the charge that his factional opponents and their followers were really Anti-Bolshevik Corps agents and dupes. There is certainly in history books a lot of skepticism and evident disapproval by Western scholars at Mao Z's blunt tactics there (a view possibly subtly encouraged by Deng Xiaoping and the capitalist restoration regime).

Thought that we should walk over this ground a bit, however, for several reasons. You know, Mao Z reminds us in one of his military essays, of the insight from von Clausewitz, that **war is different from all other human activity**.

When you check out the record, you can get the feeling that young Mao Z barely bothered to conceal how much he wanted to rip the Li Li-san faction right out of the "red" military and rural party, by any means necessary. No matter how flimsy the excuse or reason, he really didn't care. To him, the revolution had to disentangle itself, to meet a life-or-death challenge, as quickly as possible.

Check out that terrain from Mao and Chu's point of view: Just as their liberated zone of millions with its main Red Army, were feverishly preparing for a giant invasion by "White" Kuomintang armies, in the first all-out clash of the revolutionary civil war, they were also being bedeviled by several internal problems.

The first and primary one was the **pressure of disastrous orders by top party leader Li Li-san and his central headquarters group**. Profoundly incorrect orders for the guerrilla army to sacrifice the 40,000 "red" fighters that they had patiently built up, in still more quixotic attacks hurling themselves against the enemy strongholds of the big cities. Which might have by itself ended the revolution in complete defeat right there.

The other internal problem was the **unknown amount of penetration by enemy ABC agents**, who possibly had a role in the bloody factional attack on the HQ Dongguo base area. This ABC infiltration had already committed a number of assassinations and sabotage operations, it was thought, leading the army to put key personnel under heavy guard.

Suddenly, in that treacherous attack, **the two internal problems plaguing the Red Army came together, and could be dealt with by one decisive blow, as one and the *same* problem.** It was the cover of "following the leadership" of the Li Li-san line that allowed dissident officers to cajole their men into the unthinkable, to initiate an all-out military attack on their own rural Soviet headquarters base. Caught off guard, troops and party militants were killed in the surprise attack, in which the headquarters guard regiment was overcome, its woman commander, K'ang K'e-ching, and other party cadre taken captive. Just as the "White" capitalist armies were starting to move to invade the Soviet areas. Who would pick such timing, plus such bloody factional methods—except those working for the enemy or thinking like them?

Mao Z and Chu Teh weren't in suburban California, judging or dismissing cases of individuals in a civilian situation. That would be one set of circumstances. They were in a remote war zone, deep in the countryside, preparing feverishly for the largest and possibly most decisive battle any of them had ever gone through, raw soldiers and officers alike. Any disadvantage could cost them everything, while any advantage might be life-saving. That was a different set of circumstances.

The case for arrests was typically decided by deductive, and not as we might prefer inductive, reasoning. In the expanse of undeveloped rural China, in an operational territory stretching many hundreds of miles, there was little possibility of evidence in the "CSI" sense our own tv culture is familiar with. There were no fingerprints on anything or emails found on laptops, no stash of letters from the Kuomintang Anti-Bolshevik Corps hidden away, no unexplained large deposits made by anonymous electronic transfer in Swiss bank accounts. The cases were all circumstantial, except for the confessions.

While the loss of suspect cadres and fighters driven out of the movement or tried and executed was doubtlessly meaningful, to put it in perspective: it compared to only a few days' losses for the guerrilla party and army (which often lost thousands of men and women every week in the savage civil war). To aggressively prosecute the cleanup meant that both internal problems could be put behind them, as the "Chu-Mao army" began fighting against a hundred thousand enemy troops coming to kill them. Just on a pragmatic level, i can see why Mao Z and the other military commanders didn't hesitate a minute at seizing any excuse to set off the explosion. And didn't too much care what anyone thought about it.[35]

While understandably not commemorated by the party in songs and parades, the mutiny appeared to have coincided with a correction or turning point in strategic policy towards the lumpen/proletariat. Whether coincidence or not, a real tightening up began in that regard. With feelings towards the *yumin* becoming heavily salted with tougher criticism and political demands for changes in class attitude.

Particularly after the temporary loss of Xingguo county to the "Whites" Second Encirclement Campaign in 1931. During the Kuomintang's brief occupation, many cracks opened up in village society. Some peasants, poor as well as middle and rich, leaned over to inform on other peasants to the new occupation. Or looted the homes of neighbors who had been forced to temporarily flee. Communists were surprised by the numbers of peasants who agreed to join Kuomintang anti-Communist associations.

In his 1931 report on the party leadership in Xingguo county's Yongfeng district, Mao Z criticized their whole free-wheeling lumpen style as responsible for the shallow roots of the new "red" society in their territory. Operating more as a privileged club than as a people's organization: manipulating soviet government elections, granting special favors to affluent villagers, selecting only women the male leaders thought were physically attractive for party and government work, and so on. Mao had said from the very start, that army and party strata heavily dependent upon the "floating elements" had to be transformed at the first opportunity by more vigorous party recruitment of peasants and workers. In the Soviet government elections of October 1931, the new Xingguo county

party chairman issued a call definitely weighted away from the lumpen:

> *"How are we to reconstruct our local soviet governments? By cleaning out ... rich peasants, riffraff and other reactionaries, and electing good and capable representatives of the workers, agricultural laborers, poor peasants, coolies and honest and brave middle peasants and working women to carry out the work of the soviet."*

The various lumpen/proletariat were, of course, the ones most often being referred to as "riff-raff" in Chinese discourse then.

Our underlined point is the obvious: that even when that **very worst event and much else backward and negative** were said to have happened around the lumpen/proletariat in that county—not just positive things—what were revs taking home as the final result? That area in Southern Jiangxi province could really almost be taken as a negative example, there were so many problems blamed on the infusion of lumpen in the revolution. Even still, millions of people had been politically awakened there in 1927–1934 to take part in positive radical changes in some way.

Even after the Soviet area fell in a heavier way to the "White" rightist armies in late 1934, a Kuomintang investigator named Lu Xian, visiting Xingguo county right after the "Chu-Mao army" left for survival's sake on its historic Long March, could find no suitable people to trust for the anti-revolutionary schools that the new reactionary capitalist state wanted to set up there:

"The young men and women and children of this county have been deeply bandit-ized. They know only of the Soviet and do not know of the Republic of China. They know only of the Western calendar year 1934, and do not know of the twenty-third year of the Republic." He said that rightist teachers would have to be imported from other regions. An admission by the enemy that overall, the lumpen's involvement in the very setting up of the revolution in that specific locality had worked. The difficult transition, from a legal big city party to an illegal mass rural revolution, allying with them, had worked out.

This was the overall picture as well. Staying alive by allying with and recruiting large numbers of "floating people," including specific criminal secret societies, the young revolutionaries were able to build platforms reaching much larger numbers of peasants. Was this difficult, organizationally and politically? Probably both very difficult and very educational. In a countryside brought to awareness by the shock of actual person-by-person land redistribution, as well as a new kind of community life in villages and counties reorganized by the revolution, from 10,000 surviving and often scattered members in late 1927, the party had grown to 300,000 members by early 1934.

Driven largely out of the big cities, the party had in a move of logical but unprecedented boldness set up nine "Soviets"—using the Bolshevik term for workers' councils that eventually came to be a tag for that Bolshevik-run society as a whole. The Chinese used it to designate Red areas they militarily held and were socially reorganizing or governing. By 1934 there were nine such separate Soviets, stretching over a number of provinces in South China, with a population of about nine millions. The "capital," the Central Soviet Area at Ruijin, Jiangxi province, encompassed sixteen counties and had a population of three million.

The unspoken line of building on protracted peasant People's War by relying heavily on the lumpen/proletariat to play a creative role in the mix, had proven itself in the specific situation of the Chinese revolutionary crisis. They were like much of the "O.G." **Recognizing the lumpen's major role in revolutionary change was not tactical opportunism; deeper than that, it was an invaluable strategic understanding in that situation.**

9. soldiers, hooray!

Using theory as a lens to learn from the lumpen/proletariat's role in Mao's China isn't only about their past. We're catching refracted experience, giving us new angles of class understanding maybe not currently on our little screen, reflections into our own world future.

One feature of that early 20th century Chinese society was that it already had its declassed social fragments identified, grouped, and named with the basic term *youmin*—**"floating people" or "vagrants"**—long before Mao Z and revs like him were even born. The Chinese social understanding of these different people, as dissonant class fragments apart from "regular" productive and owning society, didn't come first from Marx. It had come generations before that thinker's recognition about emerging classes in euro-capitalism. So putting identification badges on the lumpen had become traditional to Chinese culture by then, in their own mainstream understanding of society.

We may pick it up only faintly in their old history, but it's when we bring our attention home to Babylon that we can appreciate how significant this was. In Mao's China the lumpen weren't wearing all the different kinds of class disguises and costumes like they so often are here in the Western metropolis, but carried their lumpen photo ID badges in plain sight. In some ways their openly hierarchical old culture's understanding of a century ago was more accurate than our own pseudo-democratic imperialism now. Where the lumpen/proletariat are only partially recognized as separate class strata, and often not at all.

So for Mao Z and his fellow revolutionaries, identifying the Chinese lumpen wasn't too difficult. The lumpen/proletariat were known by them generically as *youmin* ("vagrants") or by the more formal party terminology, *youmin wuchanjieji* ("lumpen-proletarians" or "vagrant-proletarians"). Less often they used the terms *erh liu tze* ("loafers") and *liumang* ("hoodlums"). Chinese revolutionaries back then used *youmin* as well as the term *erh liu tze* almost interchangeably to mean more or less the same thing, referring to the Marxist "partial-class" designation of lumpen/proletariat. Although *erh liu tze* was more specifically used to indicate minor offenders who weren't hardened criminals or against the revolution.

With the term *liumang* reserved as an extreme category of those lumpen/proletariat who were more evil criminals, gang bosses, or anti-revolutionary collaborators. This last grouping being differentiated by not being classified as victims of oppression like most poor lumpen, but as "Enemies of the People" themselves just like the wealthy rural landlords and capitalists. (We won't necessarily run into all these different terms a lot, but it doesn't hurt to know.)

MEN LIVING BY THE RIFLE

Every society has a somewhat different class structure, we know, with its classes having their own particular characteristics or shape. Much Chinese lumpen activity such as sex work for women or soldiering for men wasn't in itself illegal in the Old Society. Karl Marx initially felt that deserters or discharged soldiers in early 1800s Europe were driven by hopelessness to violent criminality in order to survive, thus becoming lumpen/proletarian. **But from the Chinese society's viewpoint, Karl only had a torn-off handful of incomplete analysis.** To Chinese back then, *all* soldiers and professionally armed men were seen as marginalized people engaging in irregular, dangerous and socially undesirable activity. Even police and government soldiers. *All* were considered lumpen or *"floating people"* in their terminology.

We are going into the question of the class identity of armed men making their livelihood from homicidal violence, often "eating" the societies they work in. In part because they were of special importance to this historical example of Mao Z and that revolutionary movement built on guerrilla fighters. But also because lumpen outlaws of many kinds are pushing the frontlines of change now in our own world of here and now. So the earlier examples throw light for our understanding.

About that broad class categorization of various soldiers, cops, violent criminals, and paramilitary thugs in old China, scholar Mark Selden remarked on the outwardly chaotic but in reality unified class reality of this part of the past Chinese landscape:

"In the half-century or more during which Shensi was ravaged by successive bandit and official military forces, defection became, as we have seen, a regular occurrence. The common euphemism 'returned from the northern hills' (*kuei-hui pei-shan*) was used to refer to former bandits presently serving a regular army. As Eric Teichman [British diplomat and intelligence officer—editors] observed in his travels throughout the northwest in 1917:

"'The brigands of northern Shensi are mostly ex-soldiers and Ko Lau Hui men [the secret Elder Brother Society—editors], and are composed of the same material as the provincial troops with whom they exchange*
roles from time to time. It is therefore not possible to use the latter against them. Further, they constitute in a way the reserves of the provincial army which are thus maintained without cost to the provincial government. The Shensi soldier ... serves either as a soldier or a brigand according to his own tastes and the military requirements of the local Government. In either character he is about equally obnoxious to the people.'*

"Two prime causes of defection were defeat in battle and inability of warlord armies to provide necessary supplies for their men. Military units frequently turned to outright banditry, but in several notable instances defecting troops joined partisan forces [i.e. "red" guerrillas—editors] to attack landlord and warlord hegemony. Defections in all directions occurred regularly among the forces of the *Kuominchun** and National Government, minor warlords, *Ko-lao-hui*, and other armed bandits as well as communist-led partisans. The problem of fidelity, of winning and maintaining the permanent loyalty of various military and heterodox

---

* The vaguely socialist-nationalist "Northwest Army" which had Russian Bolshevik advisors and was sympathetic to the modernizing party of Dr. Sun Yat-sen—editors.

elements, provided a continuing challenge to party and partisan leaders."[36]

Back then, back there, every soldier or strong-arm guy in China was held in some distance or even contempt, as someone deep in a stinking business. After all, the Beijing imperial military had been the foreign ethnic Manchu "bannermen" of the Qing dynasty occupation army over native Han Chinese society. The central government's Han soldiers of the "Green army" were like puppet troops serving the foreign occupation. While the local and regional militias were the next thing to lawless gangs doing the dirty work of the village and city wealthy interests. Compared to which being a roadside bandit or stickup guy seemed almost like a normal line of work. Being the violent criminal seemed little different than being the government soldier or cop. Hmm, anything familiar?

In fact, the whole mix of marauding bandit gangs on the roads, the uniformed national army soldiers, anti-landlord armed rebels of various kinds, pickup rifle-bearers in a regional warlord army, village thug militia of the landlords that might have chased those bandits we started with, as well as the traditional secret lumpen quasi-criminal societies that all of the above might have belonged to, were seen as all being part of a single lumpen class splinter. As interchangeable hats in one lower *déclassé* violent social fragment of armed men. With the same persons changing from one to another to another of such roles, as survival circumstances dictated. Especially during the long period of warlordism which became ascendant in decaying China.

About "G.I. Joe" and "Army helicopter pilot Barbie": The Western capitalist propaganda model of the idealized "citizen-soldier," who serves his or her nation for patriotic reasons for a few years in time of need—but then returns to their civilian community and their basic class life as a dairy farmer or college student or whatever—wasn't even remotely real in early 20th century China. And is hardly real here today.

If we were to superimpose something like the lumpen class matrix used by revs in Old China onto today's u.s. empire, just to see, one result would look like this:

Turning up the contrast, in our great Babylon a young euro-settler officer in the u.s. military who took part in or even commanded lethal hits on innocent villagers in any anonymous country "Whocaresistan," might be pictured in the capitalist media as a respectable or even heroic "middle-class" citizen. Like, one Wall Street hedge fund i heard about, loves to quietly recruit its rookie traders from the ranks of Israeli elite commando junior officers. One bloody hand washes the other. The bourgeoisie has always looked for useful lumpen elements to better add a super-aggressive edge to its dirty operations, even adopting some of them up into its own upper class ranks.

While a New Afrikan youth in a hoodie who jacks someone up outside our local subway station for their iPhone and wallet, is consigned down to the lower "criminal classes," as a "gangster," a lumpen. Soon to be in state prison. Thus, two professionally violent men of two different nations here are said to actually be in two widely separate classes; the first one wholesale killing for imperialism is "good," while the other much less violent person only doing it retail is designated as a marginalized "criminal" outside regular society. Remember, imperialist propaganda is just what it is, but it sure isn't our class analysis.

It was more accurate when the Chinese Old Society took those two occupationally violent types of men—the government mercenary and the illegal bandit—as both belonging to one and the same lumpen/proletarian class strata. Maybe in a parallel understanding of today's illegal "street" organizations in a Los Angeles or a Houston referring to their members as "soldiers."

X-rayed up that way, we might see our imperialist military here as divided into two broad class segments: one being the mostly "economic draftees" who, whatever their young illusions, never do become career military, and who after a term or so return to their difficult civilian lives and communities. The other class segment being the highly stratified mass of career mercenary soldiers, airmen, and naval sailors, who find their adult lives as home invaders forcibly occupying and killing while patrolling populations of alien people in distant countries around the world. The "Global village" is really just our very violent home invasion.

That first class segment retain the identity of the classes which they came from and return to. The second class segment of career mercenaries are lumpen of different types, certainly so long as they stay within the professional military world, now outside "normal" class relations of production and distribution. Having a similar relationship to the world's class economy as ethnic militias, the drug mafia commandos and assassins, or the "soldiers" of our urban street organizations. Nominal fancy tags of government service, nicey-nice uniforms and legal status not meaning too much in terms of class identity. In the long run, the lit-up White House Christmas tree is still just more cut down wood, really.

Another related characteristic of the lumpen/proletariat in old China was the existence of a whole network of various class organizations. Like all classes and class strata, the lumpen always have had their own organizations, which were and are often extremely innovative and committed. From the oceanic democracy of many Caribbean pirate ships in the 17th and early 18th centuries, to the hierarchical mass combat leagues of volunteer street fighters during Weimar Republic Germany in the 1920s–30s. Old China's examples were no less so.

Peter Linebaugh notes in his *The London Hanged*, on the steady and **spontaneous moves to self-organization by the 1700s London outlaw lumpen/proletariat**: "This picaresque proletariat was not completely lawless, however much it may have detested the courts and law-learning. When necessary it developed its own kinds of written self-organization. Some of these, like the 'articles' that John Meffs refused to sign when his transport ship was seized by pirates, were democratic and egalitarian, in which 'the supream Power lodged with the Community', in which disputes were settled by jury, officers elected, prizes distributed equally, and 'Every Man has a Vote in Affairs of the Moment'. Others may have owed more to the guildman's oath or club rules, such as the 'honorable Society' to which Jenny Diver belonged. It had four 'articles': (1) admittance was to be by consent; (2) no one was 'to presume to go upon anything by him or herself'; (3) the 'Cant Tongue' was to be spoken; and (4) if any member were incarcerated, 'a sufficient Allowance was to be given him or her in Prison.' ... "

Also for a radical reinterpretation of the "Golden era" of Atlantic piracy, see Gabriel Kuhn's *Life Under the Jolly Roger: Reflections on Golden Age Piracy*. PM Press, 2010. Oakland.

In pre-revolutionary China the largest and most powerful of those were the established secret men's societies, like *Big Sword* and *Elder Brother,* which Mao had recognized and challenged. The secret societies were all not only quasi-criminal but had developed politics, many as sworn political enemies of the Qing imperial dynasty and the oppressive semi-feudal order in the countryside. Perhaps their most obvious, though different, parallel here in the u.s. empire would have been the brilliantly post-1960s neo-Muslim "Nation of Gods and Earths," a rebellious nationalist youth subculture which spread itself on the u.s. East Coast, out of "Mecca" and "Medina."

More modest in old China were the many voluntary guilds and sects of the various "floating" professions, which were self-help and self-regulating groups, often recognizing master-apprenticeship training, for example. Strongest in the big cities and among certain clans, these organizations probably never reached more than a very small minority of the millions of lumpen.

Mainstream u.s. culture is always assuming that lumpen/proletarian organization is only two-dimensional, stereotype "gangs" and "mafias." **But inside the Black Nation, the unchecked creativity of lumpen intersects with their desperate need for communities that don't yet exist.** Malcolm X famously said that *"Prison is the Black man's university."* It's not only because for many it's one of the first opportunities to spend hours just reading and thinking.

In the state prisons, New Afrikans started finding what we might call a special concentrated level of lumpen self-organization. Where the oppressed nation as a colony always strains towards unrecognized communes and warlord micro-states both. Where it morphs outlaw formation in a deeper way. As a landless colony within the larger continent of the u.s. euro-settler empire, Black people have always had to form their own societies and their own versions of self-government wherever they go. Prison is the main extension in our lifetime of the New Afrikan community. Just as New Afrikan communities are the main extensions of the empire's vast prison system.

Real life: There was this young guy inside, who was a defendant in a major "gang-related" big murder trial. And he was talking indiscreet about it to other guys in the yard. A veteran revolutionary in that same kamp saw it happening, and wanted to tug his coat a little, take him under his wing just a little bit. Just teach him about being wise, so it didn't cause him and his street organization compatriots grief at their trial. Just for the common good against the Enemy.

But in order to do this, he first had to send a kite up the street organization to the leader. Asking permission. Cause if guys think that you are poaching on them, maybe trying to recruit out of their group, that could maybe or maybe not cost you your whole remaining life. So table

manners, you make it plain what you're doing and show respect, get permission first.

The street organization's leader, who was in another kamp but still influencing thousands of young men and boys, said okay. They were the main group in that veteran's kamp, and the clandestine reality was late at night their own small security units moved around with the keys to the cellblocks and to every individual cell, past the few guards looking the other way. Carry messages, deliver orders, drop off contraband, stab you in your chest, whatever it was that night. You weren't going to

be organizing any anything unapproved there, not in the old way anyway.

The street organizations had become like a stateless left-over army after the defeat of the Black Revolution, surrounded and moved around by their Enemy. With many lumpen and many dispossessed lower working-class strata moving from one desperate "class" choice to the other or back and forth. Out of necessity they became expansionist subcultures absorbing all the political oxygen out of the air. The same thing by simple extension had taken place in so many hardcore inner city neighborhoods. The cops always said with a big wink how they were "fighting the gangs," but really they were behind it. i mean, the drive-bys were never for them, were they?

This was just in the recent past now, since the big, big New Afrikan street organizations have been split up by the u.s. imperial government. Which tore down mass housing in the Black urban archipelago nation, and used military occupation-style arrests to empty the streets into distant kamps. Breaking down what were complex outlaw organizations of thousands which semi-governed entire neighborhoods, even reaching the level of having their own Black civil courts and reaching out for poverty grants. Down into very small, endlessly dividing sub-gangs of "knucklehead" shooters doing drive-bys on each other over a few blocks. All supervised by the police. Which is moving the street into the next phase of genocide. It's true that politicians and preachers can still talk all that "it's just like the plantation" shit, but simple colonialism wasn't like that. We have to scheme against neo-colonialism's new deals of the cards.

Like that shoeshine guy in my barbershop keeps crooning to himself: *"It's funny how Zulu and Xhosa might go to war / ... Remind me of these Compton Crip gangs that live next door."*

10. naming the lumpen/proletariat

The need by grassroots cadre and "red" village governments for more comprehensive class definitions of irregular types soon became pressing. As a rowdy rebel movement, at first they could just explain the *"floating people"* in any which way they wanted. But all along the rebels had another hat to wear, another implicit role as the core of an emerging new society. Through dialectics we see that everything contains itself and its opposite, and the Communist Party was trying to remake the population to tear down the state, while themselves becoming a state on a higher level.

Throughout the 1930s and early 1940s, in the changing and growing "inkblot" of Soviet-ruled areas, there was a continual list-keeping, a step by step adding to of Mao Z's original naming of the lumpen/proletariat. Mao's original 1926 naming of five main lumpen strata of *soldier, bandit, robber, beggar and prostitute* only pointed to familiar archetypes known to everyone. The deal coming down was always

more complex than that, as Mao Z soon would make clear even to the politically confused.

Quickly enough, more definite identifying and naming of the "rascal" lumpen was needed by the revolutionaries, for everyday practical reasons. So cadre could check a list and tell who was lumpen and not a worker or peasant. Particularly since in the large rural Soviet areas that the party and Red Army shared governing of, everything from receiving redistributed farming land to staying out of labor camps to being able to vote for local government officials and other political privileges—such as belonging to the all-important village Peasant Association—was partially determined by one's precise class designation. Their class designation was as important to them as a driver's license or a passport would be to us. Class was dead practical business, as it always is.

As early as 1930, after considerable discussion, the party's 4th Red Army and the

Minxi Soviet base area government jointly named some 30 occupations of lumpen/proletarians, the top eight of which in terms of numbers in the Soviet area were: bandits, thieves, women sex workers, soldier "riff-raff," actors, servants, gamblers, and beggars. Other expected occupations were also on the list, of course, such as local policemen, opium den bosses, runners (my first job at age ten, i nostalgically recall) and human traffickers. But there were groups on that list that might surprise us, such as freelance scholars (or literati), as well as Buddhist and Daoist monks. Like Marx's wonderful laundry list of 19th century "scum," many occupational roles from that 1930 Chinese Communist list might need cultural translation for us today.[37]

It's amusing that unlike the rest of us revs, who often are as vague or ignorant as it suits us in defining anything, particularly when it comes to the forbidding realm of theory, those older Chinese revolutionaries had the headache of defining the lumpen/proletariat in a crisp edged "legal" or official way. Which is only what you get for starting a state. In 1933, Mao's staff had issued an official definition of the *youmin*, declaring that:

> *"Workers, peasants, and other people who shortly before the uprising lost their occupations and land as a result of the oppression and exploitation by the landlord and capitalist class, and who have resorted to improper methods as their principal methods of livelihood for three consecutive years, are called idler-proletarians (customarily they are called vagabonds)."*[38]

In October 1933, Mao Z as chairman of the Central Soviet Government, issued further political guidance better defining the "gray areas" of human conduct we all know about. He said that lumpen/proletarians were only those who engaged in activities such as "theft, robbery, deception, begging, gambling, prostitution" as their *"main source of income."* Excluded from the outsider category were *"poor people"* with only *"bad habits,"* who were into these improper activities on the side.

Thus, it was better legally under that early tentative "red" law to be an amateur rather than a pro, better to smoke opium than to sell it, better to be a john or a slut rather than a sex worker. No surprise to us here in postmodern capitalism. To put this in a sharper context, though: In those years in the Soviet liberated zone, usually only specific categories of "Enemies of the People" such as Kuomintang soldiers and violent criminal gang leaders went into hard state custody, with most thieves and gamblers and prostitutes and beggars given lectures and pushed to settle down into productive livelihoods such as farming or handicraft work—or joining the revolution.[39]

By 1941, Peng Zhen, who was the party official most tasked to supervise the lumpen problem, had issued a new class list of who was officially to be identified as lumpen/proletarian. It was an effort to be more complete, and emphasized pointing out that many of those who worked for the capitalist state were themselves lumpen/proletarian parasites. Naming many more kinds of common capitalist state flunkies as well as the usual low-level hustlers: "... village policemen, township clerks, retired policemen, policemen, retired county government clerks (popularly called dog's legs), jailers, jail guards, hoodlums, gamblers, thieves, prostitutes, promiscuous women, drug runners, beggars, deserters, traffickers in human beings, funeral musicians, charlatans, witches, fortune tellers, travelling monks, professional hit men, etc."[40]

Most significant, as part of the People, the "floating element" were still defined by Mao not as "Enemies of the People," but still only as unfortunates forced for survival into "improper" livelihoods until the revolution could liberate them. This was one foundation of their mass work. This was reaffirming a distinctly warmer view of the lumpen/proletariat, of course, than what Marx once had called "that passively rotting mass."

11. beggars / work the streets

Beggars were another of Mao's five main categories of lumpen/proletarians. Although many Americans have a stereotyped picture in their minds of beggars as the poorest and dirtiest and most helpless of the poor, old China shows a reality much more complex and multi-layered. Which should alert us in general about making assumptions, in place of actual social investigation and analysis.

Even some beggars could have quite elaborate and impressive appearing organization, for instance. This is an old China lumpen fragment as meaningful, in its own way, as soldiers and bandits were in what it can teach us. The beggars were large lumpen fragments spread throughout China, and in a surprisingly wide diversity. In 1949, when the Communists captured Beijing and set it up as the capital of their People's Republic of China, they even found beggars' guilds with their own headquarters, claiming colorful origin stories many centuries old. The exact same origin stories, incidentally, were being told by beggars outside luxury hotels in contemporary Beijing in 2016.

The Qiongjiamen guild, for example, claimed to have been given an imperial mandate to beg by the founder of the Ming dynasty in the 14th century. Emperor-to-be Zhu Yuangzang was allegedly saved from starvation during hard times by the help of several beggars. After ascending the throne, the grateful Zhu gave them a carved wooden shaft as a symbol to guards and officials that they were not to be stopped or impeded in their begging. True stories or not, it was a classy act unlike the desperately tattered, down and out image we have of begging here today.

In 1949, the new Communist rulers found the Qiongjiamen in Beijing with a guildhall, where an old headman named Lu Er ruled with his deputy heads and lieutenants over a sworn "brotherhood" who were each aided by their guild in return for regular dues. These were some of the many higher category of "professional" beggars—as they were known then—as opposed to the lower category of displaced or impoverished refugees who made up the other face of begging.

Not that a guild or group guaranteed anything. The former Qiongjiamen guild beggar Zhang Hanwen testified after the revolution, that even talking about his old life was "painful": "During the day I went out to beg for food ... I never knew when I'd have food to eat ... I often went hungry. At night, where could I rest? I had no home. When I had it best, I'd huddle in doorways, or flatten myself along eaves. ...

in the winter I could hardly bear it. Once, when I was frozen solid, I tore down a wall advertisement and wrapped it around myself."[41]

The realm of "professional" beggars included some highly skilled persons—such as actors, singers, acrobats, and even Buddhist monks. We should explain: In that time and place, there were few theaters or auditoriums—usually none in the typical peasant village—where entertainers could perform for a ticket-buying audience. So from singers to musicians

to actors they largely busked right in the streets—the only "theater" there was for most—hustling for coins from the crowd.

In general, everyone who survived by soliciting money on the street was considered a beggar of one kind or another. (As opposed to sex workers and bone setters and so on, who might be on the street but were selling explicit services). Even the Buddhist monks (or hustlers pretending to be them), who as those renouncing the material world were supposed to survive by begging with an outstretched rice bowl each day. Troupes performed simple acrobatics in the street or put on short comedies for enough coins to eat that day. These free street performers were popular in a society without internet, television, movies, or enough literacy to sustain novels and comic books, and made a core of the "professional" beggars as opposed to the ever-changing destitute refugees desperately seeking to hold off death from starvation another day.

Borrowing from the beggars' tradition of simple street plays, the "reds" would later develop amateur troupes of factory workers in the Northern Soviet areas to put on comedies satirizing the Axis powers or China's many supernatural con-artists such as magical "healers." Educating people about basic world politics, medicine and sanitation and so on.

These leftist "agitation-propaganda" plays following the example of some successful performing beggars, were also always popular free entertainment.

The "professional" beggars also were known for using their group power for extortion. In rural villages, a band of "beggar-bullies" would arrive and physically take over part of the main street or public space. Harassing passing people for alms, following women and demanding food, making sales more difficult for small merchants—the "beggar-bullies" would cause so much trouble that they would eventually get paid off by the community to move on to another town. Mao Z, always single-minded, counted it as a good confidence-building victory for the new Peasant Associations when they could band together and physically drive the "beggar-bullies" off.

Even the actors and acrobats would try to extort daily contributions from storeowners in return for going away, or for not staging window-breaking "fights" by their shops, driving away customers. While Buddhist monks and Daoist priests, for their part, were also considered by the revolution to not simply be beggars, but practicing forms of what Mao Z termed "the superstitious professions." By which they meant religious professionals, spirit mediums, magicians, faith healers, diviners and others similarly fleecing ignorant people.[42]

So begging was broad strata of lumpen, with many different kinds of people in similar but varying circumstances—having in common a lack of "regular" occupation and a need to ask for coin on the streets. Including the elderly, disabled, orphaned children, refugees, and those "professional beggars" for whom this was a hereditary profession. In particular, lower begging didn't demand any particular physical strength or size. So destitute and homeless Chinese women and girls could be beggars, too, not only males.

That pattern is interesting, with the most skilled or trained minority of the "professional beggars" in old China being neither always penniless nor necessarily "down and out," but making within begging various informal or illicit crafts in their own right. Recognizing that opens a door for us to walk into a larger room—leaving behind Western stereotypes and middle-class assumptions.

It wasn't only within street begging that we saw this wide variation in fortunes and status. Even some relatively prestigious and highly skilled occupations such as mercenary generals, monastery heads, chess masters, and *wushu* martial arts experts, were formally considered

youmin, or in the "floating world," despite their status. By "mercenaries," incidentally, the "reds" usually meant something different than we might: a skilled fragment of trained officers or experienced commanders, as opposed to the much more common "army riff-raff" of penniless and often homeless "soldier" vagrant rifle-bearers.

To them it was no contradiction, to have a lumpen even as a normal member of the imperial court. As opposed to our common stereotype of the lumpen as only the worst criminals or only completely marginalized outcasts at the very bottom of society, being lumpen isn't strictly speaking determined by affluence versus poverty, or by social status. Although in that giant but impoverished Chinese neo-colony then, the overwhelming number of lumpen were indeed very poor and survived precariously. All this was in the complex class understanding of the lumpen, which other revs as well as our guy Mao Z had to carry with them under their worn coats.

WOMEN BEGGARS, TOO

One traditional beggars' guild was known for being open to women. That was the *Lijiamen* guild, which proudly traced its lineage back to that legendary 10th-century empress of the Song dynasty, who was forced to beg in the streets to survive when she was temporarily ousted by a coup of her enemies, according to story. Yet, that was a rare exception. Almost all beggars' guilds and sects banned women, and the occupation seems by numbers to have been heavily male—although there were still many women beggars, just as there were women thieves and women con-artists and so on.

A 1949 survey by the CCP of beggars in the relatively sheltered circumstances of the capital Beijing, found 8,000 beggars and petty thieves (the Communists administratively considered them as one category since they were hard to tell apart), and 80% of them were men. Women beggars there, the survey found, were usually not "professional" and were alone, unaffiliated to any guild, sect or group. This apparent major gender-class imbalance in the lumpen strata becomes a larger and larger subject of its own, something we will come back to when we have more space to let it unfold.[43]

12. practice kicks theory forward / as theory guides practice

Communist practice and theory about the lumpen were recast by Mao Z in 1926, but it was never going to stay fixed that way. Between then and the revolutionary war's end in 1949, of course the practice of millions of combatants over a generation had to bring new inventions, new problems, new corrections to the firing line. And the social reality on the ground all around them was itself not the same, being remade by the struggle itself.

One thing sticks out so much that it almost pokes you in the eye. During the whole of the active revolutionary period, the young revolutionaries almost had something like a divided consciousness about the lumpen. A heavy ambivalence. One day thinking them very good, the next day thinking them very bad. Wanting them, while distrusting them. Makes you dizzy just trying to reconcile it all.

In the arc of years between 1926 and 1949 was a distance of development, of evo-lution politically in the roles of lumpen/proletariat within the Revolution. Both entities—the lumpen and the party cad-res—ended up in positions both the same and quite different from where they once started.

Like, there was the famous encouraging but very ambivalent Mao Z quote summing up the lumpen, which was adopted by Huey and the Panthers and near the whole rebellious left in the 1960s—*"Brave fighters but apt to be destructive, they can become a revolutionary force if given proper guidance."* **Mao never actually wrote that back then, it turns out**. Which we maybe should have known, but most of us did not.

Remember, in 1926 when he penned that ground-breaking *Analysis of the Classes in Chinese Society*, Mao Z was pushing the liberating idea that counter to the contempt with which they were viewed by his society, the "dirty" lumpen were mostly victims of capitalist exploitation and oppression just like poor peasants and workers. And desperately angry people who would be good for the revolution to recruit. This was very positive, very advanced social thinking for that time in China.

So the accepted scholarly translation of what Mao really wrote in the sum-up line in that 1926 writing goes: *"These people are capable of fighting very bravely, and if a method can be found for leading them, they can become a revolutionary force."* See, straightforward, recognizing complexities of the situation, and not negative at all about them.

Mao's crucial line of 1926, however, had never actually replaced other previous theory on the lumpen, but was only his emphasized face early in the struggle in the countryside. Traditional Chinese views of the "dirty" vagrant *"floating element,"* as well as the imported Marxist negative analysis of the lumpen as *"the dangerous class,"* were both still alive as fused layers within the movement's larger theoretical mindset. Before they were all melted down and recast once more into their final form.

In 1951, Mao Z and the party in reprinting his old essays and papers quietly rewrote that final sum-up line in a more negative form: adding the *"apt to be destructive"* warning on the lumpen; as well as the only conditional acceptance of the *"if given proper guidance"* phrase. Like a warning label on a pack of alluring cigarettes. What had come down between 1926 and 1951 to settle the party's theoretical line to the more negative or traditional side?

During all this time, there was an incongruous pairing of Mao's basic line on the lumpen—that they were as a whole innocent victims of oppression forced into "improper" survival occupations—with increasing orders to distrust those lumpen who actually got close to the struggle. Seems like a contradiction, on the face of it.

So, for example, the June 1930, "The Problem of Vagabonds" resolution from the Red Fourth Army Front Committee and the Western Fujian Special Committee meeting, completely teed off on the lumpen/proletariat: "In various localities, especially in the Red Army, the problem of vagabonds has become a very grave issue as the struggle develops. Many comrades have expressed incorrect points of view regarding this problem, saying such things as 'The *youmin* know how to fight, we should not exclude them' ... 'As long as officers do a good job of leading, the organizational makeup of the troops is not important'; 'Don't attack the vagabonds right now, it won't be too late to attack them when there are general uprisings'; and so on."

They underlined characteristic "muddled class consciousness" about and by the lumpen fighters, such as "opposition to the masses," "adventurism (wanton burning, killing and looting)," as well as "roving rebelism (no concept of political power)." Then, concluding with the final smackdown:

> "*The Red Army and Red Guards are the important tools of the revolutionary masses in seizing state power and protecting it. The components of these important tools must all be workers, peasants and revolutionaries; no vagabonds can be allowed to penetrate into these organizations.*"

Yeah, well, the resolution does go through some of the military-political errors that other Mao Z writings of that early startup period hammered down on. But the paranoid conclusion, ordering that *"no vagabonds can be allowed"* in the revolutionary army that was in practice then heavily composed of and dependent upon lumpen, bore no relationship to objective reality. Totally meaningless left blah blah blah word slinging (not that i haven't done it myself—all too common when we don't have real answers to give out). We can tell how much contempt about the "dirty" lumpen there still was in the 1930 Chinese party, and how much yearning there was for that old-style orthodox Communist or old-style Imperial Chinese culture stigmatizing them and excluding them.[44]

In the same years that Mao Z was pushing the recruitment of lumpen fighters into the revolution—and pointing out how they constituted a majority of the Red Army—the party was also warning against them as a special danger. Now, all classes and peoples growing up within capitalism have flaws and bring their characteristic problems in a revolutionary context. Yes, even intellectuals, workers and peasants. This is definitely true in the real world if not in the imaginary intellectual world. Everyone is part of the problem as well as part of the solution. Only the lumpen, however, are usually painted by leftists in such a darkly negative overcast.

LUMPEN ACTIVE IN
THE GUERRILLA WAR

If many lumpen fighters and organizers were committing fundamental political errors, it was also true that many lumpen were pulling their weight and doing their job. Great changes happened for many lumpen/proletarians during this time of open revolutionary war. An important element in the class politics that were going on was the increasing self-awareness and empowerment of some lumpen themselves. Which Mao Z and other Red Army revolutionary fighters were recognizing and encouraging.

Especially with all the countless local guerrilla units, elements of the rural lumpen/proletariat continued playing an important on the ground but often unsung role in the Anti-Japanese War from 1935 to 1945. The journalist Agnes Smedley—who as always found a way to be present—was traveling behind enemy lines visiting resistance forces, during this trip as a medical aid worker. In late December 1939, she was in Central China with the Nationalist 122nd division of the Szechuen army, as the town of Juikuotan had been retaken from the Japanese army in what was said to be the first Chinese counter-offensive of the war. She tells of meeting fighters from one of the lumpen secret societies:

"Juikuotan had been taken. Forty members of the secret peasant 'Big Sword' society, the *Hwang Shih Hwei*, had led the Chinese troops along the narrow paths leading to the town. They carried long spears and huge native-made iron shears with which they cut the enemy's barbed wire. Once while they were cutting the wires a Japanese officer came to the door of a near-by house; one of the peasants rushed the building and other soldiers hurled hand-grenades into it. The Japanese soldiers fled into an underground tunnel and pulled close a steel door which could only be opened from below. The tunnel had an outlet farther along the hill, and the Chinese caught the Japanese pouring out of it, throwing off their overcoats as they fled ...

"Wounded members of the peasant secret society lay on stretchers with their long spears at their sides and the magic yellow sash of their society soaked with blood.

"'Someone said that if you wore this sash you could not be wounded and would have no fear,' I said to them. 'Do you believe that?'

"'If we had fear, we would not be fighting!' one answered; and I was silenced."[44]

Notice the passing detail that Smedley was following CCP propaganda practice in describing the lumpen outlaw society there as a "peasant" association. Mao himself believed along those lines, that many men in the traditional lumpen/proletariat were proving themselves in the fighting, and should be brought in from the cold class-wise and made more respectable.

Knowing that part of the Elder Brother Society in particular, took anti-colonial and anti-feudal politics seriously, our guy Mao Z had already personally long taken a public stand of more than just friendship towards them. It didn't hurt that in the critical areas of the large Yangzte river valley, they were also said to be the strongest of the lumpen men's outlaw organizations. They definitely were more complex than the largely negative stereotypes of lumpen/proletariat many just assume.

So Mao Z, in his role as Chairman of the Central Government of the Chinese People's Soviet Republic, even issued a historic public appeal from Yenan on July 15, 1936, to the Elder Brother Society, for a formal alliance with the lumpen/proletariat against the Japanese imperialist invaders. In this public call, he said that the Elder Brother Society was not only respected as patriotic kin by the party, but had been legalized in the Soviet area. He was trying to merge them in, as his younger comrade Gu Bo had done earlier with the lumpen Three Dots Society in his native Xingguo County:

"In the past you supported the restoration of the Han and the elimination of the Manchus; today, we support resistance to Japan and the salvation of the country. You support striking at the rich and helping the poor ... Our views and our positions are therefore quite close ... We hope and request that the lodge masters and grand masters of the various lodges in all parts of the country, and our brothers among the brave fellows on every hand, will send representatives or come themselves to discuss with us plans for saving the country."

As journalist Edgar Snow noted in his 1936 account of visiting Mao in Yenan, already a special reception bureau had been set up, to greet and give aid specifically to Elder Brother Society members coming to the Soviet area. Fleeing the harsh repression in the "White" Kuomintang and Japanese-occupied zones. Elder Brother Society members were thus registered and reunited with earlier secret society brethren already working with the "reds." Of course, they were no longer secret, no longer in practice outlaws, but had been socially reborn into the legitimate working mainstream of a new Chinese society.[45]

DISTRUSTING LUMPEN EVEN MORE

After all that, it may seem like a big contradiction, but at that same time Communist distrust of the lumpen was receiving if anything stronger emphasis. In 1939, Mao Z himself warned party cadres that it was the nature of the lumpen to *"waver"* and *"vacillate"* between the revolution and the counter-revolution. At the same time, however, he reaffirmed that at the root most lumpen/proletarians still remained innocent victims of oppression who needed the revolution's help in liberating and perhaps reforming themselves:

> *"China's colonial and semi-colonial status created a vast number of unemployed people in both the countryside and the cities. Having no legitimate way to make a living, they were forced, against their will, to seek a living through illegitimate professions. This is the origin of bandits, hooligans, beggars, prostitutes, and the many who are in the superstitious professions."*

With a different emphasis, though, Mao Z in 1939 was also less positive about the lumpen as a mostly "revolutionary force." He warned: *"While one portion is easily brought over by the reactionary forces, the other portion has the possibility of participating in the revolution."* So in this evaluation more than a decade after his original

class analysis, lumpen doing evil work for the oppressors now was a certainty; while other lumpen joining the liberation struggle was only a "possibility." The lumpen were getting a C-minus grade here.

This tough take on the "floating people" became more evident when another voice stepped to the front in Communist policy towards the lumpen/proletariat. Peng Zhen was an emerging top administrator in the Northern border areas under Soviet government. Later at War's end, in 1949 he was to become the Red mayor of Beijing, as the new Communist government was launching much-publicized campaigns to "clean up" the big cities by reforming and sending away all the lumpen street people. He was to become the leader of party programs dealing with the "lumpen stratum."

In 1941, Peng Zhen's instructions on reforming the lumpen in the Northern region summed them up harshly as a *"two-faced, vacillating stratum"* who *"obey whoever feeds them."* Though they tended to be drawn to the revolutionary struggle, he said, because "their extremely insecure social status and their half-starved existence means that they are very rarely attached to the current situation ..." In terms of the revolution, however, Peng Zhen pointed out how they caused *"a great deal of damage"* but not in return any *"sufficient amount of construction."*

Everything only pointed towards some dramatic resolution happening, and maybe a big political car wreck at that.

POLITICAL RESULTS
MAYBE NOT WHAT WAS EXPECTED

We have to put this seriously into context. Mao Z wasn't necessarily judging things our way. His whole mindset politically was, in practice, in a different orbit from our more affluent and pacified Babylon. Specifically, the results from organizing poor and oppressed lumpen/proletarians weren't necessarily what Mao had hoped for in 1926.

When Mao Z and the crew back then & there talked about organizing workers, they expected to be seeing some armed workers' militia pretty damn quick. i mean, light-footed factory or mine workers forming military units and leaving home to join the revolutionary war in the countryside, stuff like that. His whole seismographic scale of expectations was different, more tangibly about revolutionary commitment than we've been used to. He and his comrades were in a do-or-die situation strategically. No right or wrong here, just very different circumstances.

Out in "red" villages where rural people had militant peasant takeovers and had *stood up* by seizing land for redistribution, it wasn't that unusual for literally *all* the men of military age in a peasant village to leave at the same time and join the fighting. Whether as guerrillas or main force Red army, whose recruitment was always in principle voluntary. They weren't recruiting individuals so much as recruiting whole chunks of exploited classes at a time. But the sweeping class expectations Mao Z might have been used to, certainly weren't met by the lumpen.

No, that wasn't how it worked with the highly individualistic, "non-class" strata of the fragmentary lumpen/proletariat. To put all the words to it. There things were a lot more "complicated," as the Chinese revolutionaries so politely and correctly used to put it.

What everyone is often too busy to hear, was that for the lumpen/proletariat it wasn't the same time as on the clocks of the working class and peasantry and intellectuals. For those other more "regular" classes, if conditions weren't favorable or a good choice didn't materialize, they could always just lay low and do daily life as normal. Patiently organizing or preparing for a better breakthrough. But so often the lumpen didn't have that choice. Their alarm clock was always ringing. If a good choice didn't open up, they often had only bad choices they had to jump into. If

239

armed revolution looked too shaky a step, then working as a criminal or serving the regime were survival options. Lumpen had no farm or factory job or schoolroom to fall back on.

Which is why Mao Z warned his comrades that they shouldn't just shoulder the lumpen aside, or back them into a corner: *"As for the lumpenproletariat ... we should never compel them to go over to the side of the enemy and become a force in the service of the counterrevolutionaries."*[46]

Remember that Mao Z's early summary line of 1926—*"[t]hese people are capable of fighting very bravely, and if a method can be found for leading them, they can become a revolutionary force"*—had never exactly replaced previous theory on the lumpen, but only supplemented it. Both the traditional Chinese class prejudice about the *"floating element"* as "dirty" and inferior, as well as the left views of the lumpen as *"the dangerous class"* of untrustworthy elements, were running in the mix of that revolution's class mindset. Just as they might be in our left today. And in the 1930s, those years of setting up Soviet rural counter-societies, all these mindsets came increasingly into conflict.

While the lumpen/proletariat, if anything, went in the opposite direction from all uniting *en masse* with the revolution. As if in some ideal, hoped-for scenario. To the contrary, the 1935 Japanese invasion may have gradually pulled the country together on a patriotic basis as a whole, but the **increasing wartime pressures and increasing survival choices only worked to increase lumpen disunity and fragmentation.**

We can more easily grasp what this meant if we continue following the feminist journalist Agnes Smedley in her dangerous reporting with the "reds" during the Anti-Japanese War. She encountered the lumpen/proletariat on more than one occasion and in more than one way. In her 1939 notebook, for instance, she relates being with the "Fourth Detachment" guerrilla soldiers in central Anhwei Province near the Yangtze River:

> "The guerrilla detachment had recently captured a number of Chinese who had become Japanese spies. One was being held in headquarters. In the hope of saving his life, this fellow had admitted that as a result of an investigation he had made of the general headquarters of the Army to the south of the river, the whole valley in which the headquarters had been located had been bombed and over a hundred people killed or wounded. I had been in the very midst of that bombing

and, lying in a shallow ditch, had watched with horror as the planes, flying low, tried to hit the hospital. The planes had even gone after a herd of draft buffalos, machine-gunning and killing sixteen of them.

"The prisoner talked freely of a spy ring, of which he was a member. These rings were organized in groups, each headed by a 'big man', a Chinese landlord or merchant. The particular group to which the prisoner belonged had its center in Tunling, a town on the south shore near the Japanese garrison at Sunan. Ordinary spies were paid fifteen dollars a month, but sometimes the 'big men' paid poor men a dollar for each piece of military news they brought in ...

"In the evenings, Commander Yang Yun-ee and members of his staff sat in the courtyard of the peasant home where I was staying. They talked on the economic origin of banditry and treason, and of the great landlords of central Anhwei, some of whom owned thousands of acres of land. The landlords had fled far to the rear or to the port cities under foreign protection, but had left agents behind to collect the same rents and the same usurious rates on loans as before the war. The puppet Governor of the province, appointed by the Japanese, was Ni Tao-liang, a big landlord who still made use of his feudal relations with his friends and tenants to organize puppet troops. There were now about five thousand of these in the province, commanded by relatives of the puppet leaders."[47]

So a dozen years after the revolutionary civil war had begun, what was standard for lumpen men was *not* for them all to join the revolution as a tide, but to scatter in various directions as the disorder deepened and their choices as well as the dangers grew. Many lumpen/proletarians signed up to serve different conflicting groups among the combatants, although certainly most of the declassed weren't recruited into supporting any side.

While many formerly *youmin* soldiers and revolutionary cadre were still in the forefront of the Red Army, and new such men and women joined every day, their guerrilla units were now majority peasant. Still, at the same time large numbers of other lumpen worked as soldiers-for-hire or thugs for one force or another on the capitalist side. Many lumpen still filled Generalissimo Chiang Kai-shek's "White" armies and police and criminal official-dom. There were also no less lumpen willing to be employed by the remnants of the old warlord or local landlord gangs, as the number of lumpen continued to swell in the deepening chaos.

A large number of the lumpen—beggars and petty thieves and small drug dealers and sex workers and superstitious hustlers and so on—weren't recruited to either side. Indeed, weren't much wanted by any side in the revolutionary war. Were preoccupied with their little survival hustles, just trying to stay out of harm's way and survive, which in fact many didn't every year.

Even working for the Japanese imperialist invasion was acceptable to many lumpen "riff-raff," being informers or enforcers in occupied villages. Other lumpen men worked secretly, as we've heard, in "red" areas as spies for their customary "big men" landlords and merchants in return for cash.

The Japanese themselves also subsidized lumpen bandit gangs to prey on the countryside as they usually might anyway, only in a more vicious way. Robbing and killing civilians trying to move around, thus bottling up travel and trade between towns except through the official Japanese armed convoys. A more subtle and effective tactic than just announcing the empty ban on individual contact with the guerrillas or even just banning independent civilian travel.

Smedley reported on this real difference of degree between the various lumpen of the puppet occupation soldiers and the outright bandits: "But the Japanese seldom trusted the conscripted puppet soldiers to fight the Chinese guerrillas, using them instead as garrison troops in occupied towns. The puppets were bad fighters and the guerrillas had already captured and disarmed hundreds of them. Bandit gangs had been paid by the Japanese to disturb the countryside, and few people dared travel without the protection of troops. The puppet troops could be re-educated and taken into the guerrilla detachment, but the bandits seldom or never."[48]

These bandits were not the same persons that they had been in the early stages of the struggle. They were more desperate and numerous and heavily armed than before, since the mass battlefield desertions from the losing Kuomintang "White" army units attacked by the Japanese invaders had littered the rural landscape with abandoned rifles and abandoned men. Agnes Smedley reported that to civilians the "bandits ... became a menace almost as fearful as the Japanese." While the bandits by then were mostly diehard enemies to the revolution, the ordinary lumpen puppet soldiers were often willing to surrender or even switch sides if the Red Army was conveniently on the scene. Or not, was okay with them, too.[49]

These new waves of bandits were often implicitly allied to the Japanese invasion, with revolutionary guerillas as their own main targets and the civilian population as their sole source of prey for supplies and pleasure. In the Shanxi village of Changchuang, for example, the local Nationalist provincial army detachment was commanded by the rich landlord's son, Fan Tung-hsi. Far outnumbered by the occupying Japanese Army forces after the Kuomintang provincial governor reached a deal with the Japanese imperialists, Fan Tung-hsi made his own deal whereby the remnants of his unit became bandits, avoiding trouble with the invaders and basing themselves on a hilly area outside town.

Fan Tung-hsi's rag-tag rifle-bearers would attack retreating guerrillas when they were pursued by the Japanese. His fellow gentry brother-in-law and close friend Shih Jen-pao was an officer for the Japanese with the puppet Chinese militia. Together they looted and terrorized the village. During the 1942 famine, one night they sent a force of over a hundred of their lumpen soldier-bandits to turn the village upside down searching for food. They found hidden family stores which the Japanese troops hadn't discovered, and left with many carts full of corn and millet. Almost one-third of the village starved to death afterwards.[50]

While the Japanese invasion continually recruited Chinese lumpen thugs and soldiers to serve them, one informer or bandit gang or landlord militia at a time, this was only a start at accounting for their puppet Chinese support. Most came as direct switching of sides, lumpen Kuomintang Nationalist Army units joining the Japanese military, until WWII was safely over. In part as their way of continuing capitalism's primary war against the Red Army, only openly allied with the Japanese occupation itself. As one American report from China emphasized:

"In the later years of the Anti-Japanese War, years that were characterized by a stalemate on the regular battlefronts, the surrender to the Japanese of whole units intact with their arms was arranged over and over again by high-ranking Nationalist officers. The number of Kuomintang commanders above the rank of major general who put their troops under Japanese command was 12 in 1941, 15 in 1942, and 42 in the peak year, 1943. By early 1944 more than 60 percent of the puppet armies, then numbering about 425,000, was composed of former Kuomintang elements.' In the Taihang Mountains General P'ang Ping-Hsun, Commander of the 24th Group Army, went over with all his troops in May 1943, and was appointed Commander-in-Chief of the Shansi-Hopei, Honan-Shantung Communist Extermination Army [of the Japanese occupation] ..."[51]

That entire Chinese mercenary regiments and divisions of lumpen soldiers by the many tens of thousands were corruptly going over to serve the Japanese invasion, certainly didn't lead Mao Z and the revolutionary movement to think any better of the lumpen/proletariat as drinking buddies. So the lumpen were well represented on all sides, good and evil, of every conflict in China at the same time. A gritty but morally easy going, non-denominational reality. As successful as the Red Army's "flipping" of enemy lumpen soldiers into being its own recruits had been, now the

Japanese imperialists were rivaling the Communists as recruiters. The very optimistic class analysis of the lumpen in 1926 probably wasn't at the top of Mao Z's theoretical mind at that moment.

CHANGING THE RULES OF THE GAME

Talking about theory, those developments we've been discussing that had been going on with the party's relationship to the lumpen in a low-key way, finally started emerging on the surface. **To sum it up, Mao Z appeared to want to change the whole way the lumpen were handled by the party.** Piecemeal practical changes driven by the needs of the struggle, from what we can figure. This is only a guesstimate to label what wasn't always explained publicly, but connecting all the visible dots this is what seems likely.

Remember that Mao Z's fresh 1926 theoretical take on the various actors of the lumpen/proletariat wasn't like big characters painted on a clean slate. It was never the only message, but always mixed with other characters on the splatter of the crowded walls. No matter how persuasive Mao was, other viewpoints were continually shouting in everyone's minds, too. The two other views about the lumpen that held considerable influence not only in the public mind but also very much inside the party—that they were "dirty" in the eyes of traditional Chinese culture, and that they were "dangerous" and politically untrustworthy in Marxist culture—hadn't been wiped clean but instead only reinforced each other.

In the traditional Old Society culture, one main part of that superstructure was the ruling class Confucian-Buddhist indoctrination that one's station in life was only predestined. That if you were poor and wretched or living "improperly," it could only be because in a previous incarnation you had been evil and did many wrong things. Thus your karma from past lives has only caught up with you and cannot be avoided. So the suffering of the most wretched was only "just," in fact what they "deserved." Conversely, the idle luxuriating of the wealthy landlords and merchants and high-born was also only what they had "earned" in an earlier life by their supposed good deeds, and also supposedly couldn't be changed. A very convenient ideology for the exploiters and rulers, the angry rebels thought. One reason Mao Z and his comrades had little tolerance for the many superstitious hustlers and spiritual believers Old China teemed with.

One result of the negative pressure in this highly skewed situation, was

that our guy Mao Z started rearranging actual political practice on who was lumpen/proletarian or not. Thereby inescapably also changing the party's theoretical structure. All the pieces were moving around the board. Follow the blinking arrow and you'll see what we mean:

So, just for starters, Mao Z had argued way back in the 1930s against the lumpen "class" category of "soldiers" or "army riff-raff" applying to the Red Army at all. Think that in his intensely practical awareness, he saw it was hard enough proletarianizing his men and women and politically raising them up to be selfless warriors for a just society—when every day they were called by a name identifying them as unrespectable and untrustworthy outcasts, and when they themselves had long been encouraged to just accept that and live that "dirty" careless way.

Juggling dirty and clean dishes at the same time, Mao Z was the waiter clearing away unhealthy food and insisting that dinner was only some new healthier sustenance not french fries. As he was ripping cadre and troops a new one in political criticisms, calling them out in detail on their no good lumpen politics which he demanded they change—he was also being their defender, insisting that they not be named part of any loser lumpen category at all. i mean, it was maybe "dialectical" more than straight "logical," since the poor guys were called both lumpen and not lumpen at the same time. But logic be damned, some nifty plays of the hand are better than logic.

Mao Z was saying that the lumpen/proletarian "non-class" category of "soldiers" (*ping*), was only correct for labeling the bad guys—"White" reactionary armies and militias and landlord thugs and cops. While, on the other hand, he insisted that *his* men and women, the revolutionary good guys, the People's Liberation Army troops and Red Guards militia themselves, weren't any lumpen "soldiers" at all. Rather, Mao argued, they were better identified as "fighters" (*chan-shih*) for the People. Who by their political choice for the Red Army were becoming proletarianized. In fact, men and women in the party and Army were actually forbidden by Mao Z to call the Red troops by the term "soldiers," and strictly ordered to always call themselves "fighters" instead.[52]

Running parallel to that, in a theoretical turning of the glove inside-out, traditional secret society men who weren't allied outright with the Kuomintang, such as the powerful Green Gang notoriously had been, were semi-legitimized and co-opted into the "red" peasant revolution.

The secret societies were given a glossier face theoretically as simple self-help associations of the poor (although it was also admitted in fine print that because of a "backward" lumpen nature they were sometimes unwittingly manipulated by the "White" counterrevolution). In other words, they had been lesser forerunners of the Communist Party itself. The secret societies' "primitive" underground was claimed to be the model for the later cell structure of the Communists in China. The CCP actually boasting that they hadn't been imitating any foreign music, most especially not that hit rock band Lenin and the Bolsheviks (i imagine they kept their fingers crossed behind their backs when they said that silly fib). A party central committee group wrote down in their 1951 explanation that the secret society men had been *"primitive secret organizations among the people. The members were mainly bankrupt peasants, unemployed handicraftsmen, and other lumpen-proletarians."*

After the relationship between the secret societies and the party had been constructed, former secret society men were often referred to by the movement publicly as respectable "peasants," not the *youmin* or lumpen they had just been and perhaps still were. A morale booster intended, no doubt, to reinforce better class identity and consciousness. Hand is quicker than the eye political moves be kind of blurry sometimes.[53]

But our guy Mao Z wasn't simply changing the rules of the game subjectively, in deciding to redefine who was lumpen/proletarian or not. **His increasing distrust and warning about the lumpen also in some real part reflected changed class realities on the ground.** In those intervening years of protracted revolutionary war, the whole human landscape had changed in material ways. Just as the bandits in 1939 were not the same persons individually or socially as the bandits the Communists had been recruiting back in 1927. Those earlier bandits had joined the armies of one side or the other, or largely died off in their rough rapidly lived lives.

The new wave of bandits cooperating so closely with the Japanese imperialist invasion were mostly hardened anti-Communist deserters from China's lumpen capitalist armies and militias and gangs. A dozen years of all-out war had reached maturity, with each side drawing people not just by chance, but whose inclinations most suited that side's basic political worldview. By attrition and evolution, the pool of uncommitted was shrinking.

If the growing number of "good" guys were always removed from the numbers of lumpen, then your class viewpoint about the lumpen only darkens as the war progresses. Thus, the lumpen class situation had fundamentally changed in their eyes, like the nature of bandits as a lumpen splinter had changed materially and politically. And Mao and the Communists reflected that in their critical class evaluations.

Separating their own fighters and cadre in class theory from the lumpen/proletariat—and then co-opting theoretically into the "peasantry" those from the traditional men's lumpen secret societies—was only a small start.

It signaled that under Mao Z's political leadership, the party had in practice divided up and sifted through the separate lumpen/proletarian fragments. Those judged immediately necessary and useful, primarily fighting men from the ranks of bandits and rival armies, were absolved of the stigma of being "rootless" lumpen. While the not immediately either useful or hostile—most beggars and drug addicts and sex workers and others hustling on the street or surviving as petty servants of the wealthy—were categorized as still lumpen/proletarian, but as innocent victims of capitalism to be dealt with later.

Whatever the pragmatic advantages of Mao Z's changing the rules of the game about the lumpen, didn't mean the gambit was that legendary beast—a "free lunch." Fact was, in cutting corners and redefining "class" as something based subjectively on a person's supposed beliefs or immediate behavior, *not* their relationship to economic production and distribution, the party was opening a Pandora's box. The price to be paid wasn't understood then, although the bill did come due later, as it always does politically.

13. lessons / drawing in pencil

To no surprise, the political lessons that became visible out of that generations-long revolutionary civil war and the lumpen/proletariat's role in it, are so large that they are like features of a big geography, easily visible even across the considerable distance of time & space that separates us. The more extensive Chinese revolutionary experience both confirmed and challenged various aspects of the initial observations of 19th century Western pioneers on this, notably Bakunin, Engels and Marx. And new realities of the lumpen were charted.

The biggest point, well, we don't have to go on & on about it: about how parts of the lumpen/proletariat played an important role in both the mass rural struggle and the revolutionary war itself. It might be useful to point out that those lumpen, though, didn't just take a ticket and get in line; over and over, they punched way above their weight in taking the initiative in the struggle. Their disproportionate

role and commitment in whatever comes down is, i think, a widespread phenomenon in societies around the world. For good or evil. That makes them unusual class strata to really understand, very practically, in terms of fighting capitalism or simply just defending ourselves.

The Chinese Revolutionary experience showed how capitalist societies can have the same rough class formations but in somewhat different shapes and consciousness. With their own particular features. The same fragments but in different capitalist societies don't have a cookie-cutter uniformity.

Mao Z's Chinese experience with the lumpen did validate the "class" solar system discoveries of Marx and Engels, but not necessarily as they had thought. For instance, while Marx & Engels had located the lumpen/proletariat in Western Europe as big city "non-class" strata, in China they existed by the millions in the countryside, mixed in with the peasantry and other rural village classes.

One surprise: that same Chinese early 20th century revolution validated Marx's suspicions of "the dangerous class" all right, but also validated Mikhail Bakunin's anarchist vision of the important revolutionary outlaws of the "destitute proletariat." The two clashing views of 19th century European revolutionary thinkers who were only starting to turn their perception on the lumpen, turned out to not be either/or contradictions, but in a deeper way two warring aspects of the same heterodox lumpen "partial-class" reality. As many declassed social fragments, the lumpen in Old China were both good and evil as well as indifferent, simultaneously.

Chinese society also held a valuable experience because it was the polar opposite from u.s. society in openly recognizing the lumpen as distinct declassed strata, which they had called *yumin* or the "floating people." This made it much easier for young revolutionaries such as Mao Z to identify them and understand them in the struggle.

Also, that large-scale experience reminded us again of something basic that we surely know, but can forget: The lumpen as fallen out of class fragments are people of crisis. Dramatically changing in size and even political character in response to intensifying war and natural disasters, no less social upheavals and economic depressions of the system. The lumpen that Mao Z knew in his youth were not the same actors that he was seeing at the end of the long civil war.

One lesson we were reminded of again from that experience, is that **revolutionary activity has a natural relationship to the terrain of mass illegality and underground life.** This criminalized world is the ground that the lumpen/proletariat know as their own. No group of would-be revolutionaries can be sure that they will not have to navigate and survive on that fractured terrain. As the Chinese Communist Party discovered to their shock in 1927.

Revolution always needs to move around in the zone of illegal and outcast life anyway; to draw resources from it, to find needed people in, monitoring its near and far seismic activity for danger and opportunity, while in general respecting it and learning from it. To unthinkingly dismiss the lumpen and their shadow world matches the description of "cutting off your nose to spite your face."

Not a few groups of revolutionary intellectuals from privileged backgrounds in this country or that, have tried to make a point of what they considered their superior morality, particularly as opposed to criminals and street people. We can take this as the petty self-delusion it was.

Like the Bolshevik leaders before the Russian Revolution, whose central committee was once horrified to find out that their underground administration in the South was financing the whole party with Stalin's violent bank expropriations. The stuffed shirts never did find out that the smuggling of illegal revolutionary flyers and books across Scandinavia into Russia was paid for by also smuggling more profitably what was then illegal pornography (i.e. condoms and explicit sex education pamphlets). For that matter, the Communist bomb factory that ran semi-underground next to Russia in Finland, in a tacit handshake with the local Finnish police, would have sent many "respectable" intellectuals in that party into a concussion.

It isn't a simple up/down question of hiding from repression. It's our larger need to operate in the *whole* social reality as it really exists, to live in the entire human spectrum. In the actually-existing modern world, drugs alone make not only a major criminal world, but set up huge portals between the "normal" legit world and the right-next-door zone of violently irregular and illegal activity.

For example, the Chinese Communist Party's stern prohibition against the drug trade and drug use—reflecting the Chinese people's bitter experience with the Western-inflicted opium epidemic—didn't stop **"red" party and army units from getting heavily involved in the opium trade** as a major economic survival activity. Much of the "red" economy depended on drug trafficking. That was during the harsh WW2 period of Chiang Kai-shek's economic blockade and the Japanese military offensive against the revolutionary Yenan center. **Familiar situation to us here, since so many revolutionaries in our country had to step across the street into the drug subculture and "alternative economy" during the 1960s–1970s revolutionary wave**—or really had been there already.

The exception there would have been women, since **in practice the Chinese lumpen were primarily of the world of men and boys**. Desperate and often short-lived as the lumpen were, Chinese women were largely unable to choose those roles because they were not free enough to be lumpen.

By the way, i always notice when the UN or some children's rights agency screams about the recruitment of "child soldiers" in some lumpen Afrikan civil war. Not that we're the same as them, but fact is that revolution is like pure mathematics—it's best for the very young. Like in desperate poverty and oppression, is it really better for kids to just sit there and die passively? Grown-up societies aren't going to save them, that's for sure.

In 1936, the average age in the Red Army was only nineteen—and **most Red fighters had joined at age 15 or 16**. Some had been the 10 or 11 year old orphan boys and girls picked up to shelter and teach by Mao's wandering army, running errands and messages, and called "little red devils." Others had joined the movement first at 13 or 14 in the revolutionary village

teenager organizations, then graduated "naturally" and eagerly into the Red Army. Think that's "too young" to come out of the Wilderness? Clarence 13X, Malcolm's equally smart compatriot, started rebuilding his oppressed community in a more radical way specifically by recruiting bands of 10 year olds.

Another lesson we saw in detail is what it means that the lumpen can't be related to as one "class." Not standard, not uniform, not one bloc marching in step. Like every other comrade, for convenience sake i talk about "the lumpen," but technically there is no such thing. There

are many, many different kinds of lumpen. Especially if we go worldwide, with politics and activity ranging from far right to far left on scales that don't have to be the same as the rest of society. They are splinters, noncontiguous bits socially "unplugged" from the class structure of production and distribution. Fallen out of many different classes and strata into widely differing social fragments.

So our guy was eventually disillusioned with many of them. Mao Z had hoped in the beginning to get essentially all the lumpen the revs wanted, just as they eventually got the class support of the peasantry and the working class almost as entire class blocs. But the Chinese revolution never sewed up the support of the lumpen/proletariat as a whole, or anything even close to it. Because they weren't one thing or one "class." Maybe several million or more lumpen had fought for Generalissimo Chiang Kai-shek's right-wing "White" armies or were gangsters, informers, cops and petty officials allied to the Right; while many others ignored the civil war as much as possible, just like the two warring sides ignored them, and focused on their little hustles to keep their heads above water.

Even when for rebellion of some kind, many lumpen men were wedded to reactionary culture. During the 1927 "Northern Expedition," when the united front army was gradually sweeping its way across the country to absorb the warlord semi-states, women militants became particular targets. One feminist history recounts:

"The launching of a military campaign into Henan in the Spring of 1927 created the possibility of expanding the women's movement into this unfavorable social terrain. Many women students of the Wuhan Central Military and Political Institute, including Xie Bingying, were assigned to this operation. The women army propagandists, however, encountered a host of difficulties, particularly from the Red Spear Society. In Xinyang, southern Henan, this secret society spread rumors to the effect that the National Revolutionary Army 'shared wives' and thus constituted a danger to the community. It also orchestrated the murdering of some members of the propaganda team. In Xindian, the Red Spear Society shut down the offices of the local women's association because it had attracted more than three hundred members through its training program, its promotion of unbinding women's feet, and its emancipation of child-brides."[54]

Yet, the many lumpen who *did* join the revolution tipped the balance, particularly in the early years, and gave enough energy to help secure the victory over world capitalism in 1949. **A real part of the lumpen were enough for the struggle to win, they didn't have to get all or most of those outcast class fragments. That's an important practical lesson just by itself.**

When we say that the lumpen can't be just labeled together as one class, there's something specific we've got stuck in our throats and gotta cough up. There's an off-target tendency to define lumpen/proletarian as deviant *behavior*, another way of saying someone is a psychopath or amoral or something. Because of the whole dissing and social bias against the lumpen. Like, believing the lumpen are really the down and out who've been driven out of their own humanity—who are nasty, amoral, treacherous, like a Brandon Darby or your enemy going off on you any moment. That's true for some really messed up poor people i've run into, absolutely—but just as true for some middle-class types we've known (to say nothing of the capitalists, who always take the big prize for individualistic, amoral and vicious).

Lumpen/proletarian isn't a *behavior*, it isn't good or bad, it's a certain kind of objective relationship to the regular structure of economic production and distribution. Being *out* of that whole "normal" class structure thing, that is, and having a different consciousness because of it. Mao is always quoted talking about lumpen as "brave fighters," and the stereotype of them is macho, is of militants, gunmen, soldiers, and the like. But in protest politics here, for instance, it wasn't unusual to find lumpen as organizers, fundraisers, public speakers, political leaders, or sympathizers quietly doing behind-the-scenes practical work, to say nothing of the con-artists and hustlers attracted to the action—the whole wide range of political activism good and bad. To be sure, most here in the u.s.a. weren't admitting to being lumpen but held up cardboard class identities over their faces. That's Western culture for you.

Mao Z was so good at working with them politically because he **recognized their specific lived politics as real**, whether right or wrong by leftist standards, rather than thinking of them in an abstract way as an unrespectable "class."

For example: Seeing that widespread desertions especially after Red Army defeats were like the norm, the cultural standard (and if you can see it that way, a kind of self-protective "job change" career move in their desperate soldier-for-hire subculture), Mao in the early years forbid executing or severely punishing deserters. Which was an innovation then in China.

His angle was to **flow *with* the subculture** not fight against its weight. He bet that if soldiers were apt to "flip" and change sides, then the revolutionary army could relax and just be better at it. "Flipping" more deserters than the abusive enemy military did. Developing a whole program of persuasion, the revolutionaries were soon doing most of their recruiting from captured enemy soldiers— so the more soldiers sent against them, the more recruits the Red Army could potentially have (provided that you actually won that last battle, of course, always a bottom line in life—i mean, *"What da ya want for nothing? ... a rubber biscuit?"*).

The Communist fighters really got into that "flip" thing. Revolutionary soldiers who got physically lost on the chaos of **rapidly changing battlefields** were under orders to get clear and then simply use a cover story and join *any* military, especially the mercenary, messed up, helter-skelter Kuomintang army. Since enemy divisions would sooner or later always be heading over to attack the Reds. Then, the lost soldier could rejoin the revolutionary forces by simply deserting back once they got close (preferably with a few new friends or rifles). This was a standard field procedure for them. Again, working *with*

the flow of how things happened in that lumpen subculture to fashion a new small tactic, not refusing to dip your toe in the river.

(Guiding a scared young soldier, at the edge of a battlefield and lost from his unit, that was using a tiny electron of revolutionary theory, too.)

By the time they had gotten their feet under them and could take in the whole social landscape, **the Chinese comrades were also seeing a much larger lumpen/proletariat. Declassed strata they identified as much of the capitalist state apparatus and the direct servants of the ruling classes.**

So not just some capitalist thugs reclothed in the guise of soldiers and police, but many among the criminal civil servants, officials, judges, prison guards, lawyers, big and petty officials, key strategists, as well as private security and aides for the bosses themselves—were all lumpen in the "reds" intensified class vision. Which then could be seen as layers much closer around the pumping heart of capitalism, more central, not simply some marginalized poor outcasts and vagabonds at the social edges.

This raises questions for us. Certainly have run into government employees here in my city, from poverty program officials to some government clerical workers and on down to cops, who have struck me as declassed parasitic hustlers. Not talking about the capitalist state in general right now, but only what i've directly seen where i live. Obviously, in the massive bureaucratic state which tries to hold decaying capitalism together as it falls, questions of masks and faces, camouflage and identity, are complex. Questioning all this was a learning experience for me.

As we noted before, dealing with Mao Z's theory on the lumpen/proletariat turns out to be a whole different mess of fish than dealing with earlier radical theorists. Which means that different questions can come to us that had never occurred to comrades with only their little starter kit a century before.

The chaos of seemingly being without boundaries, that many lumpen brought with them into the struggle, was and is a complex gift. It's not always a curse, you know, it's also a gift. Those vastly more experienced Chinese comrades were only giving us the narrowest view of that. We know, in the ancient Greek legend of the first woman, Pandora, she could not resist curiosity, and opened the box that Zeus gave her with orders to never take off the lid. When Pandora opened it anyway, all the evils we know flew out and escaped into the world. "Disease" and "Hate" and "Death" and all the others. Leaving only, at the bottom of the box, the gift of "Hope" for us. That's the legend, anyway. i've come to think that beneath even that, the very last gift at the bottom of Pandora's box was "Do-It-Yourself." That's what was left for us, anyway. We've picked up the thread of this investigation into class understanding, to see where it leads us.

This is only a start, of course. We're moving towards the lumpen/proletariat in the 21st century politics of our own terrain.

"Little Red Devil" of North Shensi

postscript / coming home: reforming the lumpen/proletariat

One of the contradictions in the startup of the new liberated society was the awkward persistence of the lumpen. From the start, Mao Z had boldly committed the revolution to completely eliminating the lumpen/proletariat's outcast strata as part of society. They would no longer exist individually or collectively under China's new socialism. Not only in ending capitalism's "social parasites," but recognizing the mass of lumpen as only victims of oppression who needed systematic help in restarting their lives as honest and productive citizens. This was an unprecedented social project, as massive in scale as building the Great Wall or the Pyramids had been.

With mercenary soldiers and bandits being swept away as the Revolution took power, the main challenge was the overwhelming numbers of the then-remaining street lumpen; who were primarily classed as beggars, thieves and sex workers (the party actually ordered its cadre to stop calling these women "prostitutes," or talk to them in any implicitly insulting or backward language from the bad old days).

This energetic outcast melting down and recasting had started back at the beginning of the first liberated territory and the new Soviets. It only accelerated after 1935–36, as soon as the new Soviet zone had firmly been established around Yenan, at the legendary journey's end of that army's historic Long March. That remote and extremely poor Northern border region had a major problem with lumpen. In 1937, according to party social investigators, the town of Yenan itself had a population of only 3,000—but 500 of them were *erliuzi* or lumpen "loafers" and "idlers." The figure for that border region in 1935, when the Red Army's Long March survivors arrived, was much more shocking—estimated to be 70,000 *erliuzi* or almost half the population, out of a total area population of around 140,000.

Party cadre then were almost certainly way over-estimating the numbers of lumpen/proletariat there, although their numbers were clearly sizeable. The mistake would have happened in part because the cadres approached it from the backside methodologically. Everyone who was not seen being active in production with farming or in service work or handicraft production automatically seemed to have been swept into the lumpen statistically. That didn't take into account the effect of large numbers of opium addicts—said to be about 13% of the population in some large areas—and the numbers partially idled in a formal sense by landlessness and the dysfunction of the old economy in that remote area.[55]

Many different kinds of party programs were initiated to bring those marginalized back into full participation in economic production. From farming "labor exchange brigades" (i.e. labor co-ops) where peasants formed labor teams of their choosing to work their separate plots in turn together—to propaganda campaigns tugging at opium addicts to join new "mutual aid groups" where they could talk about their problems and encourage each other to get clean. This wasn't social work in the old way, but a main element of the party's economic program in the newly liberated territory. Which was under economic blockade from the "White" regime and the Japanese invaders. Villages were organized to share the burden, giving returning lumpen shelter and food while the local "red" cadre found handicraft making equipment and materials or small pieces of farmland for them.

Mass political pressures were piled on, to be sure, to straighten out those lumpen who still resisted laboring, those still too used to the addictive crooked path and living by their wits. Harrison Foreman, a veteran war correspondent for NBC radio and the *New York Times*, found their reforming of "rascal" lumpen one of the most interesting stories in his 1940s travel behind the lines through the Red areas:

"The worst thing you can call one in the Border Region today is an *erh liu tze*—a loafer. In their struggle for self-sufficiency—almost a matter of life and death—these blockaded people have little patience with the *erh liu tze*. Loafers were not merely parasites. Their wayward habits, their laziness, gambling, cheating, lying, and stealing are sources of demoralization for others, and have no place in the vigorous society for which the Communists are striving.

"Of the estimated 70,000 loafers in the Border Region when the Communists arrived in 1935, all but 9,554 were reformed by the beginning of 1943, and those were particularly hardened cases. But the government was determined to solve the problem completely. An intensive reform campaign was instituted; and by the beginning of 1944 all but 3,967 loafers were reformed, these diehards resisting all pressure directed against them. When pleas, bribes, even threats, proved of no avail, the people decided to take the law more or less into their own hands: every loafer had to wear a big white badge inscribed *'erh liu tze'*—to be jeered at, hooted, and incessantly humiliated in the campaign to shame him into reform.

"The [Red] Government, meanwhile, was employing subtler methods. At a recent convention of Labor Heroes, five hardened loafers were chosen by the Government and invited to attend ... On arrival at Yenan the five loafers were astonished to find themselves accorded the same courtesies extended to the heroes. As they entered the big auditorium they were applauded loudly and ushered to the platform to be seated with the honored guests. They were served with wine, cakes, and sweetmeats, and were called on to participate in all discussions on an equal footing with the Labor Heroes. By the end of the convention, all five announced their determination to reform— whereupon they were vigorously acclaimed ... The Government, on its part, offered them grants of land and loaned them farm implements, seeds, and animals. By this time the five loafers declared, 'If we fail in this reform, we shall no longer consider ourselves human beings!'"

In part, the revolutionaries felt they needed these public campaigns and displays, to help turn around existing mass prejudice against the dispossessed. Sympathetic real life "speaking bitterness" stories of selected lumpen/proletarians were spread nationally. In particular, first-hand stories by poor women beggars and sex workers. That was a major aim of the whole campaign, as well as to prove the superiority of the revolution by its ability to take on and eliminate the kind of mass suffering which even the most affluent Western cities did nothing about.

The soon visible lack of street begging and sex workers in the Soviet areas— which everyone could see for themselves— was always contrasted to what couldn't be denied in the still-capitalist strongholds.

In a typical example, a March 1948 headline in a revolutionary publication was "Life in Beijing Is Like Hell on Earth." The story underneath said:

> "There are a huge number of beggars and prostitutes in Beijing. On every street there are people kowtowing and raising their clasped hands in pleas for money or food. On every street there are emaciated prostitutes calling out pitifully, '3,000 for a night, I'll take 1,000.' 1,000 yuan will buy you two *taels* of corn flour."* [56]

IN THE JUNGLE OF THE CITIES

When the young revolutionaries finally started taking the cities at the end of World War II, the approach towards transforming the lumpen was both similar to and quite different from their campaigns in the Soviet rural areas. Partly because in the peasant villages and towns the lumpen were already where they were supposed to be, but in the cities they were not.

As anti-imperialists, the Chinese Communists actively saw the center of the challenge of transforming modern society as the problem of parasitism. In an imperialist world, the extreme inequality and looting of exploited millions allowed not merely a tiny elite of rich classes, but mass social sectors and entire societies that consumed but barely produced. Even in a poor neo-colony such as old China, urban centers of both international commerce and national capitalist headquarters spun large decadent layers of non-productive persons around them, of all kinds, from rich to poor. Glittering parasites upon rural peasant and worker China, who were living and laboring in the mud.

In that liberation year of 1949, a Shanghai newspaper summed up their situation as a foreign trade center: *"Shanghai is a non-productive city. It is a parasitic city."* The party newspaper *People's Daily* said in that Summer: *"In old China, that semifeudal, semicolonial country, all of the cities inhabited by the ruling classes (such as Beijing) were predominantly consumption cities."* So they underlined that a revolutionary future made necessary, *"transforming consuming cities into producing cities."*

In Beijing, the ancient imperial capital, of course the number of non-producing

---

* A *tael* was an Asian measurement used in general markets and for precious metals, varying somewhat by time and country—in China it was often a weight approximately one and one-third ounces.

persons was extremely large. After their 1949 taking of the capital, CCP cadres estimated that out of the total population of 2 million, an astonishing 700,000 people were non-productive, occupying parasitic niches whether in affluence or poverty. Not only capitalists and imperial bureaucrats and servants and judges and armed guards, but street criminals and moneylender clerks and entertainers and opium den staff and brothel workers and so on. So their programs to transform the urban lumpen into self-supporting workers and peasants revolved around two principles.[57]

The main universal in those Communist re-education programs for the lumpen/proletariat was the principle that "Labor is glorious!" As the title of one pamphlet the cadres handed out to prostitutes living and studying in a re-education center went, *"Production, labor and earning one's own living are glorious; not laboring is shameful."* To say that many lumpen then instinctively reacted against this idea would be an understatement, for sure.

The other imperative in their raising up the lumpen/proletariat and eliminating bourgeois culture was directly ending "parasite cities." Moving unemployed and non-productive poor out of the distorted cities where there were many more people than useful jobs. This was a time right after the war's end, when party cadre were having to make urgent decisions about social reconstruction on the fly. Sending groups of jobless people to fill labor needs all over the country. The lumpen sex workers and beggars and street thieves were only a part of this great out-migration and social transformation.

In contrast to the earlier rural campaigns where the revolutionaries used massed people's voluntary activity, in the cities the revolutionaries had no such organized political base and so used major mandatory state programs instead. In December 1949, after months of investigation, interviewing lumpen and planning, in Beijing Red Army infantry closed off streets in the early hours, while People's Security Bureau police and Civil Action cadres swept "red-light districts" and beggars' favored locations. Beijing was to be the "model," whose programs would be tested out and then replicated in all other Chinese cities.

Thousands of people staying on the streets were picked up, of course, filling chaotic holding areas. Those able-bodied without criminal charges were given transportation aid to return to their native villages. Drug addicts were moved to new residential health centers, while traveling peddlers and honorably discharged soldiers and migrant workers and the like were also sent back to their rural villages.

Hundreds of women sex workers picked up eventually found places as medical workers, approved theatre performers, or as workers in light industry. Several hundred of the women agreed to party-arranged instant marriages, often to veteran Red infantrymen and the new policemen, which may seem to us like sex work simply wearing a different dress. Unemployed male job-seekers without a family to return to were sometimes drafted into the many major rural infrastructure projects, filling labor crews living in tents in the countryside and helping build highways and dams. Known violent criminals and crime bosses were sent off to re-education through forced labor camps, while some few worst case criminals and brothel owners were executed. The lumpen were, indeed, being systematically emptied out of the city.[58]

What remained were stubborn beggars, petty thieves, and sex workers, who were the main subjects of new residential re-education centers, the cadres teaching them to become housewives, peasants and factory workers living with them there. The lumpen were often the farthest thing from obedient pupils. There was considerable bottom-up criticism and resistance for years by sex workers, to everything from the cadres' politics to the sufficient but very plain meals to the revolutionary re-education itself. They had been taken into long-term custody as the brothels and red-light districts were closed down. The Communist cadres discovered first-hand that people who feel able to act for themselves don't necessarily do what reformers who aren't risking anything themselves want them to do.

A former Beijing sex worker, Li Hongyu, wrote in 1950 about their alarm at "liberation" by being captured in large-scale police actions: *"When they rounded us up, I thought, 'Why didn't they give us more warning? They just show up and demand we leave immediately?' I was really afraid and I thought, 'Where are they taking us?' ... We weren't even allowed out the front door! I hated the comrades. Weren't we liberated? Why couldn't we do as we pleased? Armed guards paced back and forth in the doorway."*

The cadre Pei Di, an educated 25 year old woman who had just joined the party, experienced the re-education center for prostitutes as her first assignment: She was upset when the first morning at the new center, a former major brothel where the cadre re-educators ate and lived with the sex workers, "... one of the newly-interned prostitutes opened her dressing gown and flashed the soldier guarding the door. When the young sentry averted his eyes, 'the half-naked prostitute cried, "Sisters, run! The People's Liberation Army won't dare fire on us!"' The cadres and the soldiers tried to prevent the escape, but they 'couldn't stop the frenzied prostitutes who were pouring out the front door.'"

> "Pei claimed that she ran after them, yelling, 'You can run away, but you'll just be sent back! If you dare to engage in prostitution out there, you'll be sent back today! Where can you run?' Pei's supervisor, Ke Yan, reported that after the incident, 'the People's Liberation Army soldiers were also very upset' because the prostitutes were not only flashing and trying to seduce their guards as a ruse to escape; the women were also reputedly taunting, berating, and punching the soldiers."[59]

Far from being awed by the revolutionary cadres or grateful for their involuntary "liberation," many of the lumpen held for re-education set to work complaining and maneuvering to get back as close as possible to their old lives. Many sex workers said that if prostitution was being banned, then they would instead like to be concubines to affluent men, actresses, or taxi dancers. When the cadres broke the news that they would be expected to take factory jobs or emigrate to poor villages to be peasants, common replies were like, "Wouldn't I die of exhaustion?" While in the other Beijing centers for male beggars and thieves, the men would reminisce about their "undisciplined life" and worried that laboring would be bad since it would "limit their freedom." You could say that they had a healthy distrust of government programs and official promises.

That was only round one, of course, and what we would only expect from any self-respecting lumpen. It's easy to imagine the cadres beating their heads against the wall. Contrary to the new authority's trusting expectations, reform and "liberation" was not universally welcomed. The initial difficulty of the Communist state in accurately measuring the lumpen for new work suits was not a surprise, really. And the subsequent step, of figuring out where to fit their irregular pieces into the larger puzzle of the just-overturned class structure, also got unofficially stuck. These small problems were settled by using the larger power of the state to just "make it so." This surprisingly became a matter that wasn't tactical anymore but of strategic significance. The results as illuminating for us as the initial lessons of the lumpen in China's revolutionary war had been. Just very different.[60]

endnotes

SW = Selected Works of Mao Tse-tung. Volume 1. Foreign Languages Press, 1965.

1. Edgar Snow. *Red Star Over China.* Revised and Enlarged Edition. Grove Press. N.Y., 1968. Pages 214–215.

2. Stuart R. Schram. "Mao Tse-tung and Secret Societies." In *China Quarterly* No. 27. July–September 1966. This writing by Mao Z is the first and slightly fuller version of essentially the same although shorter text which also appears in his more often quoted 1926 "Analysis of Classes in Chinese Society."

3. Mao Tse-tung. "Analysis of the Classes in Chinese Society." In *Selected Works of Mao Tse-tung.* Vol. 1. Foreign Languages Press, 1965. Peking. *(SW)* Page 19.

4. Snow. Op cit. Page 135.

5. Ibid. Page 141.

6. See Mao's own account of that time in: Ibid. Pages 163–171; also Schram, Op cit.

7. Phillip C.C. Huang. "The Jiangxi Period: An Introduction." In *China Research Monographs Number Thirteen. Chinese Communists and Rural Society 1927–1934.* Center for Chinese Studies, University of California at Berkeley. August 1978. Pages 11–12; Agnes Smedley. *The Great Road: The Life and Times of Chu Teh.* Monthly Review, 1956. N.Y. Pages 88–89, 124–133; Snow. Op cit. Pages 333–334.

8. Snow. Op cit.. Pages 78–79.

9. Agnes Smedley. *Battle Hymn of China.* Alfred A. Knopf. 1943. Pages 156–157; Smedley. *The Great Road: The Life and Times of Chu Teh.* Page 184.

10. Mao Tse-tung. "Report on an Investigation of the Peasant Movement in Hunan." In *SW.* Page 33. Mao Zedong. *Report From Xunwu.* Translated and edited by Roger R. Thompson. Stanford University Press, 1990. Pages 116 and 122.

11. Snow. Op cit. Pages 161–162.

12. John E. Rue. *Mao Tse-Tung in Opposition 1927–1935.* Hoover Institution on War, Revolution and Peace, 1966. Stanford. Page 99.

13. Mao Tse-tung. "Report on an Investigation of the Peasant Movement in Hunan." In *SW*. Page 33.

14. Lynda Schaefer Bell. "Agricultural Laborers and the Rural Revolution." In Philip C.C. Huang. Editor. *China Research Monographs Number Thirteen: Chinese Communists and Rural Society, 1927–1934.* Center for Chinese Studies, University of California at Berkeley. 1978. Mao Zedong. Op cit. Pages 116 and 122.

15. Mao Zedong. Op cit. Pages 45–46.

16. Ibid. Pages 45–46.

17. Roger R. Thompson. *Introduction*. In Ibid. Pages 3–41.

18. Mao Zedong. Op cit. Pages 116–117.

19. Ibid. Pages 104–105.

20. Ibid. Pages 112–113.

21. Ibid. Pages 202–203.

22. Gail Hershatter. *Dangerous Pleasures: prostitution and modernity in twentieth-century Shanghai.* University of California Press, 1997. Berkeley and Los Angeles. Pages 39–41, 194.

23. Mao Zedong. Op cit. Page 15–17.

24. Christina Kelly Gilmartin. *Engendering the Chinese Revolution.* University of California Press, 1995. Pages 199, 212.

25. Ibid. Pages 15–17.

26. Ibid. Page 13.

27. Huang. Loc cit. Pages 1–3.

28. Rue. Op cit. Page 98.

29. Ibid. Page 99.

30. Phillip C. C. Huang. "Intellectuals, Lumpenproletarians, Workers and Peasants in the Communist Movement: The Case of Xingguo County, 1927–1934." In Huang. Op cit. Pages 2–28.

31. Ibid.

32. Ibid.

33. Discussion of Southern Jiangxi province events in this section from: Ibid. Pages 2–28; Stephen C. Averill. "The Origins of the Futian Incident." In Tony Saich and Hans van de Ven. Editors. *New Perspectives on the Chinese Communist Revolution.* M.E. Sharpe. Armonk and London, 1995. Pages 79–115.

34. Rue. Op cit. Page 235.

35. Sources for "Futian Incident" events in this section other than from those given above, from: Averill. Loc cit. Pages 79–115; Snow. Op cit. Pages 176–177: Smedley. *The Great Road*. Pages 280–283; Rue. Op cit. Pages 231–235.

There are many other sources with various points of view for the "Futian

Incident"—perhaps the most controversial event in the history of the revolution. Scholarly writings about it don't appear to be in any shortage. Some i personally don't consider legitimate, but i am not going to even pretend to have kept up with it all, as i am certainly not a China scholar. All that is not, however, in the main focal area of this book. Here my modest intent is to only give a brief factual summary of the "incident" so its whatever repercussions can be understood.

36. Mark Selden. *The Yenan Way in Revolutionary China.* Harvard East Asian Series 62. Harvard University Press, 1971. Page 32.

37. Aminda M. Smith. *Thought Reform and China's Dangerous Classes: Reeducation, Resistance and the People.* Rowman & Littlefield. Plymouth, 2013. Pages 24 and 53.

38. Mao Zedong. Op cit. Page 242.

39. Smith. Op cit. Page 32.

40. Ibid. Page 18.

41. Ibid. Page 128.

42. Ibid. Pages 18, 70–71; Harrison Forman. *Report From Red China.* Henry Holt, 1943. Pages 89–93; Mao Tse-Tung. Op cit. Page 51.

43. Smith. Op Cit. Pages 69–70.

44. Mao Zedong. Stuart R. Schram & Nancy J. Hodes, Editors. *Mao's Road to Power. Revolutionary Writings 1912–1949. Vol. III. From the Jingangshan to the Establishment of the Jiangxi Soviets July 1927–December 1930.* M.E. Sharpe, 1995. Armonk & London. Pages 450–453; Rue. Op cit. Page 48.

45. Smedley. *Battle Hymn of China.* Pages 438–439.

46. Snow. Op cit. Page 221; Schram, "Mao Tse-tung and Secret Societies."

47. Smith. Op cit. Page 4.

48. Smedley. *Battle Hymn of China.* Pages 319–320.

49. Ibid.

50. Ibid. Page 477.

51. William Hinton. *Fanshen: Documentary of Revolution in a Chinese Village.* N.Y. 1966. Vintage Books. Pages 77–78.

52. Ibid. Page 79. Hinton is in part quoting from the report of Israel Epstein. *The Unfinished Revolution in China.* Boston. Little Brown & Co. 1947. Page 317.

53. Snow. Op cit. Page 259.

54. Mao Tse-tung. "Analysis of the Classes in Chinese Society." In *SW.* Page 21.

55. Gilmartin. Op cit. Page 196.

56. Harrison Forman. *Report From Red China*. N.Y. 1945. Henry Holt & Co. Page 70–71; Suzanne Pepper. *Civil War in China*. Berkeley, 1978. University of California Press. Pages 346 & 354.

57. Smith. Op cit. Page 64.

58. Ibid. Pages 142–143.

59. Ibid. Pages 155–157.

60. Ibid. Pages 108–109.

61. Ibid. Page 144.

blackstone rangers:
u.s. experiment using "gangs" to
repress black community rebellion

preface (2017)

The following investigation in using class analysis to cut into current politics was written in the early fall of 1976. Even though the capitalist state is always running different trial projects in violently repressing the Black community, seldom can we document the political details. Often they are clandestine, of course. So this was a rare opportunity to do that.

My politics then were more standard Marxist on a theoretical level, and this paper reflects those primary criticisms of the lumpen/proletariat as a parasitic class easily bought off by capitalism against its own people. In practice, my political life was somewhat different even at that time; both in anti-war activity and in revolutionary working class organizing, i was simultaneously working closely *with* and also working *against* an assortment of lumpen guys both white and New Afrikan. My own theoretical view of the lumpen/proletariat has shifted its angle of vision since then, though much of what i analyzed in this situation in 1976 was

obviously factually true. We decided to leave this writing as it originally was, as an example of that thorny period politically.

What hasn't been said is that on a personal level while writing, i was really pissed at the practice of street organizations like that. Their development was obviously brilliant, but also like a terrorism enforced on the Woodlawn community and the New Afrikan working people there. It was like a white supremacist fantasy come true. The final exasperating touch was that both the white liberal community and the white left in town were strongly pro-gang. Excusing every misdeed, hoping mostly to opportunistically cash in somehow on the paramilitary rise of the lumpen-led organizations. It wasn't such a nice time for families caught in the beat down, as the state happily experimented in using Black to step on Black. Woodlawn was also, coincidentally, where i had graduated from Wadsworth elementary school (my one academic degree), and where i went to the same secondary

276

school as Jeff Fort, the founder and leader of the Blackstone Rangers.

One morning a co-worker who sat at the next desk at my job, came in obviously upset. Earlier that morning, while getting ready for school, her young daughter had glanced out the window only to see two Blackstone Ranger soldiers casually pull out guns and kill another youth right on the sidewalk outside. The daughter was completely terrified and refusing to leave their apartment for any reason. Her mom was equally frightened that the organization would somehow find out that her kid was a witness to it all. She was crying and not believing my assurances that even the street organization didn't have x-ray vision like Superman, or any magical means of discovering her daughter. That's the kind of fear that capitalism unleashes to disconnect people from their own strengths and mess up their lives. It was hard for me to romanticize that away as so many movement people were doing politically.

Lastly, I have to acknowledge the comradeship and practical assistance of the Chicago Repression Research Group, who skillfully managed to liberate from the u.s. government several file boxes of correspondence, grant applications, assorted documents and departmental reports. Again, my thanks.

blackstone rangers:
u.s. experiment using "gangs" to repress black community rebellion (1976)

A central confusion within the Movement ten years ago was the question of class. Who are the revolutionary forces? Who are the reactionary forces? Typical of that chaotic time of trying on different ideologies as one tries on clothes of different styles, was the confusion over the lumpen-proletariat and the "street people."

The lumpenproletariat, long viewed by Marxists as an unstable and "dangerous" class, were suddenly praised by many revolutionaries. In 1969, when the Black Panther Party was explaining the forcible ouster of disruptive white leftists from their Oakland United Front Against Fascism Conference, the BPP defined the ouster as "lumpenproletarian discipline."[1] Eldridge Cleaver, acting as one of the chief ideologists of the Panther Party, acclaimed the "Black urban lumpen-proletariat" to be "the vanguard of the proletariat."[2] This confused trend of hailing "the Lumpen" as the most revolutionary strata in U.S. society was widespread in various third world movements and the "New Left" Students for a Democratic Society.

In this study we show how the capitalist state, in the form of a reform "poverty program," reached down into the very mass of the oppressed in one community in Chicago to recruit a force to keep a repressive order for it. It was the leadership role played by lumpen/proletarian elements within that organization of oppressed that gave the government its leverage. Further, the situation was both masked and confused by a split within the state, with certain police elements savagely turning on their newly-bought "Lumpen" allies. During this time the Movement was able neither to successfully intervene nor even to expose this deadly maneuver, because of our confused ideas about the "lumpen." This resulted in a situation where the De Facto public emphasis of the Movement towards this development was to support the repression. As startling as this may seem, it underlines the practical necessity of class analysis in guiding our immediate work.

When radicals in the '60s spoke of "the lumpen" they were usually talking about what they also called "street people" as a whole. So that a high-school-age gang member, an unemployed veteran just back from Vietnam, and an aspiring pimp or heroin pusher might be classed together as "lumpen." Often, a personal involvement with violence and crime was regarded as immediate proof of high potential for revolutionary work. This confusion about class had tragic results. Lack of a precise understanding about the lumpenproletariat is still so dangerous because it blinds us to a key factor in the development of repression against the oppressed.

Marxists have traditionally made a sharp distinction between the poorest, most oppressed layers of the working class—who are propertyless and often jobless—and the lumpenproletariat. The latter, existing on the bottom edge of society, no longer have any relation to the means of production and distribution. They owe no loyalty save to their own personal interests, and, far from having solidarity with any class they are all too willing to live as parasites preying on their own people. At times this point is obscured since the "lumpen" are traditional victims of police activity.

In a famous passage in the *Manifesto*, Marx and Engels wrote: "The 'dangerous class,' the social scum, that passively rotting mass thrown off by the lowest layers of old society, may, here and there, be swept into the movement by a proletarian revolution; its conditions of life, however, prepare it far more for the part of a bribed tool of reactionary intrigue."[3] That analysis is still accurate, and helps us understand how organizations of "street people" are successfully used by the ruling class.

A CASE STUDY IN CHICAGO

In 1965–70, national attention was focused on the explosive political growth of Black youth gangs in Chicago, Illinois. Two Southside gangs in particular, the Black P. Stone Nation and their rivals, The Disciples rapidly became empires; thousands of youth could be mobilized wearing either the red berets of the "Stones" or the blue berets of the "Ds." Immediately, both the Civil Rights Movement and the white liberal community saw these gangs as ready-made organizations to advance the interests of social reform. Both believed that police harassment of ghetto youth and the poverty of gang members opened the door to recruiting these gang structures en masse into the Movement.

The Black P. Stone Nation, the largest of the two youth gangs, was perhaps the most successfully publicized organization of its kind in the U.S. From its origins as a grammar school marching group for the Annual Bud Billiken Day (a traditional celebration sponsored by the *Chicago Defender* and participated in by tens of thousands of Chicago Blacks), the "Stones" soon grew into a local Woodlawn gang. In the early sixties that gang, the Blackstone Rangers, became the "General Motors" of Southside Chicago gangs. It found the key to growth by becoming a "conglomerate" of gangs by convincing local gangs to affiliate into the Blackstone structure. The local gang leaders were represented on the "Main 21," the leadership council of what later became known as the Black P. Stone Nation. At their peak the "Stones" had most of the gang youth on the Southside from 23rd Street to the City's southern edge, with additional affiliates in the Black suburbs, the Westside and Northside, and claimed membership was between 5,000–7,000.

The Disciples ("Ds") were generally conceded to be fewer in number, more of a "fighting gang" and less political than the "Stones." They were dominant in the Englewood area, west of Woodlawn. Their membership was generally put at around 1,000.

In the Spring of 1966, Rev. Martin Luther King, James Bevel, Al Sampson and other S.C.L.C. staff started holding meetings with over thirty Chicago youth gangs. In May, Rev. Bevel addressed 400 "Stones" in the First Presbyterian Church of Woodlawn, stressing that a campaign by all the thousands of gang youth against the white establishment could "immobilize" the city.[4] The alluring prospect of real power was repeatedly held up for gang leaders. That June 11th, S.C.L.C., and the A.C.L.U., the street ministers of the Urban Training Center, the Y.M.C.A. and other social agencies held an all-day conference for the leaders of eight major gangs in the swank Sheraton-Blackstone Hotel. Comically named, the "Turfmasters First Annual Convention," this meeting once again tried to enlist the gangs into the liberal movement.[5]

Although the Blackstone Rangers and the Disciples soon lost interest in the rhetoric of the Southern Christian Leadership Conference, interest in them was far from over. Liberals and church progressives continued to view the gangs as important levers for social reform in Chicago. Rev. John Fry and the First Presbyterian Church encouraged the "Stones" to use the church as a center, and Fry himself became a controversial public defender of the gangs. Police harassment was countered by a well-financed defense program. Right-wing insuranceman Clement Stone, Charles Merrill, Jr. (of the founding family of Merrill, Lynch, etc.), Charles F. Kettering II, (who gave $260,000 out of GM profits) and other capitalists built up a sizeable fund for bail and legal expenses.[6]

The Illinois Black Panther Party was also trying hard to enlist the gangs, temporarily achieving a well-publicized alliance with the Disciples. The "Stones" and "Ds" were widely viewed as latent revolutionary organizations. This trend achieved its purest expression in the realm of literature, in Sam Greenlee's *The Spook Who Sat by the Door*.[7] In this best-selling novel, a Southside Chicago youth gang is secretly reorganized by a Black rebel who learned guerrilla warfare within the C.I.A. The novel ends in a powerful, but doomed, all-out armed assault by the gang against the U.S. Army.

In a recent interview, Greenlee confirms that his novel was a fictional vehicle for a "serious study to the revolutionary potential in the Black community." He says the gangs had "... the greatest revolutionary potential. All they lacked was orientation and leadership. I think they had more revolutionary potential than the Panthers, for instance."[8] Greenlee is only expressive of what many people believed a few years ago—and perhaps many still believe.

GANG LEADERSHIP NOT REVOLUTIONARY

Contrary to the myth so often projected, the Blackstone Rangers and the Disciples were never "revolutionary," or even usually militant. The youth gang leadership openly and honestly looked to their own interest, bargaining and maneuvering with all sides to get the best "deal." Andrew Barret, Youth Director of the National Conference of Christians and Jews (and a former street worker with a "Stone" affiliate), summed it up very concisely:

> "The Rangers are becoming highly politically oriented. They are interested in getting a piece of the action, not tearing down the system."[9]

As Greenlee himself points out:

> "Most of street gang activity is antisocial, and it is and was a serious problem to the community. They weren't robinhoods; they weren't robbing from the rich to feed the poor. Their rip-offs weren't taking place in Highland Park, they were taking place in Woodlawn and Lawndale. They were ripping off their friends, neighbors, mothers, fathers and daughters."[10]

While the Black liberation organizations have always had to fight the repressive police structures, to publicize their racist crimes and organize against them, the "Stones" and "Ds" leadership had a policy of submission to the police. Time and again they hoped that cooperation with the police might earn them favors, particularly personal protection from arrests.

What was the exact nature of that cooperation with the Chicago Police Department? The gang leadership, particularly elements of the "Main 21" of Blackstone, served the police as informers and enforcers, suppressing sparks of Black unrest. 1966, 1967, and 1968 all saw massive Black "riots," rebellions in the Chicago Ghetto. All three years the "Stones" leadership worked with the police to keep the Woodlawn community "quiet." In a grant application to the O.E.O., the Woodlawn Organization gave an example of this activity:

> "... Ranger activity during the widely publicized westside riots in Chicago during the summer of 1966. At the time the riots were underway, the Rangers were under considerable pressure to join the rioters because of their alliances with Westside groups.

> "The Ranger leadership met and decided not to participate in the riots but, more importantly, decided to make an organized effort to prevent similar violence in Woodlawn. The following plan was developed and carried out by the Rangers in conjunction with the Chicago Police Department, the Woodlawn Organization, and the First Presbyterian Church.

> "First, the Ranger leadership manned a twenty-four hour phone service at the Church during the time the riots were taking place in the Westside. T.W.O. workers and police officers

were called into service every time there was any possibility of gang youth becoming involved in a disturbance. The Ranger leadership, in response to calls, went to the site of possible disturbances and dispersed the youth involved. There were over 30 such calls concerned with possible unilateral action by a member handled by the Rangers.

"Secondly, Ranger members were instructed to call if approached by anyone inciting them to riot. There was one such incident in which the person inciting to riot was identified and his name turned over to the Police ... . The Rangers' action was one of the most relevant reasons that the on-going riots were prevented from taking place in Woodlawn."[11]

Many Black organizations in various cities, fearing the destruction of these rebellions and viewing them as a futile direction, worked to "cool" their communities (the B.P.P. itself did so in Oakland, California, for example). But to these particular gang leaders this "riot prevention" took the form of close cooperation with the police, and was only the most visible tip of their submission to the state apparatus.

FEDERAL RECOGNITION OF THE GANGS

On May 30, 1967, Theodore Berry of the Community Action Program, Office of Economic Opportunity (O.E.O.) formally approved a $927,341 Federal Grant to the Woodlawn Organization.[12] This decision funded an experimental project to give basic literacy and job-skill training to 800 Black gang members. The real point of this experiment, however, was that the leadership of the Blackstone Nation and the Disciples were in reality full partners in the grant, sharing in the money and the staff positions. Within a year this project was a national scandal, the subject of intense police repression and on the verge of closing down. The political coup de grace was delivered by Senator McClellan, who in July, 1968, held a Senate inquisition designed to stir up headlines and racist stereotypes.[13] This federal grant was the highwater mark of the influence of the Blackstone Nation and its best-known leader, Jeff Fort.

It is quite easy to evaluate the effectiveness of the grant. As of June, 1968, only 105 youth had been placed in jobs during the previous year, of whom 65 were still employed.[14] Microscopic results for a million-dollar project. The reason, of course, is that there is a shortage of jobs in the U.S. for Black youth. This is particularly true for youth with police records and a gang history. An internal O.E.O. memorandum, dated April 2, 1968, admitted that the lack of jobs was "the most glaring problem."[15]

The only area where the grant showed practical results was in the reduction of gang violence between "Stones" and "Ds." Youth gang murders dropped 44% in the 3rd Police District between the Summers of 1966 and 1967, as gang leadership restrained fighting lest it endanger the flow of O.E.O. dollars.

It is important to understand that for the government, the success or failure of this project had little to do with how many Black youth found jobs, or didn't kill each other. This O.E.O. grant was a disguised Vietnam-style counterinsurgency program, an experiment in enlisting lumpenproletarian gang elements to help police the ghetto. In the early Spring of 1967, a quiet meeting was held at the Woodlawn Organization offices on East 63rd Street in Chicago. Six men, representing T.W.O., Chicago Urban League and the Office of Economic Opportunity, took part in this meeting. The Chicagoans wanted to make certain there were no misunderstandings about the proposed gang project. In particular, they wanted it understood in advance that the "Main 21"

and the "Ds" leadership would use their power to "rip-off" funds from the project. There was no other way the project could work.

The senior O.E.O. representative replied that he understood quite well and that it posed no problems for Washington. He then went ahead to sketch out, "Off the record," the dynamics of the project. The real goal of the project was to help create a "Black Mafia." O.E.O. knew that the Blackstone "Main 21" had fantasies of becoming another syndicate, taking over control of drugs, numbers, prostitution and protection in the Southside ghetto. O.E.O., by giving them hundreds of thousands of dollars, job patronage for their members, Federal "legitimization" and helping arrange police connections, would give them at least a chance at their goal. Since white ethnic groups had advanced themselves through organized crime, O.E.O. was willing to help Blacks do the same. All the participants agreed that the "Main 21" had poor odds for success, but that they owed it to the Black community to try and help them.

Many believe that promoting Black control of organized crime is an important step upwards for the Black community, but it's hard to imagine the government acting from that motive. It would make much more sense to assume that a large, stable criminal organization would be created by the government because they saw it as an important tool for social control. All the evidence bears this out.

In his prepared testimony before the McClellan Subcommittee in 1968, Jerome S. Bernstein, O.E.O. Project Manager for the Woodlawn grant, proudly cited the political fruits of funding the Rangers and Disciples:

> "These two youth gangs were responsible for preventing a Black Panther meeting on August 1, 1967 which was to be held on the Westside of Chicago for the express purpose of forging a coalition of youth gangs to collectively 'take on the City' during the summer of 1967. These two gangs proclaimed that there would be no riots and that there would be no Black Panther meeting. There were no riots and there was no Black Panther meeting. On more than one occasion these youth took over the streets of Woodlawn and prevented bloodshed and property destruction when police control over the situation had seriously deteriorated."[16]

What could be more clear? As one Disciple leader told a Black newspaper: "We can control and police our people better than the police and the Army."[17] Even more pointed was the private memorandum Bernstein wrote on his return to Washington from Chicago in July, 1967. Bernstein had oriented the "Main 21" to their new role by bringing in as teachers three "Black Power Militants" from Watts who were working in O.E.O. Poverty Programs. These "Black Power Militants" were, of course very friendly to the government and "vehemently opposed to Black Nationalist movements."[18]

Bernstein soon got a report from Rev. Arthur Brazier, President of T.W.O., that their new pupils had learned their lessons quickly:

> "Rev. Brazier informed us that the meeting of the Rangers with the Watts group had a profound effect on both gangs. He stated that, whereas, on Tuesday; the day before, the gangs were ready to shoot it out in the street, the first thing Wednesday morning, the two leaders of each gang came into T.W.O. 'arm in arm'. They informed Rev. Brazier that they were opposed to any rioting in Chicago and that they would not permit any riots to take place in their 'hood'. They stated that they would not tolerate outside agitators coming into their community to provoke riots and that they would run them out of Woodlawn, and, if necessary, shoot them …

"Rev. Brazier informed me that he had received a call from Commander Griffin who was concerned about a rumor that an agitator from Detroit had arrived in Chicago to foment riots and that he was operating in South Chicago. Commander Griffin stated that his men could not identify who this individual was nor could his men locate him. Rev. Brazier transmitted this information to the Rangers who later that day identified the individual and informed the police of his name and whereabouts, and he was subsequently apprehended and, I believe, sent out of the City (I do not know if this information was transmitted to Commander Griffin through T.W.O. or not)."[19]

This is what the government was paying for, and even at a million dollars a year it was a bargain. In Vietnam, the U.S. was paying much more for native counterinsurgency troops and not getting half the service. It should be clear that in return for government favors it was expected that the gangs would use the threat of violence to keep Blacks in their place. The defense of white business property—capital, in other words—was a top priority. This project was so important to O.E.O.'s own procedures it became the only project in Chicago funded directly from O.E.O. to the community, bypassing City Hall.

A letter from Rev. Brazier to Jerome Bernstein on August 3, 1967, gives us a good example of this.[20] According to the letter and supporting newspaper accounts, the new Woodlawn grant passed a practical test of its effectiveness. The previous Tuesday, August 1st, Nicholas J. Nickolaou, owner of Big Jim's Cut-Rate Liquors at 67th Street and Cottage Grove, shot a Black man and killed him. The white merchant had accused a Black child of breaking his store window and had confiscated the child's bike. The child's father angrily came and confronted Nickolaou, who then shot him twice as he was leaving, claiming self-defense.

Since the killing was witnessed, community anger quickly rose as the news spread. Within 45 minutes of the killing, Leon Finney of T.W.O. received an urgent telephone call from George Collar, President of The Woodlawn Businessmen's Association. Finney went out to the scene to help police pacify the crowd of angry residents. Parents from the area refused to be dispersed and were talking about burning the white-owned liquor store out. Finally, Finney got Nick Lorenzo, a leader of the Disciples, to take action with 50 of his members. To quote Finney,

"The Disciples walked up to the corner in a body and demanded to have the corner clean. In a few seconds, all the adults quietly dispersed and went home."

Lorenzo boasted to the *Chicago Daily News*: "The people in the neighborhood know our strength. They moved. Yesterday it was quiet and today it's quiet."[21] Brazier, whose organization was complimented by the police and the daily newspapers, was quite pleased over the incident. As he wrote to O.E.O.: "I think that without a doubt the constructive activity of the group in this situation can be traced directly to the O.E.O. Youth Grant."[22]

Instead of organizing protests against the white merchants or taking action against racists themselves or even just standing aside and letting some rough justice be attempted, T.W.O. and the gangs had to act as police auxiliaries and protect white business property. In both Brazier's letter to O.E.O. and Finney's statements to the press the spotlight is on how the T.W.O.-gang combination prevented the liquor store from being destroyed; in both accounts one is struck by how unimportant the murder of a Black father seems. In the congratulatory newspaper editorials, statements by liberal politicians, memos to Washington, etc. the use of the threat of violence by a gang against community residents—clearly illegal by existing laws—is warmly applauded. This reveals the essence of capitalist "Law and order."

Such cooperation with the police against the people was condition of the grant, and built into the program. Every day project staff met with Sgt. Wilson, 3rd District Chicago Police Department to exchange information. Twice a month, Commander Griffin of the 3rd District met with Rev. Brazier and other project officials at a "monitoring meeting" at Regional O.E.O. offices.[23] T.W.O. was trusted sufficiently by the police to be given copies of the reports turned in by police informers inside the gangs themselves.[24]

THE POLITICS OF THE GANG LEADERSHIP

It would be wrong to view the lumpenproletarian gang leadership as politically passive, a tabula rasa, willing to go in whatever direction the momentary advantage directed. On the surface that seems true, with the Rangers and Disciples flirting with both sides. They went to the Poor Peoples Campaign in Washington, they swelled the ranks of Rev. Jesse Jackson's campaign about job discrimination, they joined any temporary liberal cause or event that promised publicity and/or money. In a deeper sense, however, these gang leaders had several important points of political unity with the government.

First, the gang leaders had a strong natural orientation towards protecting white business in Woodlawn. They viewed the community—people and commerce and real estate—as a resource to be mined for its profitability. Every white businessman who left the area simply meant a source of potential income lost. When the liquor store incident happened the Rangers and Disciples met and assessed the situation. According to Nick Lorenzo, "We agreed that this community is ours and we're going to keep it."[25]

An interesting example of this attitude was the Red Rooster Super Markets, which had a large store at 62nd Street and Dorchester, in the center of Woodlawn. Red Rooster was infamous for its unrestrained consumer fraud tactics, and over the years gathered many slap-on-the-wrist violations for rigged scales, etc. A favorite Red Rooster fraud was soaking packaged meat in water, then freezing the whole mess. Result: with each package of meat the Black shopper also paid for as much as one-half pound of ice.

In March, 1969, Rev. Jesse Jackson's Operation Breadbasket started picketing Red Rooster over these abuses. The protest was soon settled by the Red Rooster chain hiring twenty-two "Stones," including Jeff Fort, Mickey Cogwell and other "Main 21." The jobs appear to have been mostly a pay-off to let Red Rooster go on exploiting the Black community.[26]

In the same way, every time a major rebellion broke out in Chicago's ghetto, the "Main 21" would move to protect Woodlawn's white businesses with "do not touch" signs. Black homeowners were also important to the "Stones," since they could be encouraged to buy "window insurance." Small wonder that when the police accused the Blackstone Rangers of extorting protection money, both the Woodlawn Businessmen's Association and the Jackson Park Businessmen's Association held a press conference to defend and praise the "Stones." At that meeting, Father Tracy O'Sullivan of St. Cyril Church said: "The youths really delivered, and this attack by the police was the thanks they got."[27]

While movements of the oppressed usually clash with exploitative business interests, this was not true with the gangs. We could say that white business interests and the gang leadership got along so well because they both viewed the Black community in the same way.

Secondly, the gang leadership shared with the government an opposition to grassroots Black organization. After all, a successful mass Black organization in Woodlawn would have crowded the "Stones," even recruited people away from them. So that as their troubles increased, as police arrests and court cases piled up, as Fort and others were indicted on federal charges of embezzling O.E.O. funds, the gang leadership was paralyzed. By 1968, the police repression was so heavy against the "Stones" as to be crushing. Fort himself was arrested one hundred fifty times in six months—almost once a day!

All the "Main 21" could do was to keep cooperating with the police, begging for favors. We know that members of the "Main 21" secretly kept the police informed about Black Panther Party activity, pointing out as they did so how useful they could be to the police if the police let them survive. It was only pathetic in January 1969, when Leonard Sengali of the Black P. Stones announced that the gang was starting a whole new program of protecting Blacks from crime. Sengali said that "Stones" would don green uniforms (the same color as the official Community Police Aides paid for by Model Cities Poverty Funds) and patrol the community, reporting all suspicious activity to the police.[28]

The Chicago Police Department was inexorably putting the "Stones" out of business, literally. Even then, the leadership was so submissive that the police could repress them and use them at the same time. In August, 1968, when Mayor Daley and his Machine were girding to put down the expected mass demonstrations at the Democratic National Convention, the police arranged to have bail suddenly lowered for a number of the "Main 21" who were in jail. The secret condition was that the "Stones" would forcibly stop Dick Gregory from leading an announced march thru "Stones" territory. The Machine was frightened that Gregory's protest march might touch off mass demonstrations or "rioting" by Blacks. Once released, the "Main 21" threatened Gregory with death if his march entered their areas, and indeed, the march plans were hastily changed. Of course, once their usefulness was over, these gang leaders soon found themselves back in jail.

In April, 1969, Illinois National Guard were once again called out as the Chicago ghetto verged on open rebellion and once again, the "Stones" and the Disciples patrolled Woodlawn to help the police keep the lid on. By this time Commander Griffin of the 3rd District knew he could rely completely on the gangs. Each gang patrol had official 3rd District Police shoulder patches to wear on their jackets so that cops on the beat could identify them.[29] Naive people still wonder at how the Nazis could recruit Jewish police to control the ghetto for them.

THE SPLIT OVER REPRESSIVE STRATEGY

The open police harassment of the gangs and their O.E.O. project was so obviously illegal that it became itself a major political issue. Church offices sympathetic to the gang youth were repeatedly raided, to the background music of breaking doors and ripped-apart furniture. Youth Action, "a streetwork project funded by the four most prestigious social agencies in Chicago," was raided three times. During the raid on their Auburn Highland Center, two staff members were "roughed up" and $2,500 property damage was done—although the police found no weapons or drugs and made no arrests. Gang members themselves were often arrested and rearrested on any pretext. Fighting and retaliation raids between the "Stones" and "Ds" were carefully promoted and touched off by the police Gang Intelligence Unit (GIU).[30]

This open display of police power aroused many sectors of Chicago's liberal and Black communities. Youth Action, T.W.O., the Urban League, Chicago Theological Seminary, the A.C.L.U., the Better Boys Foundation, 5th Ward Alderman Leon Depres and 6th Ward Alderman "Sammy" Rayner (both anti-Daley independents) and many other liberal institutions and personalities protested these police activities. Many genuinely were infuriated at the police persecution of these Black youth from "poverty backgrounds." Out of this clash came a mythology which has been widely accepted: the picture is of poverty-stricken gang youth trying to move away from "Anti-social behavior" towards constructive community concerns, being crushed by the racist machine of Mayor Richard Daley because the city couldn't tolerate any threat of independent organization. This familiar all-American scenario is incomplete and misleading. The full story of this living interplay between federal government, the local city machine, the police and the gangs is far richer in lessons, although more complex, than the mythology of good guys vs. bad guys.

It is widely assumed that Mayor Richard Daley viewed the O.E.O. grant and the gangs as a threat to his Machine and that he therefore used repression to crush them. On the contrary, Mayor Daley always appreciated how useful the gangs could be. In 1966, Jeff Fort was given a job at the City's Woodlawn Urban Progress Center. At that time, Denton Brooks, head of the City's "Anti-Poverty" program (Chicago Committee on Urban Opportunity) took Fort and other "Main 21" to lunch and suggested that the "Stones" submit a proposal for an "anti-poverty" grant.[31] Black youth gangs had previously been used by the Chicago Police Dept. in order to harass and drive out Black community organizers. In 1965, Chicago SNCC's attempt to do "grassroots" organizing came under heavy attack from local gangs, with vandalization of the SNCC office, intimidation of children at the SNCC "Freedom School" and beatings of SNCC workers contributing to the death of the project. It was alleged that this conflict was caused by the police, who gave the gangs a "license" to commit crimes in return for attacking SNCC.

To be sure, Mayor Daley was enraged about the gang leaders floating their O.E.O. grant with T.W.O., rather than with the City's agency, C.C.U.O. (which would have poured part of those funds into patronage channels). But Daley never opposed that grant, despite what the liberals said. He was, among other things under heavy pressure from Washington to "OK" the grant.

As Jerome Bernstein pointed out to the McClellan Subcommittee (a point that went studiously unreported in the Chicago media):

"For the record, the Mayor did, in fact, concur in the funding of the program and did so in the form of a telephone call which he, Mayor Daley, initiated to Sargent Shriver, then Director of O.E.O. To be more explicit, the T.W.O. 'program' would not have been funded at all without the support of Mayor Daley. Sargent Shriver stated so on several occasions and held up funding of the program for two weeks pending communication of the Mayor's support for the program. The T.W.O. program in the sense was in reality as much the result of actions of Mayor Daley as those of T.W.O. and O.E.O. The Mayor's support for funding of the program is a matter of written record which is both known to the Subcommittee and the Acting Director of O.E.O."[32]

Washington Post columnists Rowland Evans and Robert Novak made the same point a full year earlier, as they revealed "The deep split among the authorities over how to deal with the deepening riot problem."

"Highly respected Police Superintendent Orlando Wilson (who has just retired) led the anti-gang faction in opposing the grant. He was joined by local Poverty Program officials, who view The Woodlawn Organization as far too radical.

"Although anathema to Negro radicals, Daley happens to be a pragmatic politician ... fearing a bloody summer, he was willing to give the liberals a chance at doing business with the gangs."[33]

Further, it turns out that the Chicago police themselves were split exactly as Evans and Novak discussed. Commander Griffin of the 3rd District warmly supported the grant. He communicated this support to O.E.O. and agreed that his men would take part in it. The 3rd District after all, had practical experience at how useful the gangs were in controlling the Black community.

Griffin was at odds with Lt. Buckney of the new Gang Intelligence Unit, who from the start was out to destroy the gangs. Buckney was so fanatical that his men twice took Jerome Bernstein of O.E.O. into custody. During a meeting with O.E.O., this disagreement within the Chicago Police came out:

"At the mention of Buckney's name, Griffin threw up his hands and stated that Buckney did not understand his job, he did not know what he was doing, and that something had to be done about him."[34]

On August 9, 1967, Rev. Brazier and Leon Finney of T.W.O. met with Superintendent Conlisk and seven other Chicago police brass. According to Rev. Brazier, Commander Griffin argued that the police should take advantage of "the beneficial effects of the youth project on the gang youth in Woodlawn." Lt. Buckney, Gang Intelligence Unit, disagreed and pointed to Jeff Fort as a problem (Fort had been arrested by G.I.U. for probation violation), Commander Griffin defended Fort, and then pointed out that "At the time of Jeff's arrest, Commander Griffin was waiting to meet with Jeff in his office to discuss with Jeff and some of his associates ways and means of preventing riot agitators from circulating in the Woodlawn community." Superintendent Conlisk then promised that the police Dept. wouldn't oppose Fort's defense when they testified at his parole rehearing, and that the gang project would receive police "cooperation and support."[35]

It was Captain Edward N. Buckney (promoted a year after that meeting) and his Gang Intelligence Unit which initiated and led the campaign to repress the "Stones" and Disciples. This was the unit that led the raids, made the constant arrests, maintained informers inside the gangs and tried to get them to war on each other. Buckney did so not to carry out orders from Mayor Daley, but despite his orders. Again, it was Robert Novak who revealed that the entire Senate inquisition into the O.E.O. project by Senator McClellan had been initiated by Gang Intelligence Unit "without authorization by the Mayor." And by helping Congressional reactionaries create a national scandal, Buckney and G.I.U. forced the Mayor into a position of open opposition to the gangs and the O.E.O. project.[36]

As late as May, 1968, Rev. Brazier and Mayor Daley were still trying to work out a deal over the O.E.O. project. At an April 22, 1968 meeting, Rev. Brazier was asked by Mayor Daley to keep the project going until at least next September, as Brazier was threatening to close it before the Summer. Daley asked Rev. Brazier if T.W.O. could "come under the C.C.U.O. umbrella." Brazier offered Mayor Daley the right to "pick the Project Director," but said that working under Deton Brooks and C.C.U.O. was unacceptable. Brazier then "reminded the Mayor that T.W.O. had never directly attacked the Mayor publically." Mayor Daley ended the meeting by urging Brazier and Brooks to work something out.[37] All this maneuvering was, of course, torpedoed by the Senate investigation and its publicity.

The question of why Lt. Buckney and his G.I.U. played such a role is an interesting one. It was true that the Black satraps of the Democratic Party Machine viewed the Black gangs as potential rivals too close to home, so as to speak.

Having more weight is the influence of the Syndicate. Some who worked within the O.E.O. project believe that it was precisely the Rangers' dream of a ghetto organized crime empire that led to their downfall. They believe that the Syndicate, seeing a powerfully organized rival, demanded that the police "deliver" some repression for all the protection money they were being paid. A reader who believes this is an exaggeratedly cynical view of police-Syndicate relations has not factually studied this subject. To take just one publically documented fact out of many: Commissioner Orlando Wilson's Chief Assistant, Paul Quinn, was demoted when it was revealed that he was one of the Syndicate pay-off coordinators within the C.P.D. There were clear channels of possible Syndicate influence on the policy of the G.I.U.

It is important to see that there was a sharp split in the white government over how to pacify the ghetto. The gang project, an advanced counterinsurgency program with certain real similarities to U.S. programs in Vietnam and the Philippines, brought this split out in the open. In Vietnam, we saw this split between the "civic action" programs of the U.S. Special Forces, which sought to use bribes/reforms to recruit ethnic minority native forces to fight the communist insurgency, vs. the conventional warfare of annihilation using massive levels of U.S. regular troops and firepower so clumsily wielded by General Westmoreland and his clan. The analogy lends insight to Chicago. The liberals wanted to use reforms to recruit "native" forces to pacify the ghetto, while the conservatives wanted to turn the police loose to repress anything Black that lifted its head. Some wanted to do both, which is what happened both in Vietnam and Chicago.

Evans and Novak commented in 1967:

"The Negro slums of America today comprise a secret arsenal of firearms, zip-guns and knives ready for use at a moment's notice. Besides, police officers who practice diplomacy in making an arrest in the Negro slums are just as apt to trigger a riot as their heavy-handed brethren.

"In fact, those who know the Negro slums best are pessimistic. They are sure only that **the sole force of discipline in those slums are the anonymous gang leaders** [our emphasis]. Thus, the split of the white establishment over how to deal with these gangs, as seen in Chicago, is still further cause for pessimism."[38]

This split in the capitalist government made for not a few ironies. Jerome Bernstein, the "Godfather" of the very successful gang project, was fired from O.E.O. by Sargent Shriver for having become too politically controversial. Bernstein was frustrated at, as he repeatedly explained, being fired for producing the only successful federal "anti-riot" program for the ghetto. He futilely pointed out how Woodlawn was kept from exploding, unlike Watts, Detroit, Newark, Harlem ... and Chicago's Westside.[39]

Both liberals and conservatives (inadequate categories in this case) got to try their strategies for repression. This produces the irony of gang leaders having "delivered the goods" for the government, now serving time in a federal prison for "conspiracy to commit fraud" in handling O.E.O. funds. Of course, the government officials and Black community leaders who got the gangs involved in this project, who gave them informal approval to "rip-off" funds, who virtually set them up, walked away clean after the project collapsed.

The final irony came with President Richard Nixon's inauguration in January, 1969. During this triumphant celebration of Republican victory the gangs weren't forgotten. Jeff Fort, already under Federal Investigation, received a formal invitation to Nixon's Inaugural Ball! Fort sent Mickey Cogwell and Bobby Jennings, complete with "white ties and tails," as Ranger representatives to the Inaugural Ball. The white public in Chicago was astonished. Veteran Black journalist Lou Palmer saw it as the Nixon Administration's recognition of the potential vote power: "Nixon squeaked into the Presidency with few Black votes. The Black P. Stones had campaigned to persuade Blacks to boycott the polls."[40] Naturally, vote boycotts of predominantly Democratic Black voters could only help Nixon and the Republicans, and Nixon had encouraged such campaigns.

CONCLUSION

We should now be able to see clearly what Marx and Engels meant when they said that the lumpenproletariat **"... May, here and there be swept into the Movement ... Its conditions of life, however, prepare it far more for the part of a bribed tool of reactionary intrigue."**

Groupings of the oppressed must be understood in terms of class. Black gangs are composed primarily of working-class youth, many of whose families are in what Marx referred to as the "Reserve Army" of the unemployed. These youths, because of their colonial and class oppression, are logically pulled towards rebellion. We know that some members of the Black P. Stones and Disciples participated enthusiastically in the defense of the literally besieged Black community of Cairo, Illinois. Some joined the Black Panther Party and other organizations. At least part of the leadership was at one time strongly motivated to drive heroin pushers out of the "turf." The gang structure effectively "locked up" this pull towards rebellion. The gang leadership not only used the power of their own organizations to "police" the ghetto, but, most importantly of all, neutralized within their organizations the critical strata of the most oppressed working-class youth.

There is, of course, no precise dividing line "on the streets" between the lumpenproletariat and the lower working class. Further, elements of the "lumpen"—angry, desperate—have always been drawn into the struggle, usually during its most militant or violent stages. All previous Marxist experience, internationally, has taught us to use these elements but not build primarily on them. Many organizers here in the U.S. have long since come to a similar conclusion. The B.L.A., to take one example, has seriously taken up the discussion of this question:

> "It is clear to us that the so-called lumpen class cannot carry our liberation struggle forward on its own. This is because of their class nature: undisciplined, dogmatic, and easily prone to diversion. This class however will supply some of the most dedicated comrades to the struggle. But we must clarify our view of the lumpen class as a whole. The traditional concept of lumpen as a category of the lowest social strata in an industrialized society, unemployed, etc., is a description that fits not only brothers and sisters that hang out in the street all day long and survive in that fashion, but it also fits a great segment of black people who are marginally employed and who for various socio-economical reasons think essentially the same as the classical 'lumpen'. Therefore, we must make a clear distinction between the economic definition of lumpen (the relationship of that class to the means of production) and the attitudinal, behavioral definition which can readily apply to a larger proportion of our people. When we use the term lumpen we are using a broad definition."[41]

It is interesting to notice that the B.L.A., like much of the white "New Left," mistakenly defines the "lumpen" to equate to the unemployed and marginally employed. This blurs our class analysis, since it uses the word "lumpenproletariat" to include both that class and the lowest stratas of the working class "reserve army." Thus a teen-age "Stone" who joined out of group loyalty or friendship or survival protection would be placed in the same class as Mickey Cogwell on the "Main 21." Cogwell "joined" by bringing the gangs in the Robert Taylor-Washington Park Projects into the Blackstone Rangers—in return for $5,000. After the gang hustle collapsed he then went to work for the Syndicate's Hotel and Restaurant Employees and Bartenders Union. In 1973, Cogwell got an exclusive franchise for all Black areas in Chicago, and worked at extorting "dues" money out of Blacks to be split between him and the white Syndicate.[42] This is a classic lumpenproletarian career of preying on the working class. Clearly, the need for this class analysis is as acute today as a decade ago, and applies sharply to the prison struggle and proliferation of "militant" community organizations.

The other point that emerges is how liberals and conservatives, for all their antagonisms, remain united in the common defense of capitalism by repression against the oppressed. It was, after all, the activist liberals—Black as well as white—who promoted the use of youth gangs to strong-arm the ghetto into "peace." This is the bitter fruit of liberal social pacification. Only with a class understanding of the concrete situation can we effectively grasp who are the revolutionary forces.

postscript (2017)

This research paper was originally written only for other revolutionaries, working in oppressed communities, to better help rebels protect themselves from state repression. It was never thought of for any general distribution, even within the left. Published initially in a small anti-imperialist journal, its largest readership probably came when a Puerto Rican revolutionary group reprinted it as part of the study materials at a national anti-grand jury repression conference. At some point, a cheap pamphlet edition was done, solely for convenience in answering the occasional requests for copies. So this paper has remained largely unknown, just like the federal counterinsurgency project itself. A recent favorably reviewed book on the history of the Blackstone Rangers, by two Chicago African-American journalists, barely mentions the government repression project, while giving a false, "white-wash" impression of what it was.

In a number of ways, this novel but logically evil experiment in structuring pay-offs for street gangs in return for their crushing any anti-white rebellions, was a project built around the schemes of the Black bourgeoisie. This is alluded to in the paper, but hardly analyzed seriously in any depth. In retrospect, this is the weakness i find most glaring now.

T.W.O.—The Woodlawn Organization—featured prominently in our story as the main sponsoring community non-profit organization. It is closed down now. T.W.O. was first injected into a poor New Afrikan community as a highly-funded virus, designed by Saul Alinsky's Industrial Areas Foundation (I.A.F.). It was to be a spotlighted demonstration that the I.A.F.'s patented, pro-capitalist reform organizing could smother grassroots New Afrikan insurgencies. I.A.F. was, of course, where Barack Obama's white handlers sent him to learn the tactics of top-down "community organizing." Long led by Rev. Leon Finney Jr. and his wife, Georgette Greenlee, T.W.O. before its recent demise was always highly successful—at least for the Black bourgeoisie. Rev. Finney Jr. and his wife, for instance, were paid $293,000 in 2010 by the organization. Plus an additional $190,000 paid to Finney-owned companies for providing rental space and food for T.W.O. The neighborhood is now steadily gentrifying while working class New Afrikans are being driven out, so T.W.O.'s historic pacification mission is now "mission accomplished." Although the non-profit organization's end was due to the State of Illinois's findings that T.W.O. recently defrauded the state of $689,000 in various no-show grants, no criminal prosecution is yet in sight. Business as usual for neo-colonial "democracy."

Perhaps the most interesting feedback I received on the paper came from the respected revolutionary theorist and teacher, Atiba Shanna. When we discussed it at length, he said that everything written in the paper was true, but the paper as a whole still wasn't true. In his opinion, so much had been left out about the street organization and the nature of his People's community that it was too unbalanced. In Shanna's view, in their powerless community where New Afrikans are tightly ruled but have no governing of their own, any self-organized New Afrikan body is positive, no matter how confused or off-course it may be at one time.

He spoke about this gang in its El Rukn stage, with the ex-theater building turned into a large "Moorish temple" where they would hold open court to settle disputes between community residents on the spot, from marital discord to auto accidents. Just as the Taliban does in Afghanistan villages despite the u.s.-backed government and its "legal" courts. Also important to the picture but largely left out, Shanna continued, was the fact that most of the street organization soldiers were simply poor working-class teenage boys, who have no chance of ever finding a real job. i agreed readily to the partial weight of his points, but stated that it was hardly my task to put together any overall understanding of the bloody contradictions of the street organizations. It was his movement's job, which they had largely avoided, in my belief. We parted with respectful snarls of disagreement.

Last words: That familiar cliché— "Those who don't learn from history are doomed to repeat it"—not true here. No, it won't be even that good.

endnotes

1. "Lumpenproletarian Discipline Vs. Bourgeois Reaction," *Black Panther*, August 9, 1969.

2. Eldridge Cleaver, "On the Ideology of the Black Panther Party," *Black Panther*, June 6, 1970.

3. Karl Marx and Frederick Engels, "Manifesto of the Community Party," *Selected Works*, International Publishers, 1972. Page 44.

4. John Fry, *Fire and Blackstone*, J.B. Lippincott & Co., 1969. Page 5.

5. *Daily Defender*, June 13, 1966. *Chicago Sun-Times*, June 12, 1966.

6. *Chicago Tribune*, August 23, 1970. *Chicago Tribune*, September 24, 1970.

7. Sam Greenlee, *The Spook Who Sat by the Door*, Bantam, 1970.

8. *Reader*, November 21, 1975.

9. *Chicago Tribune*, June 16, 1969.

10. *Reader*, November 21, 1975.

11. Untitled grant proposal from T.W.O. to Community Action Program, O.E.O., but clearly 1967. Page 10.

12. "Two-Track Manpower Demonstration for 800 Unemployed Disadvantaged Young Adults," C.A.P. Project No. (G8734/A/O).

13. *Riots, Civil and Criminal Disorders*, Part 9–17. Hearings held by the U.S. Senate Committee on Government Operations, Permanent Subcommittee on Investigations.

14. "Two Major Issues (Charges and Answers)." Page 5. (This is an O.E.O. background paper, written in anticipation of the McClelland Hearings and given to Senators Muskie, Javits and Harris.)

15. C.A.P. Memorandum from Dennis Porter to Donald K. Hess, April 2, 1968. Page 10.

16. Statement of Jerome S. Bernstein. Page 12.

17. *Daily Defender*, April 9, 1968.

18. Jerome S. Bernstein, "Memorandum For the Record. T.W.O. Field Trip of July 25–27, 1967," August 12, 1967. Page 3.

19. Ibid. p. 25.

20. Letter to Jerome S. Bernstein from Rev. Arthur Brazier, August 3, 1967.

21. *Chicago Sun-Times*, August 2, 1967. *Chicago Daily News*, August 4, 1967.

22. Letter to Jerome S. Bernstein from Rev. Arthur Brazier, August 3, 1967.

23. "Two Major Issues (Charges and Answers)." Page 5. Monthly reports from Rev. Brazier to O.E.O. confirm these frequent meetings with the Chicago Police Department.

24. *Chicago Sun-Times*, March 15, 1972.

25. *Chicago Daily News*, August 4, 1967.

26. *Chicago Tribune*, March 8, 1970.

27. *Daily Defender*, April 17, 1968.

28. *Chicago American*, January 25, 1969.

29. Henry De Zutter, "The Press: Loyal Troops in the City's War on Gangs," *Chicago Journalism Review*, June, 1969.

30. For a good liberal account of this police harassment, see *Chicago Journalism Review*, January, 1969 and June, 1969.

31. *Chicago Journalism Review*, November–December, 1968.

32. Bernstein Testimony. Page 19.

33. Rowland Evans and Robert Novak, "Inside Report," *Washington Post*, July 5, 1967.

34. "Memorandum For the Record," August 12, 1967. Page 24.

35. Letter to Jerome Bernstein from Rev. Arthur Brazier, August 15, 1967.

36. Robert Novak, "The Story Behind the Rangers Probe," *Chicago Sun-Times*, July 12, 1968.

37. "Memo to the Acting Director, O.E.O., from Community Action Program," April 29, 1968.

38. *Washington Post*, July 5, 1967.

39. *Chicago Tribune*, March 30, 1972.

40. *Chicago Daily News*, January 21, 1969, L.F. Palmer, Jr., "Behind the Inaugural Invitation."

41. Coordinating Committee of the Black Liberation Army, *Message to the Black Movement*, 1975. Page 10.

42. *Chicago Tribune*, November 3, 1974.

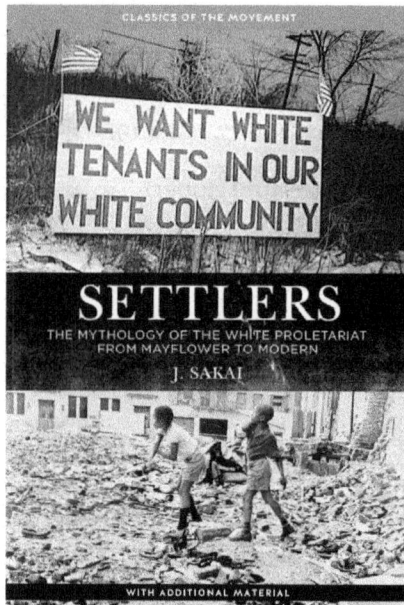

Settlers: The Mythology of the White Proletariat from Mayflower to Modern

The United States is a country built on the theft of Indigenous lands and Afrikan labor, on the robbery of the northern third of Mexico, the colonization of Puerto Rico, and the expropriation of the Asian working class, with each of these crimes being accompanied by violence. In fact, America's white citizenry have never supported themselves but have always resorted to exploitation and theft, culminating in acts of genocide to maintain their culture and way of life. This movement classic lays it all out, taking us through this painful but important history.

This new edition includes "Cash & Genocide: The True Story of Japanese-American Reparations" and an interview with author J. Sakai by Ernesto Aguilar.

BY J. SAKAI

PM PRESS & KERSPLEBEDEB

ISBN 9781629630373

456 PAGES • $20.00

"Settlers is a critical analysis of the colonization of the Americas that overturns the 'official' narrative of poor and dispossessed European settlers to reveal the true nature of genocidal invasion and land theft that has occurred for over five hundred years. If you want to understand the present, you must know the past, and this book is a vital contribution to that effort."

Gord Hill, author of
500 Years of Indigenous Resistance

"Great works measure up, inspire higher standards of intellectual and moral honesty, and, when appreciated for what they are, serve as a guide for those among us who intend a transformation of reality. Settlers should serve as a reminder (to anyone who needs one) of the genocidal tendencies of the empire, the traitorous interplay between settler-capitalist, settler-nondescript, and colonial flunkies."

Kuwasi Balagoon, Black Liberation Army

"When Settlers hit the tiers of San Quentin, back in 1986, it totally exploded our ideas about what we as a new class of revolutionaries thought we knew about a so-called 'united working class' in amerika. And what's more, it brought the actual contradictions of national oppression and imperialism into sharp focus. It was my first, and as such my truest, study of the actual mechanics behind the expertly fabricated illusion of an amerikan proletariat."

Sanyika Shakur, author of *Monster: The Autobiography of an L.A. Gang Member*

Jailbreak Out of History: the Re-Biography of Harriet Tubman & "The Evil of Female Loaferism"

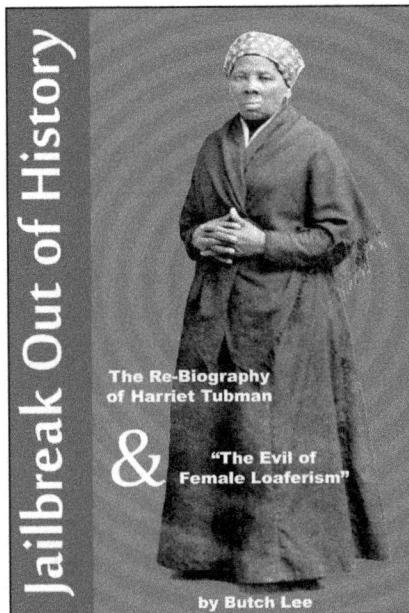

BY BUTCH LEE

KERSPLEBEDEB

ISBN 9781894946704
169 PAGES • $14.95

Anticolonial struggles of New Afrikan/Black women were central to the unfolding of 19th century amerika, both during and "after" slavery. "The Re-Biography of Harriet Tubman", recounts the life and politics of Harriet Tubman, who waged and eventually lead the war against the capitalist slave system. A second text in this second edition volume, "The Evil of Female Loaferism," details New Afrikan women's attempts to withdraw from and evade capitalist colonialism, an unofficial but massive labor strike which threw the capitalists North and South into a panic. The ruling class response consisted of the "Black Codes," Jim Crow, re-enslavement through prison labor, mass violence, and ... the establishment of a neo-colonial Black patriarchy, whose task it was to make New Afrikan women subordinate to New Afrikan men, just as New Afrika was supposed to be subordinate to white amerika.

Race is notoriously slippery, awkward to hold onto as a subject, yet totally all around us. Totally. All the time, every day, we breathe it; after all, it is us, so we can't ever be far from it. This seeming contradiction of what should be so simple being endlessly complicated in society is because how we think about race, how we talk about race ... capitalism is constantly trying to police this. They don't want to neaten it, they actually want to constrict it and keep remaking it in their own distorted images and stamping it on our faces.

So in u.s. society ... capitalism pushes thinking and talking about race into the dominant form of a white/Black paradigm. Where everything is supposed to be arranged according to the relationship between white men—who are defined as: What's "normal," the standard—and New Afrikan people—who are indirectly or covertly depicted as incomplete or deficient models of the first. So that the supposed goal of capitalistic "antiracism" is that eventually at some point everyone will be exactly like white men.

Well, we don't have to comment really on that.

Into this paradigm, everyone else—"unimportant minorities"—are essentially crammed and flattened into that two-dimensional story, according to some always shifting order that they have, judging by how important or unimportant they think we are.

This raises a question: What is an unimportant minority? Am not going to answer that, but let me point you in a certain direction ...

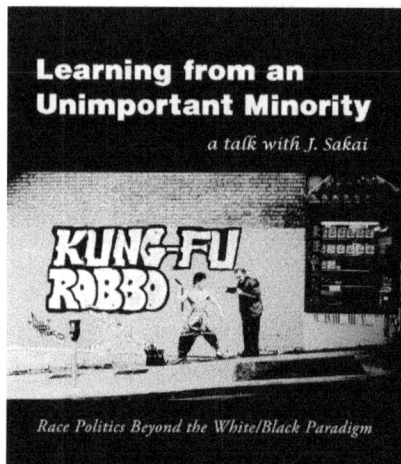

Learning from an Unimportant Minority: Race Politics Beyond the White/Black Paradigm

In this talk given at the 2014 Montreal Anarchist Bookfair, J. Sakai shares experiences from his own life as a revolutionary in the united states, exploring what it means to belong to an "unimportant minority."

BY J. SAKAI

KERSPLEBEDEB

ISBN 9781894946605
118 PAGES • $10.00

When Race Burns Class: Settlers Revisited

An interview with author J. Sakai about his ground-breaking work *Settlers: Mythology of the White Proletariat*, accompanied by Kuwasi Balagoon's essay "The Continuing Appeal of Imperialism." Amongst other things, Sakai discusses how he came to write *Settlers*, the relationship of settlerism to racism, and between race and class, the prospects for organizing within the white working class, and of the rise of the far right.

When Race Burns Class: Settlers Revisited

A Critical Assessment of the U.S. White Working Class

an interview with author J. Sakai and "The Continuing Appeal of Anti-Imperialism" by New Afrikan anarchist Kuwasi Balagoon

BY J. SAKAI

KERSPLEBEDEB

ISBN 9781894820264
32 PAGES • $4.00

Since 1998 Kersplebedeb has been an important source of radical literature and agit prop materials.

The project has a non-exclusive focus on anti-patriarchal and anti-imperialist politics, framed within an anticapitalist perspective. A special priority is given to writings regarding armed struggle in the metropole, the continuing struggles of political prisoners and prisoners of war, and the political economy of imperialism.

The Kersplebedeb website presents historical and contemporary writings by revolutionary thinkers from the anarchist and communist traditions. At the same time, the leftwingbooks.net website serves as Kersplebedeb's storefront, with well over a thousand progressive books and pamphlets available for mail-order.

Kersplebedeb can be contacted at:

Kersplebedeb
CP 63560, CCCP Van Horne
Montreal, Quebec
Canada
H3W 3H8

email: info@kersplebedeb.com
web: www.kersplebedeb.com
            www.leftwingbooks.net

Kersplebedeb

www.ingramcontent.com/pod-product-compliance
Lightning Source LLC
Chambersburg PA
CBHW080402270326
41927CB00015B/3314